Eyes of a Pedophile
Detecting Child Predators

Table of Contents

Betty J. Kuffel, MD
Fellow American College
of Physicians

An asterisk (*) denotes names
changed to protect privacy.

Praise for Eyes of a Pedophile
By Betty J. Kuffel, MD

Dr. Kuffel's remarkable book is both readable and informative. Her story of the life of an SVP—Sexually Violent Predator—David Brown aka Nathanael Bar-Jonah, should be required reading for all parents, judges, law enforcement, and especially mental health professionals. Her discussion of how this very dangerous predator was turned loose on society ... is especially poignant. Scientific research consistently informs us that these dangerous men–the worst of the worst sex offenders–cannot be changed.

By turning the spotlight on the havoc and personal destruction brought about by David Brown, Dr. Kuffel clearly shows us that the first priority of the courts and the psychologists must be to protect public safety by keeping these dangerous men confined.

Dr. Joseph Nevotti, Forensic Psychologist

Introduction

Great Falls, Montana 1996

Early one February morning, ten-year-old Zachary Ramsay got up and dressed in his favorite blue jersey with "Ramsay" printed in gold across the back. The third grader looked terrific for the special Good Guy Breakfast. Many fathers would be at Whittier Elementary to join their kids, but Zach's dad wouldn't be there. After losing a contentious custody battle, his military father lived in another state. His mother's boyfriend recently moved out, so he couldn't be there either to see Zach being honored for his artwork.

Zach went alone.

Weighing in at ninety pounds, Zach resembled a young football star as he walked out the front door of his apartment building sporting his team jacket. The boy took his usual six block route along a narrow alley. He passed familiar cluttered backyards and derelict cars. In the 46-degree weather, a brisk west wind ruffled his curly black hair.

The bright artistic student had many friends at school. Being with them distracted him from problems at home. Zach was so distressed one day that he ran away from home. It wasn't long before he called his mom and was back with his little brother and sister.

Zach hurried on to school alone—but he wasn't alone.

That morning, the attractive boy became a target in the eyes of a pedophile.

When Zach didn't show up for class, his friends worried. The concerned teacher telephoned Zach's mother. One hour later, she called police and reported her son missing.

Zachary Ramsay has never been found.

Author Note

An evidence video of Zachary Ramsay's route to school scanned the alley like Zach's eyes would have that morning. Jerky movements seemed to follow the boy's jaunty step, stopping occasionally and then proceeding. As I watched, I sensed I was walking behind Zach, watching him through the eyes of a stalking predator—a hunter waiting for the right time to strike.

As pedophiles stalk victims, sexual fantasies dominate their thoughts. Like other hunters, they target specific prey. Pedophiles hunt children.

To achieve sexual arousal and gratification, these predators choose children of a specific age, appearance and gender with the thrill of acting out fantasies undetected. They live among us in plain view, often working close to children. In positions of power, they ingratiate themselves to parents and groom children to trust them.

Most attackers are not strangers.

This book examines David Brown's life from his religious beginnings to becoming the violent pedophile Nathanael Bar-Jonah. His deciphered coded writings and letters from prison, legal documents, testimony of his victims and those who knew him unravel the chilling crime history. Bar-Jonah harmed many children. His coded writings reveal he killed and cannibalized Zachary Ramsay.

At the time of Bar-Jonah's arrest, I was working as an emergency physician in a hospital located across the street from his residence. My close proximity and access to information through cooperation from law enforcement and legal teams enhanced my ability to accurately detail this case. Consolidating information from many sources and extensive research on pedophile and sexual predatory behavior provides the foundation for this book.

My purpose is to educate people about child predators. I have seen terror in the eyes of innocent children raped by pedophiles and deep emotional scars in my sister, cousin and friends from unreported childhood rapes. I hope the information opens eyes and minds to the importance of reporting and prosecuting pedophiles. If it saves even one child from harm, my time has been well spent.

Chapter 1 Evolution to Violence

Abuse victims often become abusers themselves but not always. Attorney author Andrew Vachess aptly stated: "While early childhood experiences may impel, they do not compel. In the end, *evil is a matter of choice.*"

In the *cycle of abuse*, the prey becomes the predator. In Bar-Jonah's case, he is a victim of abuse who exemplifies the *cycle*. Above average intelligence and without obvious psychopathology, he learned to fit in well. He didn't look or act like what most people envision when they think of a "crazy" person. But pedophilia is a mental illness, defined as a Paraphilia in the Diagnostic and Statistical Manual of Mental Disorders (DSM). Evidence of the disorder only becomes apparent when they offend.

If you had met Nathanael Bar-Jonah, you would understand how mothers came to trust their children in his care. His loving mother taught him appropriate social skills and ways of the church, but the dark side of their "perfect family" eventually surfaced.

From the beginning, Phil Brown resented his wife Tyra's pregnancy. Over forty-years-of-age at the time, it is likely her pregnancy was a surprise and unplanned. After David's birth, Phil's disdain turned to horror when he looked into his son's face. The healthy blond boy had one blue eye and one brown eye, the same strange eyes as Phil's father, a man who spent most of his life as a mumbling vagrant eating from garbage cans.

David said he never met his outcast grandfather and maintained his own eyes changed color after birth. Heterochromia iridum (different colored irises) is an inherited variation in eye pigment common in dogs and other mammals but not prevalent in humans. Nor is it associated with mental illness, but Phil may have thought otherwise.

Growing up believing he was flawed, David felt inferior. Every time he looked in a mirror, David was reminded he was different. Later he used his wild eyes as powerful weapons.

When David's mother visited a woman and her two daughters who lived on the first floor of their three-story apartment building, they welcomed her. Through babysitting, the girls and their mother got to know the Brown family well. Phil's mean streak was no secret to them. One girl described Tyra as "a sweet, simple woman with the patience of a saint" who would invite them to stay for dinner. They rarely accepted her offer because of Phil. Her sister said, "Phil would come home irritated. I would leave quickly. He had a weird look about him...I was afraid of him. The anger in his eyes frightened me. If I heard him coming up the stairs, I'd go out through the back window and climb down the big apple tree so I wouldn't have to see him."

With little income as an automobile mechanic and another mouth to feed, Phil moved the family to Florida seeking better employment. A Florida photograph shows six-year-old David standing in a suggestive pose, wearing a girl's two-piece swimsuit and a blond wig. The photo could be an indication of early gender confusion sometimes seen in sexual predators.

When David continued to wet the bed after age two, an age when most children are trained, Phil beat him with a belt. Little David tried to stop wetting, but he couldn't. Tyra didn't stop Phil's beatings; instead, she coddled her son with food.

A Seattle Times newspaper article noted the prolific Green River killer, Gary Ridgway, had the bed-wetting problem, too. Growing up, he experienced demeaning ritual genital cleansing at the hands of his mother. Many sexual deviants reported they suffered punishment for bed-wetting. In both Ridgway and Bar-Jonah, childhood violence against them for bed-wetting may have skewed normal development resulting in abnormal sexual imprinting requiring violence to reach orgasm.

Bed-wetting (enuresis) is an involuntary behavior that is embarrassing to a child and frustrating to parents. It may be due to inadequate neurological connections between the immature brain and a full bladder signal, something the child cannot control. The cause is unknown, but experts agree children should not be spanked for bed-wetting.

Similar to other sexual predators, David had low self esteem and no love from his father, only beatings. Beatings he submitted to for problems he couldn't control. Nothing David did was good enough for Phil. Like his babysitters, David hid from the man, isolating himself in his bedroom or the garage to avoid his father's wrath.

At the time of his birth, David's siblings, Lois and Bob were much older. At ages eight and nine, there was little camaraderie and no indication they protected their little brother from Phil's beatings. David's escalating frustration erupted in violent outbursts. When playing with a small neighbor girl his age, he flew into a rage over an Ouija board. David attacked and choked her. Tyra heard the commotion and came running. The obese volatile six-year-old experienced the thrill of overpowering his playmate. After that incident, Tyra told her friends, "I don't know how to control him."

When David later described the incident, he smiled, savoring the story, "Mother screamed over and over for me to stop. She might have screamed twenty times before I let the girl loose."

On David's personal record of victims, he listed this little girl as number one.

A U.S. Department of Justice bulletin noted most serious and chronic offenders show signs of abnormal and violent behavior as early as preschool age. David learned thrusting the humiliation and pain he endured at the hands of his father onto smaller children provided a feeling of power and relief. As with other sexual deviants, bullying younger children became his pattern.

After the financially strapped family returned to Massachusetts, Tyra took David to programs at the Assembly of God Church. There he found friends and later became a youth leader in charge of younger boys. Like other pedophiles who enjoy the company of young children, David began seeking positions in control of children. At home, he was powerless. At church, David was in charge.

David's mother enrolled him in "Park Ave" elementary. The single-story sprawling brick structure sits in a lush neighborhood where large trees form a canopy over the street. A second-grade classmate described David as "chubby and odd," and without friends. Even as a seven-year-old, his appearance and behavior brought attention and unhappiness to him. As David's abduction patterns matured, the Park Ave neighborhood and other elementary schools became successful hunting grounds.

As soon as his siblings could leave home, they did, abandoning David to their father's harsh treatment. When Phil was no longer able to work because of a bad heart, Tyra took a job and left David with Phil's undivided attention.

In FBI interviews with convicted sex offenders many of them reported growing up in violent households. Throughout childhood, David's world was not safe. He was stressed and fearful except in his bedroom or in the garage where, in isolation, he found solace.

Like other pedophiles, he collected toys and learned his toy collection brought children to him. At the neighborhood garage sales, David purchased games and toys to sell at his own garage for profit. He enjoyed both the company of children and the extra money.

Because his siblings were so much older, David was like an only child. At age seven, his doting mother began teaching him to cook. Rejected and beaten by Phil, David found comfort in the kitchen with Tyra. With continued bed-wetting and his weight ballooning, David isolated himself more and more. In the safety of his room, he began copying long lists of names from telephone directories. Tyra noted David also began hoarding recipes and food. Compulsive behaviors continued throughout his life.

Obsessive Compulsive Disorder (OCD) exists in one percent of the general population and half of these are considered severe. Many people suffer from compulsions such as a need to be orderly, but when taken to extremes, ritual collecting, and repetitive behaviors disrupt lives. Like an addiction, they can't stop. With pedophiles, some compulsions appear more ominous than frequent hand washing. They collect pictures—sometimes explicit photos of adults in sexual contact with children. They often photograph themselves with children, clothed or unclothed, then organize and tediously log photos of children who fit the age and sex of the child in their erotic fantasies. Some purchase the photos or download them from the Internet, but because child pornography is illegal and prison sentences are stiff, pedophiles try desperately to hide their secrets and protect their collections. If you identify inappropriate photographs or computer images, this ominous behavior must be reported.

While looking at pictures or souvenirs they've kept, pedophiles relive encounters with children they molested. Years later, when the victimized child is an adult, the photo remains a treasure because it captured the child at the pedophile's desired age and the photo refreshes erotic feelings.

The face and memories are locked in time. For David, treasured collections filled the void of human interactions and the photos fueled secret fantasies.

When David was eight years old his family moved to nearby Webster. In this scenic neighborhood on the shores of Lake Webster his sexual aberrations and violence matured. To most, the neighborhood looked serene but like its unpronounceable Indian name there was a clear message in its interpretation: "The Boundary Fishing Place-Neutral Meeting Ground" or "You fish on your side, I'll fish on mine and nobody fishes in the middle."

The same uneasy truce existed in the neighborhood of Bonnette Acres from the time the Browns moved there. Wildflowers and bushes covered vacant lots near the Brown's white one-story home on Elaine Street. Colorful rhododendrons bloomed along the house and large trees shaded the swimming pool at the back of the house where David played alone. The location was a magnificent improvement from their previous residence, but from the start an undercurrent of turmoil churned beneath the peaceful surface.

Neighborhood feuds occurred and continued for years. If a ball strayed into the Brown's yard, Phil snatched and kept it. He threatened both kids and dogs who entered their yard. Even though the Browns lived next door to the Duponts for years, brothers Kevin and Alan only remember being invited inside the Brown's house once. On that visit, they watched home movies under Phil's threatening glare, an experience so uncomfortable the boys never returned. Kevin and Alan recalled Phil had ordered them to stay out of the kitchen. They remembered thinking it was an odd demand, certainly not like in their home with many other siblings. News about Phil's unwelcome treatment spread through the neighborhood.

Maybe his thin small-stature father was trying to control David's eating by placing the kitchen off limits. The strange command is something David carried to adulthood. He also forbade people to enter the kitchen in his apartment in Montana. But then it wasn't to keep them from eating his food. In his case, the curtain over the doorway hid a sinister rope dangling from the ceiling over a pulley.

David's joy in eating added to his weight and his problems. When kids called him names, his mother told him, "Do God's will, David. Turn the other cheek."

David's only friends were imaginary.

When the Duponts' beloved white poodle named Snow was poisoned and died in the arms of Kevin and Alan's mother, they all suspected David. The grieving family buried the little dog in a corner of their backyard. A few days later, they were shocked to find the grave disturbed and Snow's corpse missing.

Cruelty to animals is an early step in progression to violence against humans. Like Jeffrey Dahmer, a sexual predator cannibal who kidnapped and drugged young men before killing them, many violent predators began by killing and dissecting animals.

If a child shows violence against animals, early intervention and a full psychological evaluation might interrupt the journey to violence against humans.

David vehemently denied knowing anything about Snow's death and disappearance. His lies were convincing. With practice, David became adept at lying. Through the years, lying worked well. He covered his trails with lies.

After more squabbles with the Browns, the Duponts returned home one day to find their beautiful row of property-line pine trees disfigured. On the Dupont side the trees were bushy, but on the Brown side it looked as if they'd been cut straight down the middle. Phil had chopped all the limbs off flush with the trunk. Like David, the trees bore permanent scars. But David defended Phil. He explained, "If he did it, he probably wanted to make them healthier or keep them from dropping debris into our yard. Besides, my father didn't like the Duponts. He called them 'white trash.'"

After that incident, Mrs. Dupont marched straight to a lawyer but received no satisfaction. The lawyer told her a lawsuit would likely accelerate conflict. After he recommended no action, she had a tall stockade fence constructed to keep peace and physically separate the families.

As David grew older and taller, he became so obese his weight interfered with any sport he tried. A victim of ridicule, he avoided kids his age and began hanging around with boys much younger.

Unhappy at home, his self-esteem already low, teasing made David feel worse and eat more. At age ten and still bed-wetting, he was almost as big as Phil. In spite of his size, the demeaning spankings continued. Tyra didn't intervene. Instead, she comforted David and involved him in more church activities. Each summer, she sent him away to the Charlton church camp. Year after year, David camped with other children and became intimately familiar with this wooded area. A child on his victim list attended the same church camp.

From camp, David wrote letters to small neighborhood boys asking them to play with him when he returned. It was there in the dark forest where he later brought two kidnapped boys and tried to kill them. (Chapter 3)

Tyra maintained a close relationship with her own family and was active in the fundamentalist Assembly of God Church located near their home just across the Massachusetts state line in Putnam, Connecticut. Tyra was later instrumental in starting an Assembly of God Church in Webster. The religious woman instilled strict church tenets in David: no dancing, no dating, especially no contact with girls in the family's swimming pool where David often floated in the cool water talking to himself.

Fat and ridiculed, he tried to suppress his turmoil. He isolated himself and focused on his collections, but like the mirror-calm lake where storms sometimes blew up crashing tumultuous waves ashore, emotions ripped through the Brown household.

The Duponts said David was on his best behavior when Tyra had summertime church picnics in their front yard. The boys said it looked like a carnival with David barbecuing hot dogs and entertaining church children. In the garage, he devised games such as balloons with little prizes inside to pop. It was in this garage, playing with imaginary friends that his fantasies turned violent.

After the singing and prayers were over, after dark, David learned a different side of life. He sneaked down the street to the Webster Academy where he interacted with violent antisocial boys housed there under court order. His parents didn't know he visited the Academy, but David was so traumatized physically and emotionally at home that he needed an escape. In his eyes, Academy boys treated him better than the neighborhood children. There he found camaraderie and learned more about sex.

The Academy burned to the ground. The Brightwood Academy built in its place burned, too. No one knew how the suspicious fires started. Setting fires in youth correlates with adult crimes. Many serial killers have a history of the triad of animal torture, bed-wetting and fire-starting. There is no record of David starting fires but he learned other behaviors from the incorrigible boys.

Like many kids, David had fears. Intense fears and exhausting nightmares of man-eating fish in pursuit and visions of shocking electric beds occurred over years. Terrified of fish, David refused to swim in Lake Webster with neighborhood children.

Children who lived in the area played in deserted Quonset huts near swampland on the east end of Elaine Street, but they didn't venture into the swamp. Like David, they feared quicksand would swallow them without a trace. Yet, they didn't fear the dead or ghosts in a cemetery at the other end of Elaine where they played. In the summer, children took short cuts through the cemetery to a little store to buy candy. Sometimes David went with them. Alan and Kevin

Dupont recalled David talking about his Tutti-Frutti eyes as he walked along munching Good and Plenty and Tutti-Frutti candy.

In winter months, children careened on sleds through adjacent wooded slopes and down Cemetery Road. While sledding near the cemetery, David was only ten when he lured a five-year-old boy half his size into the woods away from the boy's sister and other children to urinate. The shocked preschooler experienced violence and fear which lasted a lifetime when David suddenly threw him onto his little sled and pinned him down. David sat on the child's chest. He couldn't breathe, couldn't scream and couldn't move. David exposed himself and thrust his penis into the child's mouth––then threatened him not to tell.

He didn't tell.

That same winter just before David turned eleven, he suffered a serious injury while sledding on a make-shift sled made from a piece of slick aluminum sheeting. With the edges curled up, it worked well until he struck a rock that spun him around. The metal gouged a large chunk of muscle and skin from his thigh. The wound bled profusely after nearly cutting through to his femoral artery.

Hospitalized for treatment, David said, "They forcefully held me down" for painful debridement, surgical closure and skin grafting. When David was recovering, his father tried to spank him. David recalled this as the only time Tyra stopped Phil. "She didn't want the wound to break open."

Beatings at home combined with the painful hospital bondage experience likely embedded a strange twist in his young psyche. The injury left a large, excavated defect extending across much of his upper right thigh and into the groin. Like his eyes, the scar was a constant reminder of torture and disfigurement.

After the injury healed, David knocked on doors and displayed the ugly scar near his genitals to startled neighbors. The scar bothered him physically and psychologically throughout his life. He asked young victims to rub it because it provided sexual stimulation. Years later, David told a counselor that he sometimes experienced severe pain in the scar and, "When the pain gets too bad, I sort of step aside and watch myself behave violently." This description suggests a dissociative disorder which removed him mentally from some situation. Dissociation sometimes occurs in individuals after a life-threatening trauma, rape or in child abuse and is thought to be a defense mechanism.

The graveyard had never scared the Dupont brothers until one day while playing there the boys found a stash of detective magazines filled with gory sexually explicit pictures. The stories of violence and death frighten them so much they avoided the cemetery after that. The brothers wondered who left the magazines. They thought it might have been boys from the Webster Academy, but knew the boys weren't free to mingle with local kids.

David denied ever seeing detective magazines. If he did read them, it could have been a step toward imprinting aberrant sexual behavior and violence on his young mind. Sexual predators reported to FBI researchers their fantasies became more twisted after seeing violent pictures and reading true detective stories.

David's childhood left him physically and emotionally scarred. He was fat, disfigured, had funny eyes, was physically abused by his father and taught unattainable codes of behavior by his mother. Ostracized by children his age, he isolated himself for peace and dreams. During this period, violent sexual fantasies grew. Along with masturbation, he later told counselors he experienced erections when he fantasized or acted violently. When he began molesting at age ten, he used force, fear and intimidation, all things he had personally experienced.

In his young brain, aggression and sex acts had fused.

Convicted sex offenders have reported a sense of failure and helplessness beginning at an early age. Many of them also have obvious physical traits or scars which decrease their self esteem. Fantasies helped them compensate.

David became preoccupied with violence, death and cannibalism. He enjoyed watching scary movies and savored the movie Psycho. Later, after reading about Patrick Wayne Kearney killing and dismembering gay men (the trash bag murders), David became fixated on killing. He also mentioned watching the movie Soylent Green (about cannibalism) and admitted imagining dissecting human bodies and tasting human flesh.

Former FBI profiler Roy Hazelwood describes sexual fantasy as "mental imagery of a desired event." Predators conjure up thoughts of things they want to do, acts that stimulate them sexually. They plan, and at an opportune time, they act. David harbored physical and emotional scars, but in a fantasy world he was king. There, the dreamer controls everything. Many people have fantasies, but few act on them.

David's early fantasies were precursors to his criminal behavior. Following a pattern seen in many sex offenders, fantasies can escalate into aggressive acts toward children of both genders. As sexual deviants experiment, they decide which gender and age is most stimulating. For David, it was ten-year-old boys who became his primary, though not exclusive, target. During this process, David bullied and intimidated children.

The psychiatric community has recognized bullying as a serious form of mistreatment. The victim is hurt by threats and harassment. Some bullies show a weapon, or through intimidation, force a child to do something he doesn't want to do. David's size alone was frightening. As with the little five-year-old boy he raped, all David had to do to control the child was sit on him. His weight became a weapon.

David molested the boy a second time. He observed him swinging in his yard alone and began swinging with him. Under David's weight, the swing broke. Angered, David threatened harm and forced the boy out of his mother's view. That time, David exposed himself and made the child touch his genitals.

The boy didn't tell his parents. Harboring shame and painful memories, anxiety followed him into adult years.

Practicing predators use fear, but they also use bribes, coercion, and kindness to gain the confidence of a target victim. This process of gaining the confidence of a child and parents through kindness and positive experiences is called grooming. As David matured in his deviancy, he fit the profile of a pedophile so well, it was as if he read behavioral studies and applied them. His fantasy schemes provided mental rehearsal of methods eventually used in abductions.

David claimed neighborhood boys frightened and humiliated him. In fact, many years after a described incident, David said he was "gang-raped" by a group of neighborhood boys. No one believes the story. He made it up to somehow justify his own behavior. His mother denied it happened. Some of the children he specifically named as perpetrators were as young as three years old at the time.

The Duponts have one vague recollection of boys holding David down and trying unsuccessfully to nail his clothing to an asphalt roadway.

David was too large and powerful. He got away.

"The kids in my neighborhood were cruel and racist," David exclaimed.

In a police interview, Tyra and his sister Lois disagreed. They described the area as a "white neighborhood, very white," and recalled no racial incidents.

David's violence and sexual practices began at an early age, earlier than he admitted. After a sixth-grade girl told him about sex, he wondered why his parents hadn't told him. Many years later, David told a counselor, he had witnessed peers masturbating and performing fellatio at the Webster Academy. Although he claimed he started masturbating at twelve, the twice molested five-year-old reported his first assault occurred two years prior to David's twelfth birth date.

How is the diagnosis of "Child Molester" made? *The Diagnostic and Statistical Manual of Mental Disorders, Fourth Edition, Text Revision (DSM-IV-TR)* is a frequently updated communication device which isn't perfect, but it provides a method communication for practitioners using agreed upon definitions. It lists three criteria to meet the legal definition of *Pedophilia: 1) Recurrent, intense, sexually arousing fantasies, sexual urges, or behaviors involving sexual activity with a prepubescent child or children (generally under age 13 or younger); 2) The person acts on the sexual urges, or the urges or fantasies cause marked distress or interpersonal difficulty; 3) The person is at least 16 years-of-age and at least five years older than the child or children in 1).*

In 1972, David attended Bartlett High School where he became involved in the photo club, taking action shots of athletes. David also worked on the school yearbook. These volunteer jobs placed him in close proximity to kids in sports. In his collection of yearbooks, detectives identified pictures of children David had molested. The pictures were labeled with the wrong names.

With little family income, David delivered newspapers and mowed lawns to earn money. His first real job washing dishes in the Bartlett cafeteria ended when he transferred to the new Bay Path Regional Vocational Technical High School in Charlton.

Built on the top of Muggett Hill Road, the modern school had a three-hundred-sixty-degree view of the surrounding wooded New England countryside. On this scenic piece of real estate, the large progressive school offered broad educational options for students from a seven-town area.

Bay Path provided educational opportunities to learn marketable skills for positions in the student's occupation of choice. Automobile mechanic, data processing, air conditioning and food services were among the trades offered. David decided to take data processing and math. With his fondness for food and cooking, he also learned skills in food services and became a member of DECA, the Distributive Education Club of America.

At Bay Path, DECA provided an avenue to improve career opportunities in food marketing, retail sales and management in food services. There, students received practical experience by operating a school store selling products made by students.

DECA instructor Olaf Garcia recalled, "David was like any other student. He acted normal but was a day dreamer. He was not shy, but he was not extroverted either." Garcia explained, "Culinary classes would bake cookies, and we would sell them. David did his share of the work and handled customers appropriately. There were serious problems with other students stealing money and not participating in class. But not David, he didn't get into trouble. He interacted with other students and answered questions in class. The way David talked and acted revealed nothing out of the ordinary."

Garcia further added, "David could take a joke. He was agreeable, calm and never angry. I would kid him about his weight and caution him against eating too many cookies. David would smile and forget it."

Classmates called him "Brownie," a nickname he didn't seem to mind.

A female classmate remembered David occasionally went on outings with the rest of the class. "He had no dates with girls, but he liked different girls, more as good friends." The group sometimes went to Riverside Amusement Park together. She said, "David would get a kick out of chasing girls. He liked to hear them scream."

Although finances at the Brown's were limited, David always seemed to have enough money. Sloppy jeans and T-shirts were common garb at Bay Path but David dressed in nice shirts and slacks with his hair trimmed short. A former classmate noted David looked different because he was overweight and at sixteen, always carried a briefcase clutched to his chest. "No one else carried a briefcase...If he didn't have the briefcase, it wouldn't have been David."

One classmate who said David got along well with other class members also recounted, "He didn't socialize much, but was always ready to help someone. For example, if someone forgot lunch money, he was quick to come to their assistance."

One morning in 1973, when Dupont brothers Kevin and Alan, ages nine and ten, were home from school recovering from having their tonsils removed, they walked outside to find someone had written on their sidewalk. In fluorescent green and orange chalk, messages led them along the sidewalk from the front of their house to the mailbox at the street. The messages promised: "Something good will happen to you. ...Surprise!"

The excited boys found an unsigned letter in their mailbox addressed to them. Like a ransom note one might see in a detective magazine, the words had been cut from magazines and pasted on the paper. "Meet me in the Cemetery at dark," the letter invited, "I will give you $20 a piece. Something nice will happen. Don't tell your parents."

The neighborhood cemetery dated back to a founding family who settled on the shores of Lake Webster. The almost undetectable cemetery entrance was hidden from nearby roads and homes by dense brush, large oaks and evergreens. Once past the overgrown path, the area opened and revealed weathered tombstones tilted over old sunken graves bordered by twisted iron fences. A sense of Gothic decay and foreboding permeated the site, a frightening place for children alone after dark.

After Alan and Kevin found the scary detective magazines, they had stayed away even in daylight.

When the boys showed their mother the letter, she called Webster police. Officers came to the home. They wanted Alan and Kevin to go to the cemetery and meet the anonymous person. Mrs. Dupont refused. She did not want her children at risk so kept them safely at home while police staked out the cemetery.

On the designated night, flashlight in hand, David made his way among shadowed tombstones to the appointed headstone and waited. In an ironic twist that Alfred Hitchcock might have conceived, David Brown had his first encounter with police in the Bates Family Cemetery where a fifteen-foot gray cement obelisk dominates the tiny cemetery and proclaims the family name.

Instead of meeting Kevin and Alan, David found himself surrounded by the law.

David surrendered peacefully and police ushered him home.

Later that night, with a tearful Tyra Brown in tow, officers knocked on the Duponts' front door. Tyra begged Mrs. Dupont, "You have children. You know how you feel about them. Please give mine a chance." She explained, "My husband is ill, and I don't want to upset him."

Mrs. Dupont was furious. She wanted something done about David but relented when Tyra assured her that she would see that David received counseling.

The next morning there was a knock on the Duponts' front door. The boys' small-stature mother was face to face with two-hundred-fifty-pound David. She froze. Frightened by his size and now his behavior, she barely opened the door.

David appeared to have come in peace. He was carrying a bouquet of wildflowers he had picked for her. He thrust them forward.

She asked in disbelief, "David, what are you doing here?"

He stared at her, then said, "I want the boys to go to the beach with us. We are going to Misquamicut, Rhode Island, to the ocean."

She said, "No. The boys can't go." Even with both parents along, Mrs. Dupont feared for her sons' safety.

David responded, "Well, then, can they swim in the pool in my yard with me?" He reassured her, "I won't let anyone else in with us."

She said, "No. The boys can't be with you."

He stood there, silent, staring at her; then he said menacingly, "You know what they say when you have two different colored eyes. It means something is wrong with you. You know, people with different colored eyes are crazy."

She closed the door and locked it.

The Bates Cemetery episode occurred several months after David began attending Bay Path. Classmates and his DECA teacher recalled nothing of the incident. A female classmate pointed out, "If David had a problem he could have gone to Mr. Garcia. Mr. Garcia was easy to talk to, a good teacher, supportive to his students." It was incomprehensible to her that David couldn't have gotten help if he needed it. She said, "He was fine, normal. He didn't seem to have any problems."

On the surface, predators often lead respectable lives. They can live next door and hold professional positions without raising suspicion. If they're subtle and keep desires hidden, they remain undetected for years. David was capable of normal behavior despite his deep-seated problems.

During teen years and in despair, David took long walks in the woods by himself. When he began driving, he would drive for hours and sometimes "wake up" not knowing where he'd been. Long before he was old enough for a driver's license, police records show they stopped him for speeding while driving at night.

David's nocturnal rides calmed his nerves as he trolled for victims. During this period, a number of child abductions occurred in broad daylight near his home.

The Connecticut State line cut along Elaine Street. The Browns lived on the Massachusetts side of the street but just walking across the street put them into the other state. The location caused overlapping police jurisdictions. Years later, Detective Norm Nault of the Connecticut State Police Eastern District Major Crime Squad worked on cold cases including unsolved crimes near the Massachusetts/Connecticut border. Following David's arrest, years after he had left the area, Detective Nault searched for information concerning the cold case disappearance of eight-year-old Janice Pockett. The abduction occurred on the afternoon of July 26, 1973, soon after the incident at the cemetery and just a few miles from David Brown's home.

No trace of Janice has ever been found.

Trooper Nault wondered if Brown could have been responsible for her disappearance.

Why would anyone suspect David of abducting a girl when most of his known molestation victims have been males? The answer is simple. In the process of settling on a particular victim type, every predator has to start somewhere.

On that summer day in 1973, blond, blue-eyed Janice Pockett left home in Tolland, CT, alone on her bicycle. Earlier that afternoon, Janice and her sister Mary had been playing along a road not far from home. Mary said Janice caught a beautiful butterfly. She placed it carefully under a rock for safe keeping until they were ready to return home. When the sisters arrived home, Janice remembered she'd left her butterfly behind and begged her mother to let her return to get it. Janice was seldom allowed to go anywhere by herself, but mother relented. With instructions to come right back, she let Janice go back alone.

Janice didn't return.

Hand in hand, Mary and their worried mother walked down the road looking for Janice. They found her abandoned bicycle in a wooded area not far from their house and rushed back home to report her missing.

The search for Janice began along Rhodes Road, just twenty miles from Webster. During the same time period and in the same area, police records show they stopped David half a dozen times for driving infractions.

Janice's sister Mary recalled her sad grandfather telling her, "Janice is gone."

Terrible emotional times for the family followed Janice's disappearance. Many years later, her loss remained a fresh wound. The family wants to know what happened. The knowledge would be a relief and ease their sorrow.

Less than a year after Janice's abduction, nine-year-old Mary Patrone was kidnapped in Woodstock, Massachusetts. On May 8, 1974, about four-thirty in the afternoon, Mary walked from a friend's house toward her own home a mile away, alone. Comfortable in the rural area surrounded by woods, she had frequently walked and ridden the route on her bicycle. That fateful afternoon, she recalled a car driving slowly past two or three times before stopping beside her. The man in the car said, "Hey, I work with your dad. Your mom wants you home for dinner. Hop in and I'll give you a ride."

Mary said later, "If mother said to be home, you'd better obey." Although Mary felt anxious, she got into the car with a stranger. Her fear accelerated when he quickly reached across in front of her bumping her face with his arm in the process of pressing the lock on the passenger side door. She recalled he wore a short-sleeved shirt and when his bare sweaty arm brushed her face, she hated being touched by him. They drove off, heading in the wrong direction.

As he drove to a turn-around near her friend's home, the man pointed and asked, "That's not your house, is it?"

She said, "No."

Based on that question, he must have been watching Mary and her friend but was confused about which home was hers. Mary remembered thinking he should know my house if he knows my father.

The man turned the car around and headed toward Mary's residence. Suddenly, he said, "Look!" and pointed out her window.

She turned to look, and she felt a sharp blow to her head.

Mary began crying and asked, "What did you do that for?"

He asked, "You okay?"

Mary felt something running down her face and neck. When she touched the area and looked at her hand, she screamed, "I'm bleeding!" (Mary said she made a big fuss and began screaming and crying.)

The blow caused a bloody scalp wound. When the abductor heard her screams and saw the red mess, he wanted her out of his car. He braked abruptly, threw open the passenger door and said, "Get out!" He shoved her out and drove off.

Fortunately, he had stopped near her home. Terrified, Mary ran inside. Her parents took her to the little hospital in Putnam for stitches. They summoned police and filed a report.

Mary's brutal ordeal was far from over. Her abduction occurred long before victims' rights were considered important and before Post-Traumatic Stress Disorder (PTSD) became a well-recognized condition. Back then, victims, even children, were expected to confront attackers face to face and identify them. This pattern of investigation forced victims to relive their terror in front of each suspect.

While being questioned, Mary recalled a "horse on the dash" of the car later identified as a possible light-colored Ford Pinto. She drew a picture of her attacker right after the incident. A police artist also created a composite drawing of the man.

Many years later following his arrest, Mary saw David Brown's high school graduation picture published in a newspaper. The photo sent a shock through her. With the image of his face forever imprinted in her memory, she instantly recognized him as her abductor. Both Mary's own drawing and the composite drawing done by a police artist show a remarkable resemblance to David's graduation picture. Mary still has her drawing and the memories that haunt her.

Without counseling help, Mary experienced elements of PTSD. She suffered anxiety attacks and lived in fear, afraid of passing cars and refused to ride home from babysitting jobs with a male driver. Now living in Connecticut and working as a parole officer, Mary deals with hundreds of people and reviews many criminal files and photos.

David was seventeen and in high school at Bay Path when Mary's abduction occurred. Was he experimenting to determine whether he preferred girls or boys? Was he trying out different techniques of abduction? If so, he learned two things: a blow to the head can be a bloody mess, and to knock someone out it takes more force than he had used. He needed better methods.

David said the Browns never owned a Ford. "My Dad hated them." He denied ever driving a Pinto or a Mustang. However, Phil worked on cars in his backyard. David acknowledged borrowing cars. Could he have used a car Phil was repairing for someone without his father's knowledge? Unfortunately, police reports from his stops in that era do not note the kind of car he was driving.

Just one month after Mary Patrone's abduction, in June 1974 David finished his junior year of high school and was home with his father. He thought Phil was asleep in his chair, but a closer look told David something was terribly wrong. He called an ambulance which rushed Phil to the small nearby Hubbard Regional Hospital.

Phil was dead on arrival.

Hysterical at her loss, Tyra accused neighborhood children of killing Phil. His death also traumatized David, leaving him unable to resolve the hatred he felt toward his father.

After his mother told him he was now the "man of the house," David suffered a major emotional crisis. Anger and grief boiled in his head. He exclaimed later he was not ready for that kind of responsibility.

As an adult, David rationalized some of the bad feelings from his traumatic childhood. Of his father, he said, "We butted heads a lot because we had the same personality. I only got four to five spankings that I really didn't deserve."

Even before Phil died the Browns had little income and David held garage sales to earn extra money. He said, "I worked for a crooked antique dealer who took me under his wing." From the man, he learned underhanded methods to make people believe they were getting merchandise older and more valuable than it was. Later in his career of selling collectibles, David developed a friendship with a knowledgeable woman who helped him learn the art of selling and setting up displays. He said, "She was the greatest teacher I ever had."

David learned to refinish furniture. He enjoyed the new skill and earned additional money, but it still wasn't enough to support him and Tyra. While he attended Bay Path, David also worked at McDonald's and hated it. His boss said he would never hire him back because he was a poor worker and other employees had to pick up his slack.

In the turmoil after Phil's death, David recalled a man, "...who befriended me like a father." Later, David felt betrayed after the man sold Tyra a car with serious mechanical problems. Money problems forced David and his mother to move from their home.

In a rage over all the injustices, his fantasy life of torture and revenge accelerated. From reports from his medical records, David found periodic relief associated with fantasies and sexual arousal, but it wasn't enough. On January 8, 1975, a cold winter morning during his senior year, instead of going to school, David took his mother's car and began driving, trolling for a victim. Dressed as a police officer, he planned the attack carefully–and brought a shovel.

Hunting for victims while driving is a behavior often reported by sexual predators. According to former FBI profiler John Douglas, predators in a prison survey said when inner stress became unbearable and fantasy built to a point they couldn't control it, they began hunting for desirable prey. They prowled. At an opportune time, they acted. That morning David followed the same pattern. Ready to explode from inner turmoil, he got behind the wheel and drove. Escalating personal problems fired in his brain. His emotions boiled. He needed relief and knew how to obtain it. That morning, he acted on his sexual fantasies to relieve the stress.

Large for his age and appearing much older, David had learned how to use his size. When wearing uniforms and carrying a fake badge, he enjoyed the appearance of an authority figure, a policeman. David had also learned to intimidate people by staring at them with his unusual frightening eyes.

He soon found an innocent, defenseless victim. Eight-year-old Richard O'Connor was on his way to Park Ave Elementary; the same school David had attended years earlier. Richard had missed school because of a sore throat and carried a note to the teacher explaining his recent absence. When he and a friend set out on their usual route to school, they'd cut behind another school and across some baseball fields to shorten the distance. When they were nearly to Park Ave School, Richard slipped on the ice and fell striking his face. His nose and face bloodied, he cried from the injury and returned home while his friend went on to school.

Richard's father consoled him, cleaned his young son's face and sent him back down the sidewalk toward school, this time alone.

Along Richard's route a parked car waited. Inside, the overweight officer rolled down the window. He called, "Hey you. I'm looking for a little boy running away from school."

Richard said, "I'm on my way to school."

The officer ordered him, "Get in the car! I'm taking you to the station."

Richard was afraid and didn't want to get in.

The officer scrambled out of the car, grabbed Richard by his jacket and shoved the youngster into the right front passenger seat and drove off.

Already frightened, Richard's fear accelerated when they drove past the police station. Richard didn't know where they were going.

The big man ordered the little boy, "Get down on the floor."

Richard ducked down out of sight for a while. He said, "We drove for a while, then pulled over by the lake at Memorial Beach." Then he began driving again. "He drove for a while, and then stopped in a wooded area."

Richard struggled to get away from the big man. "He dragged me into the back seat. He tried to strangle me. He choked me with his hands...He grabbed me by the throat and leaned on top of me. It was hard to breathe. I begged him, 'Please don't kill me.' He stopped but wrapped the seat belt around my neck, then drove some more and stopped the car again."

The "officer" ordered Richard to get out of the car and undress.

Richard recalled, "I thought he was going to kill me. He threw me on the ground and pulled a shovel out of the trunk. I lay on the frozen ground without clothes. He said, 'I can't keep you alive.' He stood over me, swinging the shovel back and forth...saying nothing, just swinging the shovel. I begged, 'Please don't kill me.' Finally, he stopped and put the shovel back in the trunk. He put me back in the car and wrapped the seat belt around my neck and tightened it again. I kept begging him, 'Please don't kill me.'"

Later, without an explanation, the abductor loosened the belt and ordered Richard, "Get dressed." Then he released Richard back on Whitcomb Street in his neighborhood. The abductor told Richard, "If you tell anyone, I'll come back, find you and kill you."

An old woman witnessed Richard get out of the car and was later able to identify the fake officer as David Brown.

With his shirt left in the woods, dressed only in pants, his winter coat and shoes without socks, Richard hurried home, crying. When his dad asked him what was wrong, he was afraid to tell him because of the abductor's threat. Instead, he said, "The nurse sent me home."

Richard's father peered at his little boy's face. His nose was bleeding badly; the whites of his eyes had hemorrhaged to a dark red. Red streaks and bruises circled his neck. His dad demanded the real story. Finally, Richard admitted what had happened and his father called the police. Richard's dad also called his wife at work and told her what had happened to their son.

Richard said, "She went hysterical and rushed home."

Officers came to their home to investigate the story. Richard required hospitalization at Hubbard Regional Hospital for the injuries he sustained from being choked. Broken blood vessels in his eyes and the deep bruises on his neck took weeks to heal. He had trouble talking because of throat swelling. There is no report of genital trauma, but Richard had very likely been choked to unconsciousness, stripped of his clothes and molested. The man had warned Richard that he would kill him if he told.

He told.

Richard feared for his life.

Police found David Brown and arrested him. At the police station, officers forced young Richard to face the monster.

Dressed in a disguise, the abductor wore a western outfit with a cowboy hat, but there was no doubt. Richard couldn't forget David's face. He said, "I'm sure that's him."

David Brown said coldly, "I've never seen him before in my life." As before, David lied, but he was ultimately charged with assault and battery.

Later, when Richard and his mother were eating at McDonald's, he looked out the window and was shocked to see his abductor in close proximity emptying the garbage. Richard had believed David was in jail and unable to hurt him, that he was safe. Instead, Richard sat a few feet from the man who had nearly killed him. He was so frightened he couldn't speak.

After Richard's abduction, the judge ordered a psychiatric and medical evaluation of David Brown. On March 25, 1975, David entered Harrington Memorial Hospital in Southbridge where a psychiatrist determined he had above average intelligence and no evidence of organic brain disease to account for criminal behavior. Further, there was no trace of a psychiatric disorder.

After initially denying the entire incident, David recanted and stated, "I was on my way to school passing Park Ave School. I must have blacked out. I think I tried to strangle him because he reminded me of a mechanic that ripped off my mother and me... The guy befriended me like a father, and then sold us a defective car."

Because David reported amnesia for the abduction, he was admitted to St. Vincent Hospital on April 4, where he had extensive psychological and medical evaluations. Tests included laboratory studies, x-rays, a brain-wave test for seizures and a CAT scan of his brain. All the tests were normal.

Two consulting psychiatrists supported the theory that David actually remembered everything he had done but was unable to admit it. He lied. He denied remembering the abduction, yet incongruously, he gave details of the abduction to police.

The psychiatrists recommended counseling to help him learn to express anger in a non-violent way and work through some of his feelings. David resisted therapy. He refused to cooperate and said he had nothing to discuss. Discharged with the diagnosis: hysterical neurosis, amnesic type, he had feigned amnesia and it worked.

Later David used the same defense of denial and "blackout spells" when confronted with his criminal actions.

At sentencing, David appeared at the Dudley County Court House with his mother and sister. There, he sat passively with them at his side while his victim, Richard O'Connor watched. Richard still has a vivid memory of the diminutive Tyra next to her huge son. She calmly patted David's shoulder and repeatedly reassured him, "Don't worry, David. God is with you."

For the serious crime of kidnapping and aggravated assault, David received one-year probation. This light sentence did not deter David Paul Brown. He had already embarked on a path that would shatter many lives in years to come by abducting and choking little boys while impersonating a law officer.

Haunted by his ordeal, Richard O'Connor said: "I can still see the look in his eyes as he stared at me. It's a look I will never forget as long as I live."

Chapter 2 Failure and Fantasy

Years of rejection, rage, and poor self-esteem overwhelmed David Brown. The serious juvenile offense didn't make the news. His high school classmates reported he attended school as though nothing had happened. They had no idea he was on probation for assault on a child. When he graduated from Bay Path in June 1975, his senior picture showed a good-looking young man with a half smile. He exchanged photos with classmates. On the back of one photo, he wrote: "To Karen* with love...to a real good friend...good luck forever. Love, David."

That fall, David attended Northeast Bible College in Green Lane, Pennsylvania. There he studied Christian education with a ministerial minor. One of the requirements for this college was to do outreach work with hapless people surviving in flophouses in the Bowery of New York. David spoke favorably about some experiences in New York, but he said he wasn't ready for college. He believed immaturity and distress over his childhood, coupled with his father's death, made it difficult for him to concentrate. School did not go well.

That same year, police stopped him in a roadblock near Sturbridge along I-84, not far from his mother's home. They were looking for someone involved in the abduction and murder of teenager Kathleen Terry. David told officers he "traveled all over." They thought he was squirmy and some of his responses were so bizarre, they were suspicious he might be the abductor.

Officers obtained a search warrant but found nothing tied him to the crime. The murder remained unsolved until years later when the perpetrator confessed to his mother on his deathbed and then, just before she died, she told authorities what her son had done.

On December 1, 1975, seven-year-old Patty Vassar from Putnam, Connecticut, was abducted from the roadway along Murphy Hill in a location a few miles from the Brown's residence on Elaine Street in Webster. David was very familiar with the Putnam area because he traveled to the Putnam Assembly of God for church services.

Patty had stayed after school to help one of the nuns with a project. En route home, she walked alone. Only a mile from home, a man driving what she believed was a yellow Ford Pinto pulled over and stopped beside her. Like Mary Patrone's case, the man told Patty her mother sent him to give her a ride home. It worked before, and it worked this time, too. Only now it had a new twist, the passenger side door didn't work.

The man got out of his car and told Patty she'd have to get in on the driver's side and slide across because he couldn't open the passenger door. She realized later, with the door nonfunctional, she couldn't escape.

Other abductors have disabled passenger doors. Ted Bundy, the serial rapist and murderer put to death by electric chair in Florida, used the same slick technique. He removed the interior door handle to trap victims.

Patty's abduction occurred in Connecticut a few miles south of the Massachusetts line. When he dumped her near Palmer Road and Route 29 in Sturbridge, Massachusetts, he opened the passenger door and dragged her out the same door he'd said was broken. Patty didn't know what happened after getting into the car, or what he did to her. It was as if she'd fallen asleep. Her only memory in the car was a horse emblem and that he left her on a dead-end road in the winter. Her wet dirty coat looked like she had fallen down and the bottom had dragged the street as the car traveled along. Her amnesia may be a protective dissociative mechanism for the traumatic abduction.

Three young girls abducted in this area, Patty Vassar, Mary Patrone and Janice Pockett, were about the same age and all looked alike with their strawberry blonde hair in the same boyish style with straight bangs. Patty Vassar and Mary Patrone know each other. They believe the same man abducted them. They realize how lucky they are because like Janice Pockett, they might have been murdered and never found.

After their abductions, both Patty and Mary remained fearful. Afraid to trust anyone, frightened by strangers and passing cars, afraid of things they had never feared.

In all, the recently cited cases involving Richard O'Connor, Patty Vassar, Mary Patrone and Janice Pockett, a pattern is evident. They are all of similar age and size, but most important of all, they walked alone. Predators do not want to be caught and the most vulnerable victim is an unaccompanied child. These abductions were all stranger abductions, but most pedophiles evolve to rape children they know. In

David's travels, he may have been watching these children, watching their activities, waiting for the time to attack. Because most abducted children are alone at the time of abduction, one important safety measure is to never allow a child to walk or bicycle alone.

While deciding where their real interests lie, sexual predators tend to sample ages and genders. David had almost no experience with girls his own age. It had been drilled into him in church and at home that being close to a girl, even in a swimming pool, was sinful and not allowed by church doctrine. His only heterosexual contact was a prom date. He said they had "necked," and he found her "compassionate and gentle."

The girl's mother didn't like David and put an end to their relationship.

David said, "In Bible College, the ministers scared the hell out of me. They said the only reason girls would go there (to the Bible College) was to marry a minister, and I didn't want to get married."

During his first year of college, David became a youth group leader for the Assembly of God Royal Rangers. The group is the equivalent of Christian boy scouts. To become a leader, David had to study and pass written tests. Royal Ranger leadership courses required both religious training and camping skills.

Study booklets for Royal Rangers dated December 1975 asked test questions that required little thinking. David's simplistic answers revealed minimal effort. When the minister tried to block him from becoming a leader, he was greatly distressed. Ultimately David met the requirements. He worked his way through levels of increasing responsibility starting with "Trail Blazer" and finally advanced to "Lt. Commander of the Buckaroos."

As in Boy Scouts, Royal Rangers earned recognition badges and patches for achievements. For David, reaching Lt. Commander placed him in charge of groups of boys. With easy access to the children and in a position of authority he could manipulate, intimidate and abuse with the power of the Church behind him.

While enrolled in college, David wrote a letter to victim Richard O'Connor's mother, apologizing for attacking Richard. David included religious pamphlets in the letter and claimed he'd changed.

Still furious for what he had done to her son, Mrs. O'Connor wrote back.

David said, "From the tone of her letter, I'm glad the days of the Inquisition are over or she would have had me tortured...or beheaded."

David hated Bible College and quit after one year. He tried different jobs, but in the end, moved back with his mother.

The following year, David enrolled in another strict religious college, the Tabernacle Bible Institute located in Florence, South Carolina. He had to support himself and grueling course requirements led to failure.

Although he had no musical skills, he tried his luck at selling pianos and keyboards. He made no sales. The challenging curriculum and conservative teachings of the Institute were too much for him. Unsuccessful at both work and college, after one semester, David returned home and moved back in with Tyra.

In September of that year, he attended a four-day advanced training course for Royal Ranger leaders at Camp Sherbourne in Mountainview, New York. He never talked about the course or said anything unusual happened, but something fueled his fantasies and triggered a rampage.

Chapter 3 Kidnapping and Attempted Murder

After an evening movie at White City Cinemas in Shrewsbury, Massachusetts, Alan Enrikaitis and Billy Benoit decided to walk home rather than wait for a ride with Alan's mother. That decision nearly cost the teens their lives.

Regina Enrikaitis arrived at the Cinema just after the movie ended about ten p.m. Alan was gone. One of his friends told her he'd decided to walk home with another boy. Regina hated having her son out after dark. She searched for the boys en route to their nearby home and didn't see them. Regina waited and worried.

Billy Benoit's frantic parents waited for their son, too. It wasn't like him to be late. At midnight, they could wait no longer. William Benoit Sr. called the Shrewsbury Police and reported his son missing. Officer Lizotte did his best to reassure the anxious father. He said kids often fail to do what they said they'd do and then turn up unharmed. He encouraged Mr. Benoit to be patient.

A few minutes after Mr. Benoit's call, Regina telephoned Shrewsbury Police and spoke with the same officer. With two boys missing from the same location for more than two hours, the officer broadcast a "failure to locate" radio bulletin to local law enforcement. By that time, the two small fair-haired boys who appeared younger than their ages were in handcuffs, riding in a car miles away driven by a man dressed as a police officer.

At 12:40 a.m., police received an alarming call from a home near the Assembly of God Church Camp in rural Charlton, Massachusetts. The caller reported a frightened youth in handcuffs had come to his door. The boy said he and his friend had been abducted and he thought his friend might be dead.

Charlton Patrolmen Donald Stearns and Paul Christenson, and Detective Sgt. Ronald Denault found Alan Enrikaitis with his face swollen from being struck repeatedly. Bruising finger marks ringed his neck. Alan told them a man had tried to kill him. He'd managed to escape but had left his friend behind. Police removed Alan's handcuffs, and then quickly put him in a cruiser to help locate Billy. Alan directed them to the area about half a mile away along a dirt road. Police swept a bright spotlight, scanning dark woods.

Alan spotted a dark green Plymouth with a white hard top. He exclaimed, "That's the guy!"

Strobes and sirens pierced the darkness. The Plymouth took off with police in pursuit and swung erratically onto Gould Road. After about one-half mile, it careened right onto Cemetery Road where the vehicle plunged into the brush and came to a stop.

According to Alan, Officer Stearns "ripped him [David Brown] out of the car." While handcuffing Brown, Stearns heard muffled cries coming from the locked trunk. Stearns pulled keys from Brown's pocket and opened the trunk. Still in handcuffs, Billy needed help to climb out.

In the glow of automobile headlights, officers surveyed Billy's injuries: Face swollen, his nose bloody and neck marred with purple choke marks like Alan's.

After reinforcements arrived, Trooper Stephen Bennett transported Brown to Sturbridge State Police Barracks. At 3:05 a.m. on September 24, 1977, David Paul Brown waived his Miranda Rights. He said he understood that anything he said could be used against him in court. Although Brown had the right to remain silent, he voluntarily gave police a written statement. He also told them about a previous incident; at age seventeen he had abducted and choked a child [Richard O'Connor]. Police found a speeding ticket but no record of the abduction, probably a sealed juvenile record.

In the presence of three officers, Trooper Bennett, and the two officers from the Charlton Police Department, Brown confessed. He said he'd abducted Alan and Billy and tried to kill them.

In his statement, Brown said he offered the boys a ride home from the theater. Once inside his car, he handcuffed and imprisoned them. He described a strange scene: "At Bev's Flea Market all three of us went into a tent I had put up three hours before. The boys sat down and asked to have their handcuffs removed."

Surprisingly, he took them off.

"The larger boy [Billy] began asking questions like, 'When are we going home? Why are we here? When are you going to let us go?' Stuff like that. I said, 'In a little while or so.' Then I stated...not really meaning it, 'If you want to go home bad enough, take your clothes off.'"

The boys refused.

He cuffed them again, herded them back into the car and started driving. He drove to Route 20, down Cemetery Road and along dirt roads, into the church campground he knew so well. Brown said the boys were frightened and crying as they drove into the Charlton woods.

David knew the boys could identify him. When he had abducted Richard O'Connor three years earlier, he'd made that mistake. Richard had fingered him and it cost him a year's parole and the anguish of being caught and forced into all those tests. He didn't want that to happen again. The law wouldn't be as easy on him this time so he decided to kill Alan and Billy to keep from getting caught.

David carried a large green canvas bag in the car and had tried to get one of the boys to climb into the bag. Neither of them would do it. David had an alternate plan.

"I took the smaller boy [Alan] into the woods. I started to strangle him. I guess mainly because he could identify me, and I wanted to kill him.

"I started strangling the boy and after three or four seconds, he went limp. I assumed he was dead. I went back and got the larger boy out of the car and started strangling him."

David then explained, "I stopped strangling him because I realized the stupidity of what I was doing..." With Billy in the trunk, David said he walked back down the dark road to find Alan and help him, supposedly planning to take the boys back to Shrewsbury. With Alan gone, David panicked. He realized if he couldn't find Alan, he'd be caught. His mother, family and church would learn his ugly secrets. He found a flashlight and searched furiously for Alan.

David said when he saw the police car coming down the road with a search light probing the darkness he jumped into the Plymouth and tried to escape. After the strobes and siren flipped on, he drove faster and lost control. This area of dense forests and numerous small lakes had once been a refuge for him. As a youth, he had stayed at the same church campground located not far from a small body of water named Wee Laddie Pond.

After Alan and Billy were reunited with their parents, they gave detailed written statements which correlated with David's.

Alan Enrikaitis told police that after the movie he saw Brown's green and white car drive into the parking lot. "He showed a badge going by." Then he stopped and asked, "Do you wanna ride home?"

They decided to ride with him. Alan said, "We were going about 35 mph, then he slowed down and braked hard. The car skidded. Then he put cuffs on us as we slid under the dashboard.

The man said nothing.

Alan said, "We thought we were going to the Shrewsbury Police Department, and then he took a turn to the Shrewsbury Center. We took a lot of turns."

On a dark deserted dirt road, David stopped the car and dragged out a large green bag. He told the boys to get into it. After the boys refused, Alan opened the passenger door in an escape attempt, but David shoved him back inside, cracking Alan's head on the door frame in the process.

The boys begged to have the cuffs removed.

Alan said, "David talked funny, like a California guy." He claimed he wouldn't hurt them if they just got in the bag. There was no way they were going to do that.

Alan said, "I tried to open the door again, grabbing the handle but he reached over and hit the door lock ...We passed two Shrewsbury Police cars. I was going to jump out but I would have gotten hurt...We were driving all around...stopped at a tent. He took the cuffs off. We kept asking him questions, but he kept saying 'hush up.' Then he said, 'If you want to see your parents, take off your clothes.'"

Alan said, "No way." He then explained that David snapped the cuffs on and forced them back into the car. He started driving again, this time into a wooded area and stopped. "He told Billy to stay in the car. He took me outside and had his hand over my mouth, then my nose."

In a later taped police interview, Alan reported, "He dragged me down the trail. He put his arm around my neck and squeezed. He lifted me off the ground. I was panicking, almost ready to pass out. I couldn't breathe. I went limp and dropped to the ground and laid there. I played dead." Alan explained, "I used to play 'army' and we'd play dead. I think that helped me."

David then slapped him across the face, turned around and kicked him in the ribs, side and leg. All the while Alan tried not to breathe. David stood there for a while watching him. Then he held his hand over Alan's face to see if he was breathing. Leaving him for dead, David walked away and went back to the car for Billy.

Alan lay on the cold hard ground listening and holding his breath. He heard David walking away and was greatly relieved. The car door opened, and the interior vehicle light illuminated a small area of the forest. At that moment, Alan took off into the woods. He ran awkwardly with his hands cuffed behind his back. He turned and saw David near the car with a flashlight.

Suddenly, Billy's screams pierced the silence. Loud choking and gasping sounds silenced his screams. Alan was sure David had killed Billy and knew he had to get away to save his own life. Alan pressed his body into a depression behind some bushes when he saw David's flashlight beam coming down the road toward him. The beam repeatedly swung over his hiding place. Alan said, "It swooped the perimeter then he shut off the light and stood perfectly still. It seemed like a long time. Not a bird, cricket or owl made a noise. Every minute seemed like an hour. I tried not to breathe. Then I heard him go back to the car."

At that point, Alan took the opportunity to slink quietly away. Being nimble and small, he slid his cuffed hands under his body and stepped through them. With his hands then in front, it was much easier to walk. He walked as fast as he could, running at times until he found a paved road. When a car came along, thinking it might be the abductor Alan dived into the ditch and stayed out of sight until the car passed. Alan said, "Soon I saw the lights of a house with people visible in the picture window." He made his way to the house and knocked. "They let me in and called the police."

The residents gathered around him to hear what had happened. It was so weird, they wondered if it was true. They tried to comfort him and offered him a glass of milk. He had trouble holding it with cuffs on and found it difficult to swallow because of his injuries.

Although Billy's report was nearly identical, he included more details about the routes they had taken, including driving all the way to Worcester, Massachusetts. He said David tried a couple of times to trick the boys into climbing inside the big green bag. If they had complied without a fight, the outcome likely would have been fatal for both.

Police found the bag in the back seat of the car cluttered with boxes of flea market sales items. They located the hunting knife David had brandished, a State Police ID for Robert McDougal and a "Special Police" badge. David was charged with two counts of kidnapping, two counts of assault with intent to murder, two counts of indecent assault and battery on a child, impersonating a State Police Officer, two counts of assault and battery with a dangerous weapon and numerous motor vehicle violations.

David Brown had finally succeeded in doing something heinous enough to place him behind bars.

Much to Tyra Brown's shock, the son she had tried so hard to nurture and raise to be a charitable man was on his way to prison. No longer a juvenile, at the age of twenty, the courts deemed David mentally competent and criminally responsible for his violent behavior. The judge labeled him "a lethal risk to the community."

David's recurrent violent behavior and failure to take responsibility for past actions made successful intervention unlikely. Dangerous and subject to further episodes which could result in murder, the judge believed twenty years might not be enough. He recommended indefinite commitment to a maximum-security prison. On December 15th, 1977, just 10 days before his favorite holiday, the Commonwealth of Massachusetts sentenced David Brown to 18-20 years behind bars. He appeared much older than twenty but had minimal life experience. At five-feet, eight-inches, weighing in at 258 pounds, the frightened man entered Walpole State Prison. His convictions were for aggravated kidnapping and attempted murder, but other prisoners labeled him a child molester, "cho mo" or "short eyes" in prison jargon.

In prison hierarchy, pedophiles are at the bottom.

An award-winning play on Broadway, *Short Eyes*, depicted a child molester killed by inmates. Molesters often become victims of other inmates, badgered, raped or killed like the notorious cho mos Jeffrey Dahmer and Father Geogan. Accustomed to terrorizing others, even though he was in administrative isolation, David suddenly found himself afraid for his life.

At Walpole, a prison where some of the worst reside, David stated another prisoner crushed a burning cigarette out on the nape of his neck. In response, he said, "I back handed the man...knocked him off the third story tier."

A fall from that height could have been fatal. If David had killed another prisoner, wouldn't it be on his record? Like many stories he told, there was no validity to this claim.

In the prison, David started two correspondence courses, one in real estate and the other in art. He finished neither. After one counseling session, he refused to talk.

This pattern of refusing to face his inner demons and at the same time demanding psychiatric care continued for two years. In a letter petitioning to be moved to the Bridgewater Facility for the Sexually Dangerous, he stated he trusted no one at Walpole. After that request was denied, trying to force action, he quit exercising and eating for a few days before giving up.

In another petition letter from Walpole, he stated he felt totally isolated, forgotten. Because of the distance from their home, even his mother and sister seldom visited. David said his lawyer wouldn't return his phone calls. He begged to be sent for an evaluation, "Before I go totally nuts."

Prison life terrified him. After two years in Walpole, officials granted David his wish. They transferred him to the Massachusetts Correctional Institute at Concord. There was no violation report to suggest he killed another inmate at Walpole. Concord officials again placed him in a protective custody unit where he submitted to psychiatric evaluations. There he felt safer but remained distraught over his dire predicament.

After the evaluation at Concord, examiners notified the Commissioner of Mental Health that Brown was *sexually dangerous*. Following that determination in June 1979, they moved David to the SDP (Sexually Dangerous Person) Treatment Center at Bridgewater for a sixty-day evaluation. Before acceptance, he had to meet their SDP criteria.

To meet the requirements, the Commonwealth had to prove beyond a reasonable doubt that David lacked control of his sexual impulses. Under those regulations, SDP behavior is defined by *repetitive and compulsive sexual misconduct, by either violence against any victim, or aggression against any victim under the age of sixteen years of age; ...or if a person was likely to attack victims because of uncontrolled desires.*

David met the requirements. His abductions and violence were undoubtedly sexually motivated. At a judicial hearing in October, deemed a Sexually Dangerous Person under Massachusetts law, he was placed in the Massachusetts Treatment Center under a civil commitment procedure. David was committed to the SDP Treatment Center *for a period of one day to life.* The most important aspect of this court order was the prison term of eighteen to twenty years was commuted. This means hospitalization was substituted for the prison term.

Convicted sexual deviants prefer a mental health incarceration over a prison term. Instead of spending his twenty years in prison, David had a higher probability of getting out much sooner if he played the game right—cooperate and convince counselors he had changed. David might have gotten out of Bridgewater within days instead of years if he'd "proven" to them he was no longer dangerous.

David first entered an out-dated prison psychiatric facility which was soon replaced by the new Treatment Center. The new facility didn't look like a modern hospital. The austere cement structure sat behind two rows of tall concertina razor-wire-topped fences with a forbidding dead zone between them. There was no easy escape. This Level Four Facility is two levels below the maximum restriction. Bright lights and motion detectors help sentry guards watch for problems. Photos of the ominous facility are not allowed for security reasons. Inside this facility with little hope of escape, David found relief.

David's marked social and interpersonal isolation during childhood and adolescence had given him practice adapting to prison restrictions and nocturnal lockdown. He stayed to himself, did his job and spent hours alone in his room with games and writing—just like at home.

"Easy time," he called it. Closer proximity to Webster made it more convenient for his mother to visit. He said, "Visiting was great. She could even bring food."

A multidisciplinary team of counselors, psychologists and psychiatrists, assigned to each unit assessed and treated the inmates. Major components of the program involved exploring the root of inmates' problems that had put them behind bars and helping them learn acceptable behaviors and improve their interpersonal relations. Based on the concept that *sex offenders cannot be cured*, the commitment was to modify behavior to decrease the chance of relapse and offending again. The goal was prevention, and at the right time, transition into the community.

Their strategy aimed at helping inmates identify what led to their violent episodes. The information shared with therapists and their group help individualize counseling efforts. The Violence Reduction Program taught effective communication and interpersonal problem solving along with anger management. The plan sounds reasonable for some violent offenders but has no reliable impact on sexually violent predators.

After all David's demands for counseling and a transfer to Bridgewater, he balked and resisted acknowledging his abnormal behavior. He had no remorse, took no responsibility for his actions and refused to participate in counseling.

On his tier, the other inmates incarcerated for similar problems at the Treatment Center, left him alone. With little harassment, he felt less stressed and could concentrate on things he enjoyed. He took a course in photography and correspondence courses in journalism and ministry of the gospel; all topics of interest to him. He claimed he earned a degree in journalism from a mail-order school in Pennsylvania while at Bridgewater. There is no record of it.

When David entered Bridgewater, he was twenty-two. His painful childhood and teenage years, followed by two years in Walpole took a harsh toll. Helpless in his own home, he had learned to bully and intimidate outsiders, but inside the walls he had little power. He had to learn new methods of control.

From the beginning, he displayed a rebellious attitude and did not cooperate during therapy sessions. Oppositional behavior became his way of manipulating the system. That way, he attained some personal control. He bullied guards and refused to obey orders, but compared to others, David was not viewed as much of a problem.

His pen became a more powerful weapon. Whenever something didn't go his way, David fired off a letter to influential people such as prison directors and congressmen. He threatened lawsuits against the facility and his counselors.

With no motivation to exercise, he remained obese. When medical personnel noted high blood pressure and offered him treatment he vehemently refused and accused the staff of harassment. They quit asking him to come in for evaluations and finally told him if he changed his mind, he should make an appointment.

Mandatory attendance at weekly group therapy sessions and psychiatric counseling on his tier didn't interest David. He appeared at the meetings but would not participate. He physically isolated himself from the group by placing his chair outside the circle and would read magazines while other inmates talked. David acted like a stubborn child who wanted special treatment. Sometimes he made group members uncomfortable by laughing when they shared serious problems.

His pattern of isolation and obstinacy at the Treatment Center interfered with instituting changes in behavior. One therapist pointed out that he attempted to keep everyone in the group confused when they confronted him about his past. After the therapist talked to David about his behavior, he quit attending. He said he had always been a loner and refused to share his personal thoughts with a group.

After another manipulative move when he demanded individual therapy, the administrator told him to stop wasting time and get involved in the programs. The group meetings provided a way for therapists to get to know prisoners and see for themselves how well they handled anger, feelings, and urges. Administration told him attendance at therapy was tied to gate passes and community access. Without his cooperation, David learned he would lose privileges and would not progress.

Staff found other programs for him to attend. But those were failures, too. In a Christian group, he claimed he found prisoners "exchanging homosexual favors under the table." But David had his secrets, too. Inside his Bible he carried pictures of children.

After David refused educational placement testing and declined most of the training opportunities, counselors looked for something he'd like. He attended eight hours of class work in camera and darkroom, then quit. After other tries, they hit on something that appealed to him, food. He got a job at the Treatment Center Canteen and worked there for many years. With his high school training in DECA and experience working at McDonald's, he performed his duties with minimal supervision and excelled. David considered his work as therapy. The position of power gave him respect within the facility and improved self esteem. He said, "When Frank quit, I became the inmate boss. Started out as a stocker and ended up in charge. I did all the ordering."

With little headway in treatment, counselors tried to gain his participation in other ways. After he quit attending group meetings, they sent letters stating he must attend a designated percentage of the sessions or lose privileges. That threat got him back to meet the minimum requirement, but he refused to participate verbally unless he was asked a direct question. Even then, he revealed nothing about himself or his thoughts. One time he commented he might attend more often if the group meetings didn't interfere with his job and favorite television shows.

At Bridgewater, the nocturnal lockdowns provided safety just like in his bedroom at home. Alone and at peace, he could fantasize and write to his pen pals.

His work at the Canteen and correspondence with two hundred pen pals took most of his time. He exchanged audio tapes with many people outside the prison, too. Some of them were solicited through personal ads: "Seeks only friendship! Mental Health Patient ...A/A [Any/All] Ages 4 sex, TAPE PALS ONLY!! But please write first! Thanks! Write soon! —Know the real you through numerology. I need your full name including your middle name, your date of birth and $5.00."

Low risk relationships with strangers interested him. He might have made a few dollars with numerology, but David didn't get too close to anyone.

While in the mental hospital for sex crimes and violence against children, he developed a newsletter that spoke out against child abuse. He gave helpful hints to parents whose children had been abducted. Instead of following the advice of the sex offender program and avoiding thoughts of children, David focused on abductions from a supposed legitimate position.

With improved personal pride in his Canteen work, David busied himself inventing games he hoped one day to market. He tested them on other inmates and made money selling greeting cards and gifts. Unauthorized sales activity got him in trouble. Prison officials confiscated his computer, a large recipe collection, tapes, addresses and business supplies. They stopped his newsletter and terminated him from his job.

Unhappy about his multiple losses, David was most distressed about losing his job and treasured recipes. Letters of appeal were not successful in regaining his computer but he did return to work.

After nearly seven years at Bridgewater, David longed to be free. He began plotting a new identity, but his annual reviews showed little change in cooperation. With the history of being in a prison mental hospital, it is difficult to start over.

First, he decided to change his name. He said it was not for a new identity, but because he wanted "to see what it was like to be discriminated against." That reason is incongruous because for one thing or another, he'd been discriminated against all his life. That reason wasn't the whole story because his first choice of a new last name was Bloomquist, his mother's maiden name.

She said, "No."

He told counselors he had chosen his mother's name first because she was half Jewish. When I asked him later, he said she was Swedish.

David didn't understand why Tyra didn't want him to take her maiden name. In the end, he chose Nathanael Benjamin Levi Bar-Jonah after gathering ideas for his new name from his prison friends. The final choice was his.

Why did he end up with four names?

Nathanael means "gift of God." Bar-Jonah means "son of Jonah or son of Jonas." There are various meanings including "Son of Dove." Did his new name carry an ominous twisted secret code? David liked codes. Part of his fantasy life, he used them to hide his desires. Some of his methods and deciphered codes are examined in Chapter 17.

After his name change, Nathan Bar-Jonah attended Jewish services and demanded kosher food. It might have been a ploy to be granted privileged visits outside the razor-wire fences to practice his new religion in town. Some of his personal writings show his motivation was to develop a new identity to cover his prison time. Job applications after his release stated he was in the "foreign service" and the "Israeli military" during his time in the Treatment Center. "In Israel" is a notation on the back of a picture of him wearing a black beret, standing beside his mother. The photo was taken at Bridgewater. He never traveled to Israel.

Early in his incarceration, he told a psychologist about his fantasies. Bar-Jonah claimed all of his fantasies were of a violent nature, sadistic murderous thoughts that were sexually stimulating to him. As a youth, he had watched horror movies and especially liked Alfred Hitchcock directed movie *Psycho*, and *Soylent Green* about cannibalism. A much more dire focus was his interest in the *trash bag murderer* and the Manson murders.

Nightmares plagued Bar-Jonah until he was about thirty. At that point, he said he came to terms with a childhood rape when he realized they could no longer harm him. He spoke of the rape with such animation that he appeared to enjoy sharing details of the story. He first reported it at

Bridgewater when he was in his late twenties, "I was gang-raped in the woods near the cemetery by eight kids when I was ten." He said one day he and a younger friend, aged seven, were stripped of their clothing by neighborhood children. "Six boys held me down. They tortured me sexually using tree branches. They kicked me and squeezed my jewels until I passed out." When asked about being poked with sticks, he denied anal penetration.

"The two oldest boys tortured my friend," he said. "The boys tied my friend's arms and legs between two trees, drenched him in gasoline, then they threw burning matches on him."

The reported rapists were much younger than Bar-Jonah. Interviews with some of those he named place their ages as young as three-years-old at the time. Based on their birthdates, others were ages four and five when Bar-Jonah was ten. When one of the boys on his list of perpetrators was asked as adult about the event, he laughed out loud and exclaimed, "That's crazy. It never happened."

It is difficult to visualize how children as young as those on his list could even dream up such an assault and then carry it out on someone his size. Tyra Brown recalled no incident where her son had come home upset and no one reported injuries to the seven-year-old friend who he said was set on fire. Something may have happened but this scene in its entirety was contrived.

We know many rapists and molesters were themselves abused as children and maybe something else happened to him. Something that he just couldn't face, something that triggered his predatory behaviors, something he wanted to hide forever, and this story was a more acceptable substitute in his mind.

Some believe he made up the story to justify his violent sexual behavior. He had every opportunity to discuss it when he was sixteen and in the mental hospital in Southbridge after he abducted and choked Richard O'Connor, but he didn't mention it then and refused counseling.

Bar-Jonah claimed you could obtain almost anything you wanted within the walls of Bridgewater, including sex with therapists. He said sex among inmates was encouraged as a healthy process for re-entry to society.

In 1986, officials found a large amount of contraband material including sexually explicit pictures and video tapes inside the walls of the state penal hospital for the Sexually Dangerous. Considered inappropriate and damaging to treatment, officials put a stop to the delivery of sexually oriented material to the facility.

At Bridgewater, SDP unit, Bar-Jonah was locked up with murderers and rapists but wasn't afraid for his life like at Walpole after the painful cigarette burn incident. He watched his back, but said things went well most of the time. "The people there weren't the greatest. There were guys who did unthinkable things," Bar-Jonah commented.

A frightening episode occurred after several prisoners escaped. In the shakedown that followed, guards forced Bar-Jonah to strip for a body search. He requested a medical doctor be present and they refused. The shift commander ordered him escorted to the Crisis Unit where his clothing was forcibly removed.

Bar-Jonah stated he was detained and a few hours later the "extraction team" entered and again ordered him to submit to an unclothed search. He refused. Correctional officers then removed his clothing and spread his buttocks to check for contraband. Traumatized emotionally by this standard procedure, Bar-Jonah knew the whole ordeal was video taped to protect staff members involved. Animatedly, he described it in vivid terms, as if replaying every minute as he spoke. "When I was raped the second time, in prison, it was eight guards, the goon squad. I remember the one who stuck his finger up my butt. One of them said, 'It's Nathan. Nathan never gets in trouble. What is going on?'... Then a huge Black guard edged in and a puny little one showed up and orders him to back up. With the goon squad in SWAT gear, they threw me on a bloody mattress where they had just killed a guy. * The blood on the mattress was still sticky. That's when I made my first porno flick."

After the incident, he was outraged and wrote to everyone, "the State Police, the courts, the politicians. All of them told me they were just doing their job." He said the experience triggered bad memories "from the age of ten when I was raped, with my seven-year-old friend."

David was finally upset enough to talk with his therapy group.

Each year a board of professionals at the Treatment Center met to discuss each patient, their progress and needs. Inmates were encouraged to meet with the Board. Bar-Jonah refused. Because he refused, his annual evaluations were based on input from therapists only. They gave summaries of what was gleaned from his limited participation and canteen work.

Bar-Jonah believed he was ready to be released and petitioned for discharge. His cumulative documented avoidant behavior was counterproductive. The Restrictive Integration Review Board denied his request. They said he had not addressed his self-hate during childhood, and he still harbored a deep-seated desire for revenge against children. Further, he did not take responsibility for his actions and used "blackouts" as an excuse. He was not ready for release.

*Note: There is no record of an inmate death at Bridgewater in that episode. This was just another lie.

Chapter 4 Get Out of Jail Free

In 1990, Bar-Jonah petitioned for release again. He had failed in the past but had learned. This time he was serious. He wanted out so badly that he changed his ways, at least some of them. Attendance and group participation improved. He was physically present after successfully resisting years of effort to help him understand compulsions driving him to repeat violent offenses. His fantasy life and preoccupation with murder, torture and cannibalism continued.

After the latest petition for release, the State asked Clinical Psychologists Leonard Bard and Liza Brooks to evaluate Bar-Jonah. Officials wanted them to determine if he still met the legal definition of a Sexually Dangerous Person.

Dr. Bard twice asked Bar-Jonah to meet with him. He refused. Based on past encounters, Bar-Jonah knew he couldn't manipulate Dr. Bard. He said, "Dr. Bard was a snake. I wouldn't talk to him."

This lack of cooperation forced Dr. Bard to base his psychiatric analysis on documents alone. In the doctor's review of written treatment records, he found no indication Bar-Jonah committed himself to rehabilitation. He had refused to participate in Board reviews dating back four years. His antagonistic behavior and avoidance of therapy showed no progress toward reintegration into the community.

When asked why he didn't cooperate at Bridgewater, Bar-Jonah asserted, "I participated in counseling a lot. Some counseling didn't pertain to me. I trained about fifteen psychiatrists while I was there."

As a result of his detailed record review, Dr. Bard determined Bar-Jonah still met statutory criteria for a SDP and should not be released.

Thinking he could charm Dr. Brooks, Bar-Jonah met with her on two occasions in January 1990. She found him, "engaging, vulnerable, honest and responsive." He told her of violent fantasies that began with the reported childhood rape but denied physical and psychological abuse from family members. The records showed he had participated in more therapy sessions but in her final analysis, Bar-Jonah learned Dr. Brooks wasn't the easy target he thought she'd be. Because of minimal progress and failure to address his violent fantasies and acts, like Dr. Bard, she determined he remained sexually dangerous and should not be released.

In February, the Review Board denied his petition for release because Bar-Jonah had not worked to change his behavior. Still at high risk for re-offense because of his failure to address problems, they recommended medical testing, psychological testing and an evaluation for possible medication. Specifically, they recommended self-control management, individual therapy and group therapy. Most importantly, he needed treatment to explore the meaning of his offenses against young boys. They recommended a focus on "orgasmic reconditioning."

The process of orgasmic reconditioning attempts to suppress the erotic feelings he would experience when he acted with violence against little boys. The goal is to derail abnormal sexual thoughts and substitute more appropriate thoughts and behaviors. The method involves masturbation to the point of orgasm and at that point, substitute images of age-appropriate individuals. This is not standard effective therapy

One method used to both assess and predict sexual offender reactions to visual and audio stimuli is to measure their sexual response. A small sensitive instrument attached to the penis measures increases in blood flow. Called penile plethysmography, the test is gaining acceptance. Many experts believe it is the best objective measure of arousal, but additional research is needed to document its accurate predictability of future inappropriate acts. The measurement has been used in developing criminal offender profiles, including family court incest cases. It is used on the premise that penis response to stimuli correlates with overt acts. The method may be useful for treatment but is not considered a reliable predictor of future behavior.

At Bridgewater, they were never able to assess Bar-Jonah's violence and eroticism toward young boys. If he had cooperated with treatment plans, they would have made progress in assessing the safety of returning him to life outside the prison hospital.

It didn't happen.

In August 1990, a few months after the two doctors completed their evaluations, Dr. Bard reiterated his psychiatric analysis in a written report to the presiding justice in

Worcester Country Superior Court. Both Drs. Leonard Bard and Liza Brooks regarded Nathanael Bar-Jonah as sexually dangerous. They said he was in need of further in-patient treatment and should not be released.

Bar-Jonah wasn't defeated. He had another idea. Failing with Drs. Bard and Brooks, he tried a new approach: pick your own psychologist. His brother Bob hired a Christian psychologist to evaluate Bar-Jonah for release. Suddenly, he cooperated.

Bar-Jonah met with Dr. Richard W. Ober and discussed his fantasies and problems in detail. Dr. Ober reviewed the same treatment records analyzed by Drs. Bard and Brooks but saw a different picture. He said Bar-Jonah had shown impulse control, increased socialization, improved adjustment to the institution, and enhanced self-esteem. For example, Bar-Jonah had even talked of a female pen pal and heterosexual interest. To Dr. Ober, Bar-Jonah portrayed a maturing sexual attitude and denied violent fantasies related to sexual urges that previously plagued him.

After discussing the charge of "rape" he brought against guards, Dr. Ober regarded Bar-Jonah's behavior following the incident as *an adaptive sign of recovery*. He could have become violent but didn't. Instead, he responded by talking to his therapy group and trying to get legal and political assistance through writing letters. Dr. Ober said this behavior demonstrated the ability to handle the stress induced by a traumatic incident and control his impulses.

Writing letters was not new to Bar-Jonah. He had found letters were effective in the past. It showed no change in his behavior. Writing to a female pen pal wasn't new either. He searched for women with children of his chosen age.

Considering all of his findings, Dr. Ober made his clinical decision based on the above information. He determined Bar-Jonah was *very unlikely to victimize others due to his uncontrolled desires.*

Bar-Jonah was delighted with Dr. Ober's findings, but knew he needed to find a second psychologist who would come to the same conclusion. Under Massachusetts law, if two psychologists stated a sexual predator no longer met the legal definition of a Sexually Dangerous Person, a prisoner could be freed.

In December, Bar-Jonah met with a second and very thorough psychologist, Dr. Eric Sweitzer. He reviewed all past medical and psychiatric records, analyzed tests and administered new psychological tests. In Dr. Sweitzer's review of an early MMPI (Minnesota Multiphasic Personality Inventory), he found Bar-Jonah's score within normal range. A Rorschach Inkblot Test, given in conjunction with that MMPI, revealed no evidence of sadistic thoughts or preoccupation with aggressive sexual practices. To evaluate current thought processes and determine Bar-Jonah's interpretations of other persons' feelings, Dr. Sweitzer administered another Rorschach and a TAT (Thematic Apperception Test).

On the new Rorschach, Bar-Jonah showed anxiety and focused on details but revealed no impaired thought processes. On the TAT test, pictures displayed people in various social situations, his interpretations showed emotional and interpersonal relational immaturity, but not severe pathology. Dr. Sweitzer believed Bar-Jonah showed no distortion of thought or evidence of aggression. Even though he lacked awareness of emotions portrayed by human figures in the photos, he had no tendency to react with violence. He was often wrong when interpreting a character's feelings, but there was no evidence he harbored a psychotic condition. Bar-Jonah misread social situations, but this wouldn't be unexpected considering his lack of positive social interactions and personal isolation since childhood.

Based on Bar-Jonah's offenses, Dr. Sweitzer believed he had no sadistic sexual impulses or hostility. He stated, "Having a boy disrobe did not lead to molestation." Sweitzer believed Bar-Jonah experienced aggressive fantasies regarding the boys who had molested him but did not report them until after he entered the Treatment Center. Because Bar-Jonah wouldn't talk to the Review Board or counselors, they were forced to carry the previously reported fantasies forward to the next year because they had no new information.

After his detailed examination, Dr. Sweitzer came to the conclusion Bar-Jonah's offenses were "not of a sexual nature." The psychologist reported he had shown great restraint and maturity when confronted by the aggressive search by guards. Besides, seven years of steady work at the Treatment Center Canteen required significant social interaction with inmates and this behavior offset the self-imposed isolation and lack of group participation elsewhere. Many pen pals, and a relationship with a female, confirmed improved maturity and proved he was not socially isolated.

According to Dr. Sweitzer, all of these details, in conjunction with a network of support outside the facility, made a strong case for Bar-Jonah's release. He was also convinced that Bar-Jonah's religious faith would act as a deterrent to future acts of violence.

Dr. Sweitzer determined Sexually Dangerous Person status did not apply, and like Dr. Ober, recommended his release. None of the clinical tests provide predictive validity regarding Sexually Violent Predators. Would these doctors have been comfortable with Bar-Jonah living next door to their children or grandchildren?

Bar-Jonah said, "They [Drs. Ober and Sweitzer] were a last-minute thing. We couldn't find anyone I was satisfied with. They did testing and thought I didn't belong there because I had never committed a sexual crime. The only reason I ended up there was because I begged them. They [Bridgewater Treatment Center] were the only ones that had psychiatrists."

In response to recommendations by the two latest psychologists, Walter E. Steele, Justice of the Superior Court of the Commonwealth of Massachusetts, ordered Nathanael Bar-Jonah released. He found Bar-Jonah had *resolved underlying psychological conflicts that resulted in the commission of his crimes*. The Judge cited positive aspects such as his work in the Canteen and recent group therapy attendance and commented on Ober's and Sweitzer's findings that SDP status no longer applied. Judge Steele emphasized only statements made by the psychologists hired by the Brown family. He ignored Drs. Bard's and Brooks' reports that emphatically said Bar-Jonah was still a danger to society.

Judge Steele's ruling was dated February 12, 1991.

After all the evaluations in the preceding year with two in favor of release and a judge's degree for release, Bar-Jonah remained behind razor-wire fences through an administrative snafu. Somehow the facility didn't learn about the release order and kept him incarcerated.

When the time for the 1991 annual Restrictive Integration Review of his care came due in June, the Board revealed their findings. Based on all the same information Judge Steele had when he ordered the release, the Board determined Bar-Jonah *had minimal social competence and overwhelming feelings of rage*. He was at *high risk for further offenses and should not be released*. Then, someone found Judge Steele's order contrary to the Review Board's recommendation. In spite of their fear for public safety, the Treatment Center was forced to release Bar-Jonah.

Two days later he walked out a free man.

Because he spent many extra months in prison due to administrative error, the Commonwealth of Massachusetts reportedly paid Bar-Jonah thousands of dollars in damages but he denied this.

Psychopathic sex offenders deceive clinicians on a regular basis. They talk to each other and learn what works. Then they dupe therapists into believing they've benefited from treatment and are ready for release. Effective and practiced liars, sexual offenders are believable. Their participation in therapy is convincing because they mouth the right responses. Nathanael Bar-Jonah duped Drs. Ober and Sweitzer. Judge Steele chose to listen to them instead of all the other seasoned doctors and the knowledgeable Review Board. Like many other conniving offenders, Bar-Jonah was freed to act out his fantasies.

There is no cure for pedophilia. Yet based on minimal interaction with him, the two psychologists hired by his brother said Bar-Jonah was unlikely to repeat his actions. In essence, he was cured.

After fourteen years behind bars, the Commonwealth of Massachusetts released Nathanael Bar-Jonah back to society without a community reintroduction plan.

With his prison sentence commuted, he walked out of Bridgewater Hospital for the Sexually Dangerous without restriction.

Everyone soon found that all of the Board members and the prison psychiatrists were correct. Bar-Jonah was still sexually dangerous.

Forty-three days after his release, the 260-pound bearded ex-convict pedophile got into a car with a small boy.

In front of the Oxford Post Office, the child sat alone in a car parked while his mother ran inside. When she returned a few minutes later, she opened the rear door and threw her purse in, then jumped in the front and started the motor. She looked at her son sitting in the front seat beside her and found Bar-Jonah squashed against him with the door closed. Shocked, she screamed at Bar-Jonah to get out.

He refused.

The distraught woman grabbed her son, bolted from the idling car and ran back into the Post Office.

When Bar-Jonah realized there was a big problem, he got out and walked rapidly down the street.

A man parked next to the woman's car saw the whole thing and was tempted to pursue Bar-Jonah. But seeing his size, he decided against it and called police.

In the mother's report to police, she described a heavyset Caucasian dark-haired bearded male wearing a vest with patches and a coon-skin-type cap without a tail. The data was radioed to all police cars in the area. A search of local bars and the surrounding area found no one who matched the description.

Two elderly women in Bar-Jonah's mother's apartment building located near the Post Office knew him. They saw him run across their yard, past them and upstairs. When police questioned the women, they confirmed he'd entered wearing a blue denim vest with patches on it; a few minutes later he left dressed differently.

The same man who saw Bar-Jonah at the Post Office spotted a man hitchhiking down Charlton Street in the rain and reported him. Oxford officers saw the man but he didn't match the description they'd been given. This guy was wearing blue pants, suspenders and a blue T-shirt. Officers stopped to question him anyway.

As he had many times before, Bar-Jonah lied. He didn't want to go back to prison. He denied being at the Post Office. He denied having a vest or hat like they described. But he didn't have a good answer when they asked him about his hair being dry on top and wet on the sides, and why the torso of his shirt was dry in the pattern of a vest.

When they presented him to the distraught woman, she couldn't identify him.

Officers went to Alpine Supply located across the street from the Post Office. A clerk said Bar-Jonah had worn a blue denim vest with patches a few minutes earlier when he purchased a bottle of contact cement.

Oxford Police took Bar-Jonah to the station and confronted him with witness information. They noted a bottle of glue in his pocket.

Bar-Jonah confessed. In a written statement, he said, "After leaving Alpine's, I went over to the Post Office for some certified mail slips and as I came out, I walked past these two cars, and I was going to cross the street when I decided to ask this lady if she could give me a ride. I opened the passenger's side door and sat on some of the seat next to the boy and was just about to ask if she could give me a ride when she went spastic. She was in hysterics, and I was stunned and startled. I then got scared, got out of the car and walked fast down toward Charlton Street. I went to my mom's and took off my vest and hat and then I left and began to hitchhike and got near Barton Street when a police car stopped me and then I was asked some questions. I was scared and they had witnesses come down to ID me. I was then taken to the station."

Sitting in a stranger's car doesn't sound like a big deal. But his history of violent stranger-abduction of children and attempted murder makes it much more ominous. After years of counseling that stressed pedophiles should avoid risk situations and stay away from children, he got into a car with a little boy he didn't know—he hadn't learned.

The incident provided a clear opportunity to put him back behind bars, but because his sentence had been commuted, he wasn't even on parole. There was no infraction which would automatically send him back. His release from Bridgewater was unconditional.

Between the time of the incident and his arraignment, Bar-Jonah stalked the mother and child. They saw him drive past their house and take taxis through the area. He walked and bicycled past their home. He had them in his eyes. His intimidating behavior terrified them. Bar-Jonah enjoyed the power. Years later he explained, "The lady kept calling the police saying I was outside her house. After that, my family thought I should leave the state."

Charged with assault and battery, breaking and entering a motor vehicle with intent to commit a felony, and placing a person in fear, he was arraigned before Justice John C. Geenty on August 21, 1991. The judge ordered a psychiatric evaluation. The three witness statements should have been in the file, but the following day when Bar-Jonah appeared before Judge Sarius Teshoian, there was no mention of them.

The Dudley County Courthouse file did not contain the witness statements.

The docket sheet for his court appearance stated Bar-Jonah had an indefinite prison sentence suspended after two years. It said nothing of his transfer to Bridgewater Treatment Center and twelve years of incarceration as a Sexually Dangerous Person.

The Judge Teshoian ordered him out of the town of Oxford and a "strict stay away order from the victim and family. —No contact."

The Brown family aimed for a plea bargain and got it. Bar-Jonah received a suspended jail sentence and two years probation to begin immediately, with the condition he receive psychiatric counseling and move to Montana where his brother had offered him lodging. The new order for counseling superseded the order issued the previous day for a psychiatric examination.

No evaluation was ever done, and he received no counseling in Massachusetts.

A newspaper article in the *Great Falls Tribune* years later quoted the woman's lawyer, saying he was unaware of the three signed witness statements. The Assistant District Attorney and the local Chief of Police had told the boy's mother her case against the man was weak, especially since she wasn't able to identify him.

In the plea agreement, Bar-Jonah's history of choking little boys was not considered. The *Tribune* also quoted Worcester County District Attorney John Conte who said prosecutors had done their best to get two years probation because the only witness was the boy, and his mother wouldn't let him testify. When asked why Bar-Jonah didn't get a tougher sentence, Conte responded, "You don't convict people on their past records." In Bar-Jonah's case there were many mitigating factors not considered and the dangerous pedophile walked out of the court room free to hunt more children.

Chapter 5 Hunting in Montana

In October 1991, Bar-Jonah boarded a jet and headed west. High above the expansive wheat land of eastern Montana, the pedophile exiled from Massachusetts anticipated a new life where his past deeds were unknown. As the jet descended, his anxiety mounted. Probably clothed in his usual attire with his obese belly straining at the seams of a food-stained T-shirt and wearing too-long pants with shredded dragging hems, his moist flesh and body odor encroached upon adjacent passengers. But the packed jet imprisoned its occupants. There was no escape. No empty seats were available to provide refuge from the disgusting scent of this man.

Bar-Jonah's anxiety continued to build as the jet approached his new home. Nearly hidden behind large, smudged lenses, his magnified eyes darted furtively. Feral eyes, one pale blue, one brown. Powerful eyes used as weapons, locked in reptilian stares, they unnerved adults and paralyzed small boys.

Waiting at the airport, his brother Bob paced. He worried about the future and about his image as a college instructor with a pedophile felon living with him. How would his wife react? It would be strange calling his little brother David by his new name "Nathan."

As the plane neared his new home, Bar-Jonah's concerns mounted. He had no job, no car. And this time, he had orders for two years of probation—what if he messed up and ended up back behind bars again?

Bar-Jonah knew he needed his mother's financial support and her calming influence but *love-hate* feelings for her ate at him, gnawing like gray rats he'd watched in the Canteen storeroom at Bridgewater.

En route to Montana, the jet engine roar intensified the noise in his brain and forced his thoughts into overdrive. On his very first flight, he had boarded with little fear about flying and with cautious anticipation of a new life. Bar-Jonah tried to calm himself when anxiety mounted as his destination drew closer. His burgeoning abdomen would have pushed back as he struggled to reach beneath the seat ahead of him. His pudgy hand searched to find the notebook and gel pen he'd brought with him. He could write while the plane brought him closer to his future of freedom in the West. Writing calmed him.

Bar-Jonah's pattern in the past had been to print with fury, pressing hard, indenting pages, writing anything that came to mind, crushing the letters together, no space between words, crushing them together like he wanted to crush the little boys, sit on them till they couldn't breathe, choke them.

Writing...writing... *davidpaulbrownnathanaelbenjamin levibarjonahlakewebstermontana*

Calming.

The Bridgewater counselors had told him he wasn't ready for discharge.

For years they'd told him to stay away from children and explained to him sex and violence were "fused in his brain." He knew he required violence to reach orgasm. His thoughts always accelerated with stress and nearing Great Falls accelerated his fantasies. On the flight, like storm clouds, vivid fantasies, chaotic erotic images swirled in his mind.

Bar-Jonah had to block the images. He continued to write. He may have practiced *slipping*. Coding by slipping letters looks like gibberish but in this simple way he could conceal his thoughts and the person sitting next to him would be none the wiser. He just moved all the letters of the alphabet a set number of positions one way or the other and he had a new alphabet no one knew. Bar-Jonah used the method to record his achievements, his victims, and gloat. When using his secret methods, no one could tell what he wrote.

Bar-Jonah may have focused on victim photographs he carried with him, images forever locked in time in his mind. Memories that calmed him.

The plane banked slightly. He strained to look out the window and visualize details on the ground. As the jet descended, the serpentine Missouri River came into view. Dust devils spun skyward like smoke rings off parched August fields. Just after crossing the river, the jet settled onto a runway located on the bluff above the city and came to a stop at the terminal.

Bob's eyes scanned the arriving passengers, looking for his large younger brother. The slender compulsively clean brother, nine years older and worlds apart from Bar-Jonah could never have imagined how bad it would be.

Bar-Jonah stepped off the flight into new hunting grounds.

After being confined behind bars since the age of twenty, Bar-Jonah's family believed at thirty-four, he could put the fourteen years behind him and start anew. It was his chance for a new life, a life where few knew about his history of abducting children. Even the probation officials were unaware of his long prison sentence for aggravated kidnapping and attempted murder. Although his convictions were not for sexual offenses, his actions had been violent and sexually motivated.

Massachusetts released him to serve out two years probation for a "minor" incident in the midst of an unsuspecting population where he could prey on little boys unhindered. Montana officials were not told he had been confined to a facility for the sexually dangerous for twelve years where mental health experts said he should not be released.

In Great Falls, Bar-Jonah was not required to register as a sex offender.

As in many cases across the country, this lapse in the legal and medical systems released an incurable sexual predator. Interstate compacts mandate approval from receiving states before ex-convicts on probation are allowed to move to the new jurisdiction. Massachusetts Department of Corrections should have notified Montana of Bar-Jonah's entire record and obtained permission to send him. That didn't happen.

When Bar-Jonah reported to the Montana parole board, he shocked the probation officer with details of his offenses. The officer had received a thin file containing the Post Office incident. It didn't cover two years in prison for attempted murder and twelve years in Bridgewater State Hospital for the Sexually Dangerous.

Montana authorities were furious. They tried to send him back. Massachusetts didn't want him. Rejected by both states, Bar-Jonah's new life had an unpleasant beginning and Montana was stuck with him.

Three years later, Massachusetts changed its law regarding sexual predator release. Many had believed courts in Massachusetts were too lenient on sex offenders but with the new law, a judge can no longer authorize a release. Cases must be heard and decided upon by a jury. The change came too late for Montanans. Bar-Jonah was free.

Law Professor Wendy Murphy, an advocate for victims of sexual violence, publicly criticized Worcester County District Attorney John J. Conte whose jurisdiction released Bar-Jonah. In an April 2002 article in the *Worcester Telegram & Gazette* newspaper, Professor Murphy said she had requested statistical information on sex crimes from Conte's office in 1999. She was quoted saying, "I want the numbers, but he won't give them to me." Conte had reported glowing claims of success on his conviction rate on drugs and other crimes but said nothing about rape and sex crimes.

Under Massachusetts's public records law, Murphy requested information about sexual assault prosecutions in Worcester, Bristol and Plymouth counties. She had hoped to improve the law's response to victims of sexual assault by identifying problems in the system. After several communications, she was finally told by Conte's office the statistics she requested were not available. Angered, she asked, "It is estimated that as many as one in four children have been assaulted by someone they know, why aren't the numbers routinely analyzed and evaluated?"

Sexual abuse of children is a problem everywhere, but in Massachusetts child abuse had been headline news after numerous Catholic pedophile priests were finally charged. The church hid their transgressions for years by moving the predatory priests from parish to parish. In roles of power and respect, protected by the church, they continued their terror for years, sometimes decades. Abuse involving hundreds of children occurred without prosecution.

Pedophiles in the priesthood are not unique. It is common practice for pedophiles to seek positions of power, and then use status in community organizations, churches and schools to target the children they desire. After gaining confidence of parents and children, they befriend and abuse the children. Once abuse begins, the children are confused by special treatment and gifts coupled with abuse, all the while knowing their parents approve of this adult.

Powerful demands of silence, intimidation, and fear of harm if they tell, places a child in an untenable trap. There is no way out. If they do tell a parent, they believe something bad may happen to them personally because the pedophile will carry out threats. Sometimes parents do not believe the child and punish them for reporting it and abandon the child to more abuse. These reasons make it essential that outsiders, teachers, friends and healthcare workers report any suspicious behavior to police so potential abuse can be investigated.

Disabled children and those from single-parent poor families are prime targets. Pedophiles develop relationships with women who have children of the age they desire sexually. Children without male protection are particularly vulnerable. Single mothers unknowingly push their sons into dangerous relationships, thinking a father-figure is important and nurturing. They don't realize their child is being victimized by a monster.

Because of fear and shame, many victimized kids don't talk about it until years later. After initial exposure of the extensive abuse within the Catholic Church in Massachusetts, boys victimized over years by other priests across the country came forward. They revealed the pervasive pattern of abuse and protection of the priests from prosecution. The same process of protecting priests occurred in European countries and finally came to light.

In Montana, Bar-Jonah followed standard rules of probation, not the more restrictive rules imposed on sexual deviants. All he had to do was report once a month, follow all laws and not carry a weapon. Work was mandatory and he had to obtain permission to travel. If he had been charged as a sex offender, his address and photo would have been published in the newspaper so others living in the area would have been alerted to his presence. No one knew a high-risk sex offender lived in their neighborhood and was mingling with children.

Bridgewater therapists stressed to pedophiles they must avoid contact with children. If the recommendation is followed, it decreases access and lowers risk for offending again. But Bar-Jonah lived with his brother and sister-in-law mere blocks from elementary schools and parks. Like a recovering alcoholic who moves in next door to a liquor store, Bar-Jonah moved in close to a grade school and went out of his way to gain access to children.

In sharp contrast to his years in prison, Bar-Jonah had wonderful new-found freedom in Montana. He lived close to the powerful Missouri River that carved through town and spilled over thundering waterfalls. He strolled slowly along the River Walk alone. The river drew him, as did nearby Gibson Park, where children swarmed over playground equipment and fed wild ducks and geese.

Thin and orderly, Bob was a polar opposite of his obese, messy brother. They had nothing in common and bore no family resemblance. Bar-Jonah was only ten years old when Bob finished high school and joined the Air Force. They had little contact for almost twenty-five years until they were thrust together under one roof. Many believed Bar-Jonah was mentally retarded by his actions and the way he'd sit and stare. He had them all fooled.

The two brothers and Bob's wife lived together for a few months before Bar-Jonah moved to a nearby older building at 1000 4th Avenue North. There, he lived alone in a top floor apartment a couple of blocks from Whittier Elementary, the school ten-year-old Zachary Ramsay was attending when he disappeared forever.

After Bob purchased a duplex in the same area of town and remodeled it, Tyra moved to Montana to live with her younger son. There, mother and son lived in one half of the attractive side-by-side stucco home. Bob rented the other half to a single woman with a young son. Like their home in Webster, the new residence with a garage in back was located on a tree-lined street in a comfortable neighborhood.

Bar-Jonah had a private room where he spent hours locked inside. The garage with a dirt floor sat along an alley. It became his haven. As soon as he and Tyra moved in, Bar-Jonah began attending garage sales and gradually increased his inventory until he had enough collectibles that he could hold his own sales.

Toy sales were perfect for Bar-Jonah. As in the past, toys attracted neighborhood children. They liked the friendly big man who laughed and played with them. They didn't know he kept frightening personal writings of torture and murder hidden from view beneath tables loaded with toys.

Bar-Jonah rented a corner at the annual antique toy sale held at the Fair Grounds. Particularly fond of Star Wars collectibles, he specialized in them, but sold many other toys including Barbie Dolls. As an added attraction, he displayed a borrowed taxidermy mount of a small bear and perfected a growl to entertain shopping children.

Bar-Jonah said he took pride in his displays and believed presentation would help him beat his competition. With his expertise in display design, he said he could easily "get a job in New York setting up windows. I was very particular about how things were displayed."

Many single mothers lived in his new neighborhood. He offered to baby sit and often cooked meals for them. Trust soon followed and the women left their children in his care. Tyra and Bar-Jonah were active in the Assembly of God Church. They attended potluck dinners at church, and he shared food he'd personally prepared. Neighbors and church members said they didn't find him threatening. The Bear Club, a group of church women interested in collecting teddy bears, had one male member, Bar-Jonah. He surrounded himself with children at church and helped with the Royal Rangers youth group just as he had in Massachusetts.

Bar-Jonah liked the dark-skinned good-looking unsuspecting child who lived in the adjacent duplex apartment. He watched the boy play in the backyard and from inside the house, took covert photos of him. Bar-Jonah frequently invited him to church events.

A fast-food restaurant within walking distance of home hired Bar-Jonah. In the part time position, he was in a familiar setting and became the "Biscuit and Chicken Man." His dream of opening a Christian shelter called the *Hobo and Trains Café* was dashed when he couldn't come up with enough money to start the business. But he didn't give up. He took great pride in his cooking and to enhance his skills, he enrolled in a gourmet cooking class held at a local high school. Bar-Jonah enjoyed the class with other adults in the community and used his growing recipe collection to share dishes at potlucks, and with friends and neighbors.

Bar-Jonah made an unforgettable grisly impression on his cooking classmates. He'd show up bedraggled in filthy clothes. Typically, he wore a stained shirt and baggy pants with shredded bottoms from dragging the street. His strange eyes, stringy long hair and bushy dark beard reminded some of Charles Manson. He didn't look like a chef or anyone clean enough to share his food.

The instructor paired him with a strait-laced retired kindergarten teacher who embodied the image of Maxine from Hallmark card fame. The tall lean woman with curly hair, bright red lipstick, dubbed "Bossy Bessy" by the class, ordered him around. The class thought she made him miserable. Overbearing and outspoken, never imagining a *Psycho* connection, she continuously called him "Norman." Based on his frowns, he hated it. Nathan corrected her, but she persisted.

Bar-Jonah recalled she was very precise and it "drove her nuts" when he wouldn't measure ingredients. He was accustomed to using a little salt dumped into his palm or a "dash" of flavoring. This wasn't her way. He claimed he enjoyed her company and didn't find her offensive.

Cooking class started each night as a sit-down gathering around a large table with friendly conversation until class started. Classmates said the strange man was quiet. One of his classmates recalled, "He almost never spoke but looked at you with an evil expression." At one point, he shared his interest in garage sales and antiques with the group. He told them he often went to sales at the end of the last day and many sellers would gladly give him the unsold stock just for carrying it away. This increased his inventory for garage sales at no cost to him.

The entertaining chef bought groceries for the whole class and they all split the cost. "Bessy" nagged at the chef about overcharging the class. One classmate said, "She drove everybody crazy but spent most of her time bossing Nathan around." The chef took mercy on Bar-Jonah and spent time talking to him.

The group cooked delicious spicy dishes. They left with an array of great new recipes including jambalaya, Italian red sauce, Italian stuffed meat loaf and Texas barbecue sauce. Later some of the classmates could not stomach the recipes after they learned their unusual friend was charged with murder and sharing gourmet dishes made from human flesh.

Chapter 6 Arrested for Molestation

Little more than two years after his arrival in Montana and barely off parole, Great Falls Police arrested Bar-Jonah for molesting an eight-year-old boy. Unsuspecting parents had left Jimmy* with him when they attended an out-of-town Christmas party. Upon return, their son told them Bar-Jonah had fondled his genitals. To the charge, Bar-Jonah responded as he had in the past, he didn't remember. "If I did it, I must have blacked out." He added, "If I fondled Jimmy, I probably would have killed him."

Prosecutors intended to try Bar-Jonah as a persistent felony offender, but Jimmy's mother didn't want her son to testify. She thought it would have an adverse effect on him, besides, she stated she didn't want Bar-Jonah to go to prison. She thought he was a nice man who needed help and said she would still be his friend.

The trial had been set for August 1994, but a year went by and nothing happened. The new County Prosecutor Brant Light received a huge case backlog including Bar-Jonah's. Processing the volume of cases soon after his transition into office was time-consuming. In the meantime, Bar-Jonah spent months in jail because the prosecutors were plagued with delays. His attorney filed a motion stating his client's right to a speedy trial had been violated. Later, Prosecutor Light was forced to drop the charges. Like Massachusetts, Montana failed to stop him.

After Bar-Jonah borrowed money from his sister and posted a $10,000 bond, he was released. Conditions of his release included living with his mother, following a 9 p.m. to 9 a.m. curfew, and checking in with his attorney three times a week.

In many molestation cases parents want to protect their children from the stress of facing the molester and refuse to let them testify. If the molester is a family member, the terrible deeds against children are often hidden to protect the family name. When that happens, the predator is able to continue the illegal destructive behavior.

Loving parents feel guilty when their child has been sexually abused. They want to end the child's emotional trauma but when they impede prosecution, they allow the molester to continue his terror.

Bar-Jonah continued his activities as he preyed on vulnerable women with needy children and pretended to help. On the surface, he was a kind generous man but beneath the facade he fantasized about their kids. With his collection of games and toys, he acted like a big kid. Many of the children appreciated the adult interaction and enjoyed special treats he served them.

Parked in front of the duplex, Bar-Jonah sat in his mother's car watching neighborhood children. He would call out and talk to passing kids. Two boys recalled spending time with him inside the duplex watching television and sharing snacks. They escaped unharmed, but after Bar-Jonah's arrest, they were frightened by the chance they'd taken. At the time, they trusted him and did not believe he was a threat.

In Bar-Jonah's eyes, something terrible happened after police charged him with molesting Jimmy. Officers visited the Assembly of God pastor and told him of Bar-Jonah's sexual predatory past and latest offense. The wise pastor removed him from the job as assistant leader of the Royal Rangers. When Bar-Jonah could no longer be alone with children at church, he was devastated.

While in jail on the molestation charge, Bar-Jonah met Doc Bauman. The retired orthopedist and Bar-Jonah shared an interest, young boys. Doc had been arrested on sex charges, *unlawful transactions with minors*. He and Bar-Jonah continued their friendship outside the Cascade County Jail. Doc was older, in failing health and troubled with progressive vision loss caused by macular degeneration. Bar-Jonah helped him with grocery shopping and invited him to dinner with Tyra.

While working at Hardee's fast-food restaurant, Bar-Jonah found another friend, Pamela Clark. With this clean, interesting, religious Black woman, he began talking of marriage and children. His new angle of attack is common with pedophiles—he'd have children of his own to molest.

He and Pam became engaged. From the very beginning, Tyra was dead set against their relationship.

The unlikely couple worked together, socialized and attended Mount Olive Christian Fellowship, Zachary Ramsay's church. Bar-Jonah claimed he didn't know Zach, but they were seen interacting.

Chapter 7 Zachary is Missing

On February 6, 1996, Zachary Xerxes Ramsay left home about 7 a.m. en route to Whittier Elementary School. As you learned earlier, the ten-year-old boy never arrived at his destination. After his mother, Rachel Howard, notified police, Great Falls Detective Bill Bellusci took charge of the investigation. The same day of the abduction, Detective Bellusci brought up Bar-Jonah's name as a possible perpetrator.

In child abduction cases, the FBI is involved. After the first FBI Special Agent transferred to Washington, D.C., James Wilson took over. In their rush to follow all leads, investigators conducted house-to-house searches along the route from Zachary's home to the school. They leveled snowbanks and scoured the river's edge but found no clues. Many people participated in the search. Between calls, ambulances cruised the neighborhood. Volunteers distributed missing-person posters with Zach's photo. Frequent television alerts helped get the information out. On the morning of the third day, bloodhounds worked the area but found nothing. Bellusci went to Bar-Jonah's house and knocked on the door. There was no answer.

Bar-Jonah stonewalled all contact with the police. He would not cooperate, and they couldn't force him to talk with them. Bellusci was aware of his stranger abductions in Massachusetts and had interrogated him over the previous molestation case. Bar-Jonah didn't like or trust the detective.

Investigators wondered if Zach had been kidnapped or killed. Had he just run away? Had his father abducted him? Was his mother the villain? Her former boyfriend?

Parental abductions are common and after the custody battle, Zachary's absentee father was an immediate suspect. Police contacted him in Colorado Springs, and he was cleared. As cruel as it seems to consider parental murder or to treat a grieving parent as a suspect, they had to investigate Rachel Howard.

Publicly, Rachel presented herself well, too well, according to some. A beautiful white woman with long dark hair and a quiet manner, she was calm. On television, she did not appear distraught over her son's disappearance. Hopeful he would be found soon, she said her faith would remain strong no matter what happened.

When officers went to Rachel's home, they found her in the process of replacing a piece of carpet. That made them more suspicious. After examining the old carpet for blood evidence and a search of her home, they cleared her, too.

Police questioned Rachel's ex-boyfriend. He was cleared of any possible link to Zach's disappearance. The man later committed suicide.

Zach's mother consulted psychics. They assured her Zachary was alive.

Many people came forward with information to help police.

Mike MacIntyre told detectives he saw a boy matching Zachary's description walking east toward Whittier School the morning he disappeared. On his route along the alley between Fourth and Fifth Avenues and Fourth and Fifth Streets North, Mike saw someone else in the alley, Nathanael Bar-Jonah.

When Mike went outside through the back door of his apartment building at Fifth Street North that morning to empty his garbage, he crossed the alley to the dumpster and noticed a man standing near it. He recognized and greeted him; it was Bar-Jonah. They had met before. MacIntyre recalled seeing him associating with children in the neighborhood.

From a vantage point near the dumpster, looking west across Fourth Street, Bar-Jonah had an unobstructed view of Zachary's front door at 414 Fourth Street North.

That same morning, Mike MacIntyre took his own daughter to the Good Guy Breakfast at Whittier School.

A little farther east along the route, the Henry family saw Zach, too. About 7:15 a.m., they were leaving for school. Mrs. Henry usually drove the children. That morning she used her husband's pickup which was parked behind their house near the alley route Zach took to school. Just after her two kids got in and she was pulling out, they all saw him. They remembered Zach well because he was nearly struck by a car as he darted across the street.

Mrs. Henry said it appeared as though the boy looked for traffic and didn't see any. But when he started across, a light-colored car almost hit him. She assumed the driver wasn't paying attention. The boy made it into the next alley and at that point was about four blocks from school. She had to get her children to school and herself to work before 7:30, so drove off. Later that day they realized the boy they'd seen was the missing Zachary and called police.

Another woman resident in the area also told police she saw Zach walking near her home en route to school.

One block farther east a man witnessed a crying boy being followed by an irate man. If it was Zachary that was the last time he was seen. The witness thought it was a father-son disagreement - until later.

For the next three years there was no progress in solving Zachary's disappearance.

Following Bar-Jonah's arrest on other charges in 1999, photographs of Bar-Jonah and Zachary appeared in the newspaper. Another witness came forward. At first police were not inclined to believe him. They wondered why he didn't report the incident three years earlier at the time the boy went missing.

The man, a resident of Washington State, had been visiting Great Falls in 1996. He didn't put it together until he saw the arrest photos which jarred his memory. He was absolutely certain he saw Zachary with Bar-Jonah in a light-colored car that looked like an ex-police car.

In an interview with Kim Skornogoski, reporter with the *Great Falls Tribune*, the witness told her he was driving near Whittier School when he met the other vehicle. In the front seat was a dark-haired worried-appearing boy. The driver was a man who looked like a truant officer, dressed in a dark jacket. "The kid was leaning forward in the seat as if to look around the guy's head to see me." He also recalled, "The guy [driver] was staring very hard, eye to eye."

Bar-Jonah had a car like the one described. The fearful boy could have been Zach.

Tyra and Bar-Jonah lived at 1216 First Avenue South, about seven blocks from Whittier School, south and east of it. Zach lived with his mother and a younger brother and sister, in a different direction, almost due west. What was Bar-Jonah doing standing in an alley before dawn on a cold winter morning less than a block from the Ramsay residence, a mile from his own home?

Chapter 8 Life Goes On

Following Zachary Ramsay's disappearance in 1996, Great Falls police detectives and FBI investigators searched diligently for clues but met with dead ends everywhere. They still considered Bar-Jonah a prime suspect, but he refused to talk to them and they had no evidence to obtain a search warrant. Prior to Zachary's abduction, except for a few weeks when Tyra was in Massachusetts after her sister died, Bar-Jonah had been under his mother's watchful eye. She had a calming and controlling influence on him. It was during her absence that Zachary disappeared.

Four months after Zachary's disappearance, sexual assault charges from the 1993 case against Bar-Jonah were finally dropped and Tyra could move back to Massachusetts to live near her daughter Lois. Tyra's life in Montana, living with her slovenly grown son, helping him financially, driving him around, and even helping with his yard jobs at her age, must have been difficult. After she left, he was free to do whatever he wanted and she likely felt relief being back in rural Massachusetts, far from the stress of daily life with him.

Bar-Jonah continued his relationship with Pamela Clark. By the time of his arrest in 1999, she had stopped seeing him and had moved to another state. Interviewed during the investigation that began in December 1999, she confirmed Bar-Jonah spent a lot of time in the duplex garage. "Sometimes he was out there all night long." It was set up like a "paradise for children."

Before Tyra moved back to Massachusetts, he had used her car at times. But she took the car with her, and Bar-Jonah was forced to bicycle or walk. Working part time, on such a low income, he couldn't afford a car and couldn't afford to pay rent to his brother for the duplex. Bar-Jonah moved to a new apartment across town, just off Tenth Avenue South conveniently located across the street from a hospital and less than a block from Hardee's. Pam and her daughter Mandy* lived in an adjacent building.

Bar-Jonah's high blood pressure, diagnosed in his twenties at the mental hospital, remained untreated. His weight contributed to diabetes and non-healing foot sores. He had bad teeth and no money for a dentist. Always short on money, Bar-Jonah searched for boarders to help with his rent payment.

Boarders came, but they didn't stay long after they saw and smelled his messy place. He continued sales of toys and collectibles but when he didn't have them on display, he stored them in the two-bedroom apartment. The residence was always piled high with boxes and filled with too much furniture, but the real problem was the stench. People could tolerate the clutter but not the suffocating smell that permeated the air and clung to their clothing.

For a while, Bar-Jonah rented a booth at the American Antique Mall located down the street from his apartment. It was close enough to walk and he kept the booth until 1998. A woman who shopped there said he displayed lower-end items such as fast-food promotional toys and glasses, games and junk. She had questioned him about a Barbie Doll he represented as "vintage" when it appeared used. She couldn't convince him it was not a collector's piece. The same woman had shopped at his garage sales held at the duplex and at the Collectors Club at the fairgrounds where he had the same corner table year after year. She described "strange people" hanging around him. He always appeared disheveled with dirty with long hair and untrimmed beard.

Bar-Jonah's toy sales and antique business supplemented his income. He had confidence in his ability and gained personal satisfaction designing his displays. Years of experience back in Massachusetts, beginning with flea markets as a youngster, paid off.

In September 1997, he met a new friend at the mall, Sherri Deitrich. She arrived in town driving a rented Ryder truck loaded with all her belongings. With no money and no place to stay, Bar-Jonah took pity and offered her not only a place to stay, but she paid him with her possessions which he sold at the mall.

This arrangement didn't set well with girlfriend Pam. She and Bar-Jonah did not live together, and Pam was very jealous after Sherri moved in with him. Pam was afraid this talkative white woman with dark-colored teased hair would come between her and her boyfriend. Pam and Sherri, both hefty women in their late thirties, were *not* friends. Even though they didn't like each other, when Bar-Jonah was at work, Sherri would show up at Pam's apartment and tell her stories she didn't want to hear.

Sherri warned Pam, "Nathan's a child molester. You better watch your daughter." Pam thought Sherri's stories were lies to get her out of the way so Sherri could claim him for herself.

Over time, Sherri's stories became more frightening. Pam didn't want to believe them, but she continued to listen. One day when Sherri was sitting with Mandy and Pam, she started in about him again. She said, "Nathan tied a little boy to a plywood board and killed him."

They were shocked and found it difficult to believe. He was such a nice man. Even though Mandy didn't like him and wouldn't eat his cooking, she didn't think he could do anything like that. They were sure Sherri had made up the story.

After his arrest in 1999, Pam recalled Sherri's stories and wondered if they were true after all. After police located and interviewed her, she told them what she could remember. "I saw this board. It coulda had blood on it but it was brown...Sherri said he molested a little boy, chopped him up and buried him in different spots. Police would not find his body scattered through the forest."

The taped conversation went on: "Sherri showed me bloody kitchen gloves. She said a lot of bizarre things, too. She was sort of a psychologist, multiple personality. She said Nathan was a split personality, a little boy and a man."

Pam said, "I saw two ropes, one in the car and one in the closet. Nathan gave puppet shows so I didn't think anything of it."

When police asked her about the apartment, Pam said, "It had a horrible odor. I smelled death in there. It was a fearful spirit." She explained, "My daughter and I would buy room spray. We couldn't use it. He would have allergies."

Pam tried to explain the odor. "I don't know what kind of smell that is. It wasn't cigarettes. It wasn't trash. He bathed every morning, but he carried a certain odor on him that was very displeasing."

When asked about his cooking, she recalled, "His cooking was very secret. My daughter wouldn't eat it. It tasted funny. The lasagna had a twang." Regarding the meat, she said, "I think he bought it at Buttrey's grocery...I didn't see him prepare it. He prepared it at home and brought it to me."

Sherri told police while living in his apartment, Bar-Jonah frequently locked himself in his bedroom. He'd flip the deadbolt on the inside of the door. She wondered what he was hiding. One day when he was at work, she decided to see for herself. In order to repay his kindness and hospitality, she also thought it would be a nice gesture to clean the apartment thoroughly. In the process she snooped around.

She found his bedroom stuffed with packages of toilet tissue and towels. In the closet, "A jacket was hung up...a smaller jacket. The kind you wear in high school. Dark green or blue with lighter colored sleeves." She found something else, "A plastic sack of children's clothes." She had already cleaned the floor when she opened the bag and pulled the clothes out. So much dirt fell out, she had to clean again.

"There was a pair of black high-top tennis shoes. I tried them on." She added, "There were underclothes, briefs, white, not boxers, white T-shirt and crew socks.

"The clothes were ridden with dirt and sand. There was a dark pair of pants, dirty. They might have been jeans."

She said she had asked Bar-Jonah later, "Where'd you get this stuff?"

He looked startled.

She asked, "Do you want me to wash them?"

He ordered her to put them back in the sack. "They belonged to a friend of one of my roommates, a mother and boy."

She described other things in the closet: "Snow shovel, box of chains for tires, battery charger and a little box with toys. There was also a doll cap and jacket, a light colored, off-white rope, skipping rope size. Electric cord, toys in a box, molded plastic figures, a ball and little knit gloves." All of them personal items, or items he might sell. The dirty children's clothing exactly matched the description of the clothes Zachary wore the day he disappeared, right down to the black high-top tennis shoes.

In her searching, Sherri also found telltale papers showing Nathan Bar-Jonah was really David Brown. When she told Pam this, it made her more suspicious. Maybe Sherri was telling the truth. But Pam wanted to believe in Bar-Jonah. She called him a "calm and gentle man."

Pam told police, "I would not believe he could do it [kill Zachary]. I would bank my life on it. He's too meek. He's too mild." She paused thoughtfully and then added, "His life was *all* about children."

Pam said she became so suspicious after hearing Sherri's tales that she waited until Bar-Jonah was at work and looked for herself. She said she climbed in through his ground floor window. "I'm not a snooper," she told a detective. "I trust people, but I wanted to see what he was hiding." She found a wig and fingernail polish, and then wondered if he was, "trying to be a drag queen."

Regarding their relationship, she responded, "One evening, we were together like lovers will do. Nathan said, 'I hope you will marry me. Maybe if I tell you what I've done, you won't marry me.'"

It was that night Pam found out he'd been in prison. He told her, "It was over a bird that had been killed." But he didn't do it and in the process of defending someone else, he got in trouble. He also told her he'd been molested as a little boy.

After some thought, Pamela recalled, "Nathan acted like a child. He'd throw actual tantrums. To see a big guy like this have a tantrum, it was frightening."

Soon after Sherri's snooping began, Sherri, Pam and Bar-Jonah were together in his living room. Sherri started talking about Tarot Cards. Pam said, "I couldn't understand it, why he got so mad. Yeah, the violence was there. I had to stop him. He coulda killed Sherri. Sherri jumped up and ran into her bedroom. I tried to calm him down." She emphasized, "He would kill her. He was going to hurt her. I left after that, I felt danger."

Bar-Jonah decided to evict Sherri, but she wouldn't leave. He wrote notes to her. One note said, "Sherri, Smile! Your [sic] on candid camera. My room has two hidden cameras. I got you on tape going through my personal papers and also taking the toilet paper for the bathroom. You cannot be trusted any more. Nathan." Later, on October 6, 1997, he gave Sherri an eviction notice. It said, "Find another place to stay as of Nov. 1. Try not to piss me off. Shut off the damn lights when you leave. My electric bill is outrageous..."

That time Sherri moved out.

Pamela moved to a different location, too. She told police in the 1999 interview, "I have this inside ability I was born with, my inner thing would tell me things, like when to move. We broke up in 1997. My daughter said he gave her the creeps."

Just like Tyra wanted, Nathan wrote a letter to Pam breaking off their engagement. But Pam had already separated herself from him. Bar-Jonah's brother said it was because Pam's "religious beliefs were not in sync" with his brother's. Bob also commented, "I marveled that this woman was a bit above Nathan in social class. I wondered what she saw in him."

The real question is—why didn't these women contact the police in the year following Zachary's disappearance when Sherri was convinced he'd killed a boy and chopped him up?

Why did the police have to draw it out of them years later, after his arrest in 1999? Were they afraid of his wrath?

Chapter 9 The Cookie Man

Bar-Jonah realized both Pam and Sherri knew some of his dark secrets. They knew he had a prison record. Pam didn't believe the outrageous story that he was locked up for some lame excuse about a dead bird. But he was such a nice man; she didn't think it was anything too bad. He had lied and she knew it, but she had wanted to believe in him and had done her best to do so.

With Pam out of his life and Sherri out of his apartment, Bar-Jonah's stress didn't fade, in fact, it increased because he needed rent money. He had worked part-time at Hardee's for four years, but the income was inadequate to meet his needs. Other than the Treatment Center Canteen, it was his most stable work history.

On the outside, Bar-Jonah's existence appeared comfortable. He lived in a two-bedroom daylight basement apartment in a nice two-story modern brick building located less than a block from his job. Sometimes he invited male employees from Hardees over for dinner; at Christmastime, he even bought presents for other workers. It appeared he was doing well, but that was not the case. In this "normal" environment he continued to seek the companionship of young boys.

It was three years earlier that ten-year-old Zachary Ramsay had disappeared en route to school. Nathanael Bar-Jonah lived near Zachary's school and knew the boy but had refused to cooperate with police. A suspect from the beginning, Detectives and FBI investigators had followed all leads. They obtained Bar-Jonah's prison and medical records from Bridgewater. From these, they not only learned details of his violent past but of his interest in cannibalism.

Following Zachary's disappearance, their interviews raised the sickening suspicion that Bar-Jonah killed him and disposed of his body by cooking and eating it. Unsuspecting neighbors, relatives, friends and church members at potlucks had shared his special meals of chili, spaghetti, quiche and stew. They all said the meat tasted strange. But investigators had insufficient evidence for a search warrant, or arrest, so they waited.

To supplement his meager income, Bar-Jonah took a second part-time job at Fuddruckers upscale restaurant that catered to children. From his apartment, it was a two-block walk. Between September and December 1999, Bar-Jonah had the best job a hungry pedophile could desire. He was the "The Cookie Man" in the bakery department handing out free cookies to kids.

One day, Special Agent James Wilson's children stood face to face with the man their father believed was responsible for abducting and cannibalizing a ten-year-old boy. When Special Agent Wilson recognized the ex-convict handing cookies to his little children, a sickening thought raced through his mind. *He wants to eat my children.*

The job didn't last but Bar-Jonah worked there long enough to meet many children, including those of Special Agent Wilson. Wilson and his family had just finished a meal at the homey restaurant filled with kids. Laughing children gathered around large tables covered with red or blue checkered tablecloths, while others lined up at the bakery for free cookies. Adults looking for a quiet meal might think it was too noisy but energetic children found the place enjoyable. It was the perfect setting for a pedophile––being paid to be with children.

Before long, Bar-Jonah's new job was in jeopardy. At work, he spoke very seldom but fixated on one young attractive female employee. She became so fearful and uncomfortable with his stares that she refused to work with him. After more employees leveled complaints against him resulting in a reprimand, he became verbally abusive and threatened to sue the restaurant. Throughout his life, even in prison, Bar-Jonah had used threats of personal lawsuits to intimidate people. The method usually worked because no one wanted to be sued, so they would often back off and he'd get his way in the end.

This time he lost the job.

With money a problem, Bar-Jonah continued to court roommates. After living in his car, one man accepted Bar-Jonah's offer. Initially he was pleased—until he walked inside and found the apartment looked like a furniture storage shed stacked with trash bags and reeking with the foul smell of rotting garbage. Excess furniture and boxes made it difficult to walk through the living room. Two couches and a desk filled most of the floor space. Jumbled knickknacks, games and videos stuffed an entertainment center leaning against one wall. In the kitchen, mountains of empty cans, dirty dishes and glasses covered every flat surface except the stove top.

The new roommate cleaned his bedroom and covered the odor with air fresheners. After one month, he left. During that month, the roommate said he never saw Bar-Jonah cook but often noted two young boys visiting. They were "very friendly, chit-chatting like good neighbors and good friends."

The boys in his apartment building were nice kids living in a crowded upstairs apartment directly above Bar-Jonah. They enjoyed spending time downstairs with him watching television and videos. The boys relaxed on the couches eating treats of chips, pizza and pop. Initially, two half brothers, Calvin*, age fourteen and Buddy*, age five, visited Bar-Jonah. After their 9-year-old cousin Eddie* came later to stay, all three boys hung out in the basement apartment with Bar-Jonah where they even stayed over night.

Bar-Jonah groomed them with friendship and kindness. He could have lived in his lair for years, enjoying the company of his little friends. But he couldn't keep his hands off them. Like all sexual predators, he couldn't stop. His fantasies stirred, especially when his stress accelerated. After the boys learned to trust him, Bar-Jonah became bold. He walked around wearing only jockey shorts, exposed himself, molested them and using ropes, choked them. He threatened them with death if they told.

They didn't tell.

Bar-Jonah had lost his job at Fuddruckers. He had no roommates. He had no money. It was nearly Christmas and that made things worse. For his favorite holiday, his decorated apartment appeared festive, but he was in turmoil, very unhappy and alone. His mother had been a calming factor in the past, but this time there was no one to calm him. His fantasies took over and as in the past, stress had triggered abductions and violence. He fit the profile of most sexual predators, when his stress-state accelerated, his fantasies accelerated. He wouldn't be calmed until he acted.

Living two blocks from Lincoln Elementary school, many mornings, Bar-Jonah donned his authentic navy-blue police jacket with a reinforced area for his badge. In the early morning before school started, Bar-Jonah walked to the schoolyard to mingle with children.

He prowled for a victim.

Off-duty police officer Robert Burton noted a large dark-clothed figure lurking in early morning darkness near Lincoln Elementary School. Persistent icy winds off the east slope of the Rocky Mountains swirled snow and chilled little children dressed in bulky jackets and boots struggling to class. The man slowly circled the school, stalking the little children.

Officer Burton recognized him from the previous arrest for molesting a boy and knew of Bar-Jonah's violent past. He'd seen the man at Lincoln for the preceding few days and wondered what he was doing. Suspicious of the behavior, Burton called in and requested a police car be dispatched to the area.

Uniformed officers found the bearded man dressed in the dark colored police-style jacket. They aimed a spotlight on him and asked him to stop. Instead, he quickly walked away. The first officer got out of his car and this time, ordered him to stop. A second car arrived. Officers Brunk and Badgely placed Bar-Jonah in front of one of the cars in the headlights. Defiant, he stood stiffly with hands jammed in his pockets.

Asked if they should be concerned about what was in his pockets, he revealed a stun gun, two cans of pepper spray, a toy gun and fake police badge. Nathan Bar-Jonah had finally given officers a reason to arrest him. He was charged with impersonating an officer and carrying a concealed weapon.

Bar-Jonah was charged and released.

Officer Burton alerted Detective Bellusci who was in charge of investigating sexually related crimes. He was the same officer who arrested Bar-Jonah on molestation charges two years prior to Zachary's disappearance. Bellusci carried Bar-Jonah's file to Chief Prosecutor Brant Light. After impatiently waiting for many years, Light had reason to issue a warrant to search Bar-Jonah's apartment.

Chapter 10 Pack Rat Paradise

In contrast to the pleasant entrance of Bar-Jonah's apartment with pictures of Santa and an angel greeting everyone at the door, inside a rotten smell permeated the stagnant air. Agent Wilson recalled it smelled like a combination of "death and burned flesh." In spite of the putrid odor, Christmas was in the air.

A dozen little stockings decorated one wall, and a huge, wrapped object that looked like a framed picture hung on another. Many colorful gifts with blank cards attached rested beneath a television stand next to a box of addressed greeting cards ready for mailing. Another wall displayed holiday ribbons adorned with a collection of star-shaped sheriff badges.

Decorations covered every surface not piled with junk. Because of floor clutter, only a narrow pathway remained to navigate from room to room. Clothing lay strewn on the floor while empty dresser drawers stood open. Like his former roommate had described, the kitchen counter sat heaped with fast-food wrappers and dirty dishes. Bags of garbage covered the floor. Agent Wilson captured the mess on videotape before investigators disturbed anything. He took care not to miss a thing.

Photos of Santa with little children were everywhere. On a bulletin board, a note from Santa explained:

I checked my list.

I checked it twice.
I found out you were not very nice.
I thought it over and here's the scoop.
All you get is snowman poop.

In stark contrast to the silly poem and festive decorations, the next room held a collection of news articles on Zachary's abduction from three years earlier and other morbid objects. Leaning against Bar-Jonah's bedroom wall stood a large plywood board with chop marks and an ominous dark stain. It appeared to be the one that had concerned his friend Sherri.

Photos of Zachary, stacks of large albums picturing mostly boys, and many notebooks filled with handwritten strangely jumbled letters caught their attention. Agent Wilson closely examined the writing and before the day was over, had deciphered parts of the code.

The team collected and boxed an enormous amount of evidence while breathing in a stench that made it difficult to work. At the end of the day, they left with twenty-eight boxes, some containing receipts dating back twenty years.

Detectives Bellusci, Officers Grubb and Schalin, and Special Agent Wilson found thousands of child pictures and piles of spiral notebooks. Notebooks contained lists of names, some of them children of local law officers and lawyers. Even Prosecutor Brant Light's daughter was on the list. Many of the names had been taken from a stash of yearbooks from Great Falls schools. One notebook sheet carefully written in green gel pen entitled "Lake Webster" (where he started his vile activities) had a list of twenty-seven names.

Preceding each name on this ominous list was a year, a name and a number. Some names also had adjacent letters such as "BLDH/BE" or "BKH/BR."

At first, the coded meaning wasn't clear, but soon they realized the number was the child's age. The rest was a description such as, "blonde hair/blue eyes" or "black hair/brown eyes." After the description, another name followed an equal sign. It was his log to the photos of children whose names were changed. A photo album held carefully organized pictures of these children labeled with the names as noted on the list, not their real names, some known victims. Investigators feared others on the list might be dead.

Personal writings listed Zachary's name with victims. This fueled investigators' belief that Bar-Jonah had abducted the missing boy, too.

They found many samples of writing with strings of letters and no spaces. There were no obvious words, and the letter jumbles appeared meaningless. But soon Special Agent Wilson saw a cipher pattern and recognizable words jumped out at him. They were recipes for dishes made from human flesh including *stir-fried penis* and *little boy stew*.

Chapter 11 Damning Evidence

Relief swept over Bar-Jonah after his initial release from custody. He thought he'd face minor charges and no jail time. At that point, he thought he'd duped law enforcement again. They wouldn't realize he was scouting for another victim to enjoy and ease his anxiety. Nor would they suspect his activities with the kids at the apartment complex because they wouldn't tell. He'd threatened them with death. Besides, the boys and their parents liked him.

December 13th,1999, turned out to be a very unlucky day for Bar-Jonah. His arrest triggered two search warrants that unearthed massive ruinous evidence.

Elated investigators who had worked the Zachary Ramsay case for years found information that pointed to Bar-Jonah as the killer. Jumbled handwritten notes revealed recipes for human flesh. They finally knew what had happened to Zachary and why they'd found no body. After securing Bridgewater Treatment Center records that revealed Bar-Jonah's fantasies of torture and cannibalism, they were sure.

The cluttered apartment contained so many items of interest it was difficult to sort through everything. Bar-Jonah's lifetime of hoarding would be his downfall.

Once investigators sorted through everything and organized the evidence into a meaningful format, they could analyze the details. Boxes of receipts dated back twenty years.

They didn't know which ones were meaningless and which ones might carry clues to other crimes, maybe other missing children. Cancelled checks, bank notices of insufficient funds, old driver licenses, car rental agreements, gas receipts and paycheck stubs intermingled with copies of letters and prayers he had written.

A letter and poem detailed some of his intentions. Over the years, Bar-Jonah courted women through pen pal and audio tape relationships. From his apartment in Great Falls, he told them of his good cooking and wrote love poetry. The following sample of writing taken from his notes in evidence is a poem in-the-making:

"Roses are red, Violets are blue,
I'm marriage minded, how about you?
I'm looking for a lady to share my interests
And for one to share my day when the work is done.
Kids are a plus up to eleven.
My cooking will make you feel like you've died and gone to
heaven.
I am indeed uniquely maladjusted but fun to be with too.
I've got so much love to give you and your little dog, too.
I've got tutti-frutti eyes and weigh nineteen stone.
Drop me a line, a family photo, and I will too."

Bar-Jonah sounds like an innocent man, a "late bloomer" as he called himself. But he wasn't searching for a woman; he was searching for a child and companionship of boys under age eleven.

When Bob Brown heard his brother had been arrested at the school, he rushed to the apartment and took a laptop computer he'd let Bar-Jonah borrow. Bob explained to police that Bar-Jonah was computer illiterate. Bob said he was in the process of teaching his brother some computer skills and that only training files were on the laptop. Its data files contained nothing of interest to police. Bob said even the trash bin was empty. What he showed officers supported his claim.

Police didn't confiscate the computer or do a forensic evaluation of the files to see if important information had been erased, data that might have helped the investigation. The hard drive could have been reformatted leaving no apparent information behind, except to a forensic expert. Because of Internet use by pedophiles and pornographers, forensic computer experts have become instrumental in convictions.

Contrary to what Bob said, Bar-Jonah had some working knowledge of computers. He had used one at Bridgewater for years. Bar-Jonah may not have told his brother.

It took Bellusci and other investigators about a month to wade through twenty-eight boxes of evidence. Many photographs in the albums had been cut from yearbooks and meticulously pasted in with names below each picture. At a glance, detectives identified photographs of known child victims labeled with the wrong names. Later they found a logbook revealing lists which correlated bogus names with correct names.

In addition to school photos, there were other pictures, but few were sexually explicit, and none showed evidence of child pornography. They found an unsettling unlabeled photograph of a dead baby in a casket. Pictures of genitals and naked bodies had been cut from adult magazines.

Police evidence-lab personnel developed film found on two disposable cameras. The rolls contained numerous photos of a naked Bar-Jonah showing his deep eight-inch-long right thigh scar, and his penis in various stages of erection. The film also contained many pictures of unknown children, some in suggestive poses. In addition, they found videos of the same children who were later identified as his young friends from the apartment upstairs, and a photo of Zachary Ramsay taken in front of his school.

Of great interest to the investigators were stacks and boxes filled with spiral-bound notebooks. The notebooks contained amazing lists of names of people, cities, states and countries around the world. Was this mindless compulsive copying or did they also carry hidden tales of terror?

Among his papers, Special Agent Wilson found weird writings with letters compressed together without spaces. Initially they appeared meaningless but when he saw the words materialize, his interpretation and exclamation sent a shock wave through the team. There, in Bar-Jonah's own handwriting, embedded with the letters of his full name, they found little boy stew and other dishes made from human body parts. They felt ill. In disgust and anger, they issued an arrest warrant for crimes against Zachary.

Their work was far from done.

From the many boxes, Detective Bellusci moved items of high interest into a separate area. Two of importance: The "Lake Webster List" and an academic article on traditional theories of sleep and dreams. Underlined and marked with margin notes, it appeared Bar-Jonah had tried to come up with a plausible explanation that the boy he was accused of molesting in 1993 could have been dreaming. There were also photocopies of pages from a book, Sex in Dreams.

A job application showed creative thinking on his part. Bar-Jonah listed his work in the Treatment Center Canteen as "T.C. Cantina." On it, he said the supervisor/owner had closed the restaurant and was not available for a job reference. It appeared Bar-Jonah was in the process of developing a new identity, Phil Brown. His father's birth certificate had been altered to show Bar-Jonah's [David Brown's] date of birth and he used his father's name on a resume.

Numerous officers worked on the case. They tracked down as many clues as they could. Detectives made a public request asking people who knew Bar-Jonah to come forward and talk to them. A large response resulted in hundreds of interviews including many who had eaten funny meat.

Sgt. Dave Smith and Detective Tim Theisen interviewed people in many states including Wyoming where a child was missing. They had found evidence that Bar-Jonah was planning to move to Wyoming. Canadian authorities also reported the Border Patrol had turned Bar-Jonah back when he attempted to enter their country.

In April, Tim Theisen and Lead Detective Sgt. John Cameron traveled to Massachusetts where they interviewed Tyra, Bar-Jonah's sister Lois and her husband. Conversations with the Brown family revealed little. The family did not believe he was responsible for Zachary's disappearance. It was all a big mistake.

Tyra defended her son. Now very hard of hearing but outspoken in his support, she explained to officers that his trouble stemmed from a childhood incident when he was "gang raped." She said he didn't say anything about it until ten years later because he was so upset. She made it clear she wanted to know details of all the charges against him. "I don't have to be protected! I'm eighty-four," she said.

When asked if Bar-Jonah used her car, she assured them he never used it without her permission. "That I know of," she added quietly.

Theisen and Cameron informed her Bar-Jonah had used it when she was back in Massachusetts for her sister's funeral. Receipts showed he'd put gas in it at that time.

Unfortunately, the family didn't offer to let detectives search items Bar-Jonah had sent home for safekeeping, items that could have held terrible secrets. Were there journals or a video documenting Zachary's death hidden in a secure location? Bar-Jonah told me he had sent important items home, including treasured cookbooks. These have never been searched by law enforcement. Massachusetts jurisdiction allowed Montana investigators access to Tyra's car but refused to issue a search warrant for other items.

During the interview, Tyra claimed, Jimmy, the first Great Falls boy who said he was molested by Bar-Jonah, was a liar. Lois supported her mother's belief, "It was made up." Lois also said she felt sorry for her brother Bob because he worked so hard and had done his best to help his brother. Lois said Bob had been troubled by Bar-Jonah's "deep secrets, not shared." Lois said Bar-Jonah lived just like he did in prison. It was "lockdown time" at 7 p.m. He'd go to his bedroom and shut the door. She suggested the officers concentrate their search efforts in Bar-Jonah's old bedroom and the garage at Bob's duplex.

In the taped interview with the Browns, the family sounded like wonderful caring people. Lois's young granddaughter even offered a toy to Detective Theisen to carry back to Montana as a present for his child.

The family was upset by the charges against Bar-Jonah. They said they grieved for the missing boy and his family. They hoped Zachary would be found.

Back in Great Falls, detectives interviewed Bob Brown. The whole ordeal Bob had to endure, first with his brother's notoriety and then the invasion of his home for a detailed search, was difficult for him. In contrast to his untidy brother, Bob was compulsively clean. Bob had tried to give his brother a new start on life but things had not gone well for either of them.

After his wife divorced him, Bob sold the home where they'd lived and remodeled the lower level of the duplex as an apartment for himself. By the time of the arrest in 1999, Bob had finished the basement, cemented the floor and had thoroughly cleaned and painted Bar-Jonah's garage. Investigators said when they visited Bob, his apartment was in perfect order. Even books were perfectly arranged according to size.

Bob's ex-wife, Donna*, said she never saw her brother-in-law violent. When he first moved to Great Falls, he lived with them for about half a year, and then moved to the separate nearby apartment. Eventually, he moved to the duplex with Tyra. Donna recalled the young black woman with a son about age eight who lived in the other half of the side-by-side duplex adjacent to Tyra and Bar-Jonah. Detectives found evidence he watched the boy, photographed him covertly and kept track of his activities on a calendar noting when Bob had taken the boy on a fishing trip.

Donna said the most upset she'd ever seen Bar-Jonah was when "he was booted out of the Royal Rangers." That position had meant a lot to him. It was a reenactment of his younger days, a position of power. Probably most important, it removed him from easy access to little boys and provided public exposure of his dangerous behavior.

After Zachary's disappearance, Bar-Jonah's sister-in-law recalled nothing unusual. At that time, he was no longer living with them, but she said she'd observed his behavior at the duplex. "He didn't do anything different. If he wasn't in a prison cell, he went in his room and didn't come out."

In a video interview with police, Bob appeared depressed and defeated. His shoulders drooped as he sat at a table answering Detective Cameron's and Theisen's questions. With nine years separating them, Bob explained, "I didn't know Nathan. I changed his diapers, but I left home for the military at age nineteen. Shortly after I went to Turkey, Nathan went to prison."

Bob had rarely seen his brother between the ages of ten and thirty-four when he was released from prison in 1991 and moved to Montana.

The following information and quotes are from a police videotaped interview:

Bob said he got mad at his brother because he was so dirty. Bar-Jonah tracked grease onto light-colored carpets in the duplex and didn't clean up after himself. Bob also said his brother always had car trouble. "He couldn't fix even the simplest things; once the starter was hanging on by one bolt. If his car broke down, it would sit there till I had time to work on it."

He said Bar-Jonah usually had a job but never a full-time one. He rarely drank alcohol, seldom socialized and watched television endlessly. "We are different as night and day. Even when he was here, we weren't that close. Not the same life...it makes me sad it's my brother. He's the type of person that could walk into a field where there is a little pile of shit. He'd fall into it. It seems to cling to him...I would have done anything. I even offered to buy him teeth. He refused. He's very stubborn...I'm a Type A person. If there's a problem, I can find a solution." Bob said he gave up trying to help. "I decided I was just going to be his friend."

When Bar-Jonah landed a job at the Air Force Base for $6.72 per hour Bob was delighted. Finally, he had a wonderful opportunity to succeed. Two weeks later he was arrested. Bob frowned and said, "See, shit just seems to cling to this man."

Bar-Jonah shared nothing personal with his family, not even when he was seriously ill did he call his brother. Bob was shocked by a telephone call from a doctor who told him his brother was in the hospital with a heart attack. It was his second heart attack and Bob hadn't even known about the first.

Detectives asked Bob about Zachary.

Bob shook his head sadly and asked if the river had been dragged. Then he added, "It was frozen solid in February. Trying to think like Nathan, I wondered about the dump and if they'd checked dumpsters." He explained, "Nathan's not very smart. Well, he is smart, but about things like that he wouldn't be very smart. He panics easily and doesn't handle stress. He becomes angry. That's how he handles stress. If he did it, I don't think it would be hard to find the body. It's sad to say that." He explained, "My brother is very personable, like a Baby Huey, or a cuddly teddy bear. But he is fiercely independent and wants to do everything on his own. He has had many opportunities to make things better.

"If Nathan really did it, there is nothing I can do. My goal would be to get Nathan help, but he has to want it. I worry about him doing it again.

"I want the truth, for Nathan's own good, for the sake of his soul. I just can't feature him doing that. My mother, for years and years couldn't believe it, but now she's started to, but she is unaware...and things could happen right under her nose."

Bob emphasized, "This hasn't been fun for the family. He comes from a really good family. This has been heartbreaking for both families -ours and Zach's."

On December eighteenth, a warrant was issued for Nathanael Bar-Jonah's arrest. Officers found him at the unemployment office sitting on a bench with other men. Disheveled and dirty, eyes downcast, he sat motionless, as if trying to hide by blending in with the rest. When Bar-Jonah saw the officers, his shoulders slumped, and a blank look transformed to an image of fatigue and failure. Just as he had in the past, he gave up without a struggle.

Nathanael Benjamin Levi Bar-Jonah was charged with aggravated kidnapping and deliberate homicide, punishable by death. Bail was set at $2.2 million.

After her son's arrest for murder, Tyra flew to Great Falls to be with him. Bob took the devastated woman to the Cascade County Jail to visit her son. With a glass divider between them, she couldn't kiss him or even give him a hug. When she later met one of the jail nurses, Tyra begged her, "Take good care of my baby."

Chapter 12 Tracing His Steps

Webster, Massachusetts 2000

The "Lake Webster" list sent Montana investigators to Bar-Jonah's hometown of Webster and back to Bonnette Acres subdivision where he'd spent minimal time in more than thirty years. The area had changed little since his childhood. Many of the neighbors lived in the same homes. The large popular lake still drew swimmers, boaters and fishermen from southern Massachusetts. The Dupont's pine trees still bore the scars from Phil's cutting. But time had allowed enough brush overgrowth to hide the Bates Cemetery from view.

Police from Southbridge, Shrewsbury, Webster and other small towns in the area helped Montana detectives with the difficult prospect of finding all the people on the Lake Webster list. The elapsed time caused problems. People on the list and others who knew Bar-Jonah had grown up and moved away. Police found some neighborhood residents reluctant to talk.

When the sensational news of Bar-Jonah's arrest and alleged cannibalism in Montana hit a local Massachusetts newspaper The Patriot, few realized he was a person they knew. The scruffy bearded man in the arrest photo looked nothing like the clean-cut boy they'd known. After scrutinizing the high school graduation picture published with the arrest photo, they realized it was David. He'd changed his appearance and his name. David Paul Brown was now Nathanael Benjamin Levi Bar-Jonah. His old classmates and neighbors were shocked.

Ironically, two officers with the Southbridge Police Department, Detective Sgt. Norman Brodeur and Officer Mario Marcucci, remembered Bar-Jonah very well. They had attended high school with David Brown. Back then, he was a loner but someone who caused no trouble in school. Now they were involved with an unbelievable search for possible victims on his detailed "Lake Webster" list.

In Webster, Officers John Boulduc and Michaela Kelley spent hours on phone calls, visits to his old neighborhood and personal interviews. Officer Kelley stated many people she talked to denied anything had happened to them or their children, but some didn't look her in the eye. She got the impression they were not telling the truth. The officers even found parents who tried to protect their grown children by blocking police from contacting them. Some denied vehemently that their child had suffered abuse.

Other talkative parents voiced their concerns. One mother said, "He was big, you know, overweight and tall, yet he always hung out with little kids." Another said, "I wouldn't let my boy play with him after he got a letter from David. He was away at camp and wrote to my son and said he wanted to play as soon as he got back. It sounded innocent, but my son was half his age."

The first name on the Lake Webster list was Mary Paquette, age six, 1963. Mary was the first child Bar-Jonah reportedly choked when he was six. Most of the names on the list were males. The last two were known abductions that had sent him to prison at the age of twenty in 1977.

One by one, officers located people on the list. Some of them still lived in the area. The investigation opened old wounds; things people had tried to forget resurfaced. What happened to them just wasn't discussed back then. Jason Mercer*, one of the young victims, was living in another state. He learned his name was on the list and called Special Agent James Wilson in Montana.

Mercer emotionally confided that for thirty years he had told no one about how David had repeatedly molested him. Jason kept the ugly secret. He wished he hadn't, saying he might have prevented the abuse of others.

Jason Mercer was David's first known male victim. At the time of the first episode, Jason said he'd been sledding in the woods along the cemetery road with his older sister and David. David suggested the boys go deeper into the woods to urinate. When they were well out of view and earshot of Jason's sister, the unsuspecting little boy relieved himself but suddenly David pushed him backwards. Then huge David sat on the small boy's abdomen, crushing the wind out of him. Jason could barely breathe and couldn't scream as David thrust his penis into the boy's mouth. It was a year later when something happened again. Jason couldn't tell that time either.

Harboring the secret abuse took a toll on Jason's life. Angry and troubled, he had problems relating to others, especially children. Jason never told his parents or his wife of the abuse; he tried to forget and had been comforted knowing David was in prison. After learning via the investigation and Webster list of names that David had been freed and had continued his attacks on others, Jason was appalled. Repulsed by the stories he'd read, and after finally revealing his plight to James Wilson, Jason asked to testify against Bar-Jonah to keep others from being harmed.

To investigators' relief, everyone on the Webster list was accounted for. Five of them acknowledged they were sexual assault victims. Much more work lay ahead before dogged investigators could bring Bar-Jonah to justice. They needed evidence tying him to the Zachary Ramsay disappearance in Montana. The detectives wanted to conduct a search of Bar-Jonah's mother's home in the Webster area and her car, the one he had driven in Montana. They needed cooperation and permission from the Commonwealth of Massachusetts and County Prosecutor John Conte, the same prosecutor who had set Bar-Jonah loose and sent him to an unsuspecting Montana population in 1991.

Considering the sordid evidence found in his Montana apartment, their request sounded appropriate and important. Massachusetts refused to cooperate and blocked a search of the residence. A judge finally issued a search warrant for the car. He allowed Montana detectives to speak with the Brown family but refused a household search for stored items.

An FBI team carried out the automobile evidentiary search looking for hair, fibers and debris. They found strands of Tyra's gray hair but nothing of value to help solve Zachary's disappearance. Detectives returned to Great Falls disappointed. The victims in Massachusetts confirmed a pattern of violent behavior dating back to age ten but there was no information to fill gaps in the Ramsay case.

Chapter 13 Three More Victims

In July 2000, Detectives Tim Theisen and John Cameron, and Special Agent Wilson interviewed the children living in Bar-Jonah's apartment building. Bellusci had interviewed them right after the arrest in December. Later, he realized the boys in photos on the evidence rolls of film were also in videos found in Bar-Jonah's apartment. In their first interaction with the police, the boys flatly denied Bar-Jonah had done anything to them. The second time was a different story, that time Calvin* and Eddie* talked.

A journal article in his apartment revealed Bar-Jonah's organized approach to selecting vulnerable children. The article's author described children who were poor witnesses against sexual offenders. Those detailed were minority heritage, learning disabled, from low income and single parent homes. The children who lived upstairs fit the profile exactly. Nathan Bar-Jonah had specifically targeted the young Native American boys with learning disabilities.

The boys had liked Bar-Jonah. He treated them well at times, but also made them do things that made them feel dirty, secrets that couldn't be told or they might end up dead. Eventually their tearful stories exposed his exploitations.

At the age of fourteen, Calvin appeared younger. The smiley good-looking boy resembled Zach Ramsay. Even though Calvin had trouble with reading and writing, in special education classes he had mastered printing. His chubby hyperactive five-year-old half-brother Buddy* loved going to Bar-Jonah's to watch television and eat chips. Their cousin Eddie had come to live with them when his mother was hospitalized in Great Falls.

The three boys became fixtures in Bar-Jonah's apartment. The kids spent most of their time in the living room, relaxing or sleeping on the couches. He barred them from the kitchen. A blanket curtained the doorway.

Like most pedophiles, Bar-Jonah groomed the boys with kindness, taking them on trips around town, to the County Fair, and movies. The kids enjoyed his game-filled apartment stocked with snacks, a VCR and movie library. In December just before his arrest, as a special treat, Bar-Jonah had taken Calvin out for dinner. They visited Bar-Jonah's new workplace at Malmstrom Air Force Base.

Bar-Jonah also groomed their parents. A family of eleven crowded into a two-bedroom apartment. Living conditions worsened when relatives came to stay. The family had little money and lived on welfare. Parents visited with Bar-Jonah. They learned to trust him and appreciated his interest in the boys. At times, they borrowed money from him and allowed their sons to stay overnight.

Bar-Jonah never invited the boys' sisters.

Police videotapes of interviews with Calvin and Eddie revealed poignantly how much they feared Bar-Jonah. Typical of Native American culture, they were quiet with little eye contact. Calvin was shy. He didn't want to bring shame to his family by exposing the molestation, but he knew about Zachary's disappearance from television news reports and that his friend Bar-Jonah was under arrest for murdering the child. With Bar-Jonah behind bars, Calvin felt safer. He told investigators Bar-Jonah had told him and Eddie, he'd kill them if they ever told about sexual contacts with him. The first-time police asked Calvin, he couldn't tell; he feared for his life.

In the second interview months later, Calvin sobbed out the truth. The big boy's shoulders shook. He hid his face and cried for nearly an hour before he could speak. "He wanted me and Eddie to touch his wiener. 'Grab my wiener' he'd say. He forced us. He would grab us by the arm and put it by his wiener. He made me touch it. He put my hand there."

Calvin said Bar-Jonah "would lay naked on his bed and want us to lay with him or he'd get mad at us. He'd make us pull our clothes down and touch our butts with his hands.

"He had handcuffs. He would handcuff us and sit on us. He sat on me until I'd run out of breath.

"He didn't stick nothing in us. He'd grab our heinies and put it by his wiener. He wanted us to rub his scar.

"He showed us a stun gun and said, 'Let me try this on you.'

"He would make us stand by his closet and pull our clothes down. He'd touch us with his hands.

"He used handcuffs. He'd sit on us and tried to make us play with his wiener on the couch. He'd hold me down and sit on me. Sometimes Buddy was with us. Nathan would try to rub his butt, too."

Calvin went on with difficulty, "The ropes were tied around my neck and over a two-by-four in the bedroom. It was a white rope, very tight. It felt weird. I thought I was going to die...it was tight around my neck over the bed. He'd hang me about a minute then he'd let me go home.

"I saw him hang my cousin Eddie in the kitchen from a ceiling rope. Eddie was crying. Eddie tried to stick his hands inside the rope, trying not to choke. He thought he'd pass out.

"Nathan showed us a big, long steak knife. He said, 'I'll just cut you up in pieces' and laugh. Then he'd go in the bathroom and shut the door.

"He said his brother would shoot me. He'd bury me where no one could find me...I was scared, man."

Calvin explained, "I thought he'd chop me up. That's the only way you can get someone out of the house [when they're dead]."

Eddie's interview didn't go as well. Detectives had to drive across the state to reach his home. There was no neutral area there where they could talk to him. Finally, they went to a comfortable area in the school. The first time, he talked freely and spoke of many of the same things Calvin had talked about. When investigators went to play back the tape, they found no sound. The audio portion failed to record his voice. The repeat interview was a disaster. Eddie didn't want to go through it again. He finally did, but the second time he wanted his mother with him.

Interviews of this nature are usually more accurate when not stilted by the presence of a parent, but Eddie wouldn't do it without her. Eddie said Bar-Jonah put a noose around his neck and lifted him off the kitchen floor. The rope hung from the ceiling. Maybe that was why Bar-Jonah didn't want anyone in his kitchen. He wanted to hide the hole where he hung the noose. He wanted to hide his tactics, his plans, and his fantasies.

Eddie said, with the rope around his neck, he panicked. He couldn't breathe and he thought he was going to die. He struggled and gasped. When Bar-Jonah finally released him, Eddie bolted upstairs crying. Ugly red rope marks grooved his neck. His father was furious when he heard what happened. He stormed downstairs and pounded on Bar-Jonah's door. There was no answer.

After that incident, the boys said they didn't go to the apartment anymore. They were afraid for their lives.

Calvin said, at the time he had wanted to tell his mother, tell someone what Bar-Jonah had done to them. He knew it was wrong. He felt bad inside. "I wanted to let it out, but I thought Bob would shoot me." He also said, "I thought Nathan would brand me [stun gun] and bury me where no one would find me."

Detectives interviewed five-year-old Buddy, but he was so distractible and young, his reports were unclear.

Officers brought charges against Bar-Jonah related to Buddy based on what Calvin told them. Calvin said, "Nathan rubbed his butt." Once the big brother saw things happening he didn't like, he refused to let Buddy visit the apartment.

After the July interviews with Calvin, Eddie and Buddy, Great Falls police charged Bar-Jonah with a slew of additional crimes against the children, the kind that could put him behind bars for life.

Following those charges, Bar-Jonah wanted to see Calvin. The boy was petrified, but too afraid to refuse. At the Cascade County jail, Bar-Jonah asked Calvin and his family to write letters of support.

They did.

This behavior emphasizes the ambivalence both the victims and their parents felt. On one hand, the boys felt loved by Bar-Jonah. They thought he cared about them. They believed in him, and most of the time he was good to them. But, he took advantage of their trust. He intimidated and molested the boys. They couldn't tell. The predator controlled them with a complex mix of kindness and fear.

The parents believed he was good to the boys and trusted him. His arrest must have been a mistake. They wanted to help.

One of the most dangerous and ominous tactics Bar-Jonah practiced was choking children. Over many years, the method had worked. With his first victim, a six-year-old neighbor girl, he had learned choking was very effective.

From papers found in his apartment, it was clear he was interested in autoerotic asphyxia. This practice of partially hanging oneself and cutting off adequate oxygenation to the brain, combined with masturbation, heightens orgasm. It can also lead to unintentional death by asphyxia. We don't know if he practiced it on himself, but we do know choking others gave him feelings of power and sexual gratification.

It may have been more of an issue of absolute control over his victims, rendering them unconscious and without recollection of what he did to them. He used ropes, his hands and sometimes his size to subdue victims. Choking or sitting on them until they couldn't breathe provided the same end point—control and silence.

Bar-Jonah may have used ropes on Calvin and Eddie as a game at first, but then extended the length of time and increased the force. He choked both boys using a rope. On the bed, he also tied and choked Calvin. Both boys thought they were going to die and after the choking episodes were afraid for their lives. They refused to go back.

Based on Bar-Jonah's actions, his financial crisis, minimal work and no roommate to help with expenses elevated his stress level to crisis status. This revved up his fantasies and he became more aggressive with the boys while trying to calm himself and satisfy his sexual needs. Lacking continued access to the boys because they stayed away likely triggered Bar-Jonah's risky behavior to prowl for a victim at the school where he was arrested.

Chapter 13 The Prisoner and the Law Men

Great Falls, Montana

Being an experienced prisoner, Bar-Jonah understood how to manipulate the system to his benefit. With a flurry of letters to jailers and his doctors, he demanded kosher food.

It didn't work.

Threats to sue Cascade County for not providing him special food didn't work.

He did his best to get a television in his cell but failed.

Things were not going well for him. One of the most important things to Bar-Jonah was to be in control, to control his existence in some way, and in jail that was difficult. In the Cascade County Jail, he found previous methods unsuccessful.

With few visitors and no television to watch his favorite shows and coverage of his high-profile case, Bar-Jonah became angry and bored. He decided to entertain himself with trips to see the jail nurses. His history of obesity, high blood pressure and heart disease, placed him at significant risk for health problems. He learned a complaint of chest pain triggered a trip out of his cell to the infirmary for a thorough evaluation including an electrocardiogram. Nurse practitioners at the jail looked for evidence of another heart attack and found none. Obesity had tipped him into a diabetic state which added to his health problems. High blood sugars delayed healing of leg wounds he picked open and infected which prompted more visits to the nurses.

Typically, pleasant to people when he wanted something from them, jailers recognized his manipulative behavior, a common trait among prisoners. He was not a problem inmate. They seldom saw the violent side he'd learned to suppress, but he was furious after he learned Detective Cameron and the FBI had accessed his records from Bridgewater.

Following his arrest, Bar-Jonah dressed in an inmate hunter-orange jumpsuit and because of his high-risk status, they kept him shackled when being moved. Handcuffed to a chain around his waist and chained ankles limited his movements. He appeared on closed circuit television for arraignment. Close to a hundred pounds overweight, with an untrimmed beard, stringy long hair and sores on his face picked open, he appeared frightful. His piercing odd-colored eyes stared into the camera.

Most of the time, Bar-Jonah was quiet and cooperative with the jail nurses. He tried to manipulate them into authorizing what he wanted. He even pressured them to help him obtain a television. Sometimes, the nurse counselor who didn't cater to his demands would set him off. He raised his voice loud enough to penetrate the walls and alerted those nearby. Sometimes he'd throw tantrums, like his former girlfriend Pam described. In frustration, he'd try to storm out of the exam room, and comically stomp down the hall in baby-steps with ankle chains jangling.

Eventually, the nurses refused to be left alone with him. His outbursts and fear for personal safety forced them to treat him only with a guard present. After he picked his old thigh scar open and infected it, he required daily treatments. To save jailers the hassle of transporting him to the clinic every day, the nurses went to Bar-Jonah. Accompanied by a guard, they made "house calls" to his cell for daily dressing changes.

Early in his incarceration, Bar-Jonah faked injuries at the hands of other inmates, and then begged for protective isolation. He got his way. Jailers isolated him from other prisoners in an administrative segregation section called "K-Pod". The same pod contained prisoners who represented a risk to the staff, violent offenders, or like Bar-Jonah, because his crimes placed him in an undesirable jailhouse category. News of his child molester status spread within the jail. Being a "cho mo" made him a target for other inmates. Very nervous and afraid for his life, he watched his back. Bar-Jonah remained in K-pod the rest of his time in the Cascade County Jail.

Isolated like he wanted, protected from other prisoners, Bar-Jonah kept busy making trivia games like he did as a child, like he did at Bridgewater.

Not long after his lockup, police received a chilling report from a Bar-Jonah cell mate. This "cellie" reported the two were confined together for about a month. At first, he found Bar-Jonah congenial, actually charming, "a good guy." Then Bar-Jonah changed. "He had strange behaviors that frightened me. I'd wake up and he'd be just sitting there on a chair by my bunk staring at me while I was sleeping, like he was planning to do something. It would freak me out."

One day the man yelled at the guards, "Get me out of here!"

He said the guards came and asked Bar-Jonah, 'What did you do? What is your problem?'

The cellie said, "He'd say, 'Nothing, just sitting here.' Then he'd smile."

The man said Bar-Jonah talked about human flesh.

"It tasted like chicken," Bar-Jonah said.

After the police announced they'd found bones buried in the dirt floor of his garage, Bar-Jonah claimed they were dog bones. He told the cell mate the bones were buried deep. As the case unraveled, Bar-Jonah grew quiet and quit talking—except to himself.

"He played roles over and over, like talking to his victims." The man later said, "He told me things and said if I told, he'd find me when he got out and would do something bad to me. He said he'd kill me and bury me in a place where no one would find me. He didn't say exactly how."

One day Bar-Jonah told him, that he asked the kids to rub his scar because it felt good. "He asked me to touch it. It made me sick. He'd go back to his bed and say, 'Come on.' It gave me this really sick feeling. I had to get out of there."

The man also told police, "He used to lock kids in his closet and get violent... He said he'd drive and circle the school, at times wearing a blue coat and a fake badge. He said the car police talked about his having a white car was wrong, his car was red. If he zapped a kid with the stun gun, the kid couldn't say anything – 'They don't tell nobody.'"

Bar-Jonah told the man he carried handcuffs and would sit in a certain area near the school in a car. If a child needed help, the kids would approach him, and he'd be really nice. "If I tried to get Nathan to talk, he would clam up. Nathan talked about being Jewish. He said if he was in Israel, he probably wouldn't be in so much trouble. He commented, 'It's nice down there.' At first, I thought he was truthful and had lived in Bethlehem...He figured he would die in prison. He always kept a will with him."

Things changed after the cellie told Bar-Jonah he might tell what he told him. The man said, "Nathan jumped on me. He charged and we grappled. I tried to fight back but he was bigger and heavier. He took me to ground and put his weight on me. In a headlock, he sat on my chest. I could hardly breathe. His arm was across my throat from behind, my head down, face down. I finally got a guard's attention. Bar-Jonah said he was playing around...I'm afraid to go to court. I'm afraid to be in the same room with him."

This was from a statement made by an adult. Imagine Calvin's and Eddie's fears after similar threats and experiences.

Bar-Jonah frightened former roommate Casey Sullivan, too. Like many of his friends and roommates, Casey had some problems. He was a slight young man and from those who knew him, they said was likely controlled and possibly abused by Bar-Jonah.

Casey told police he was present in the living room during the episode when Bar-Jonah strung Eddie up by his neck in the kitchen. Casey heard Eddie choking and crying. Casey didn't know what to do. He didn't want to get in trouble with the police, so he just went to his room. He hadn't offered to talk with police after Bar-Jonah's arrest because he thought he'd be criticized for not helping the kids. When he was finally interviewed about the incident, Casey told police what he had seen. He wasn't afraid then because Bar-Jonah was in jail awaiting trial for assaults on the three boys.

When Bar-Jonah's lawyers told him about Casey's testimony, he wrote the following letter to him. (A copy of the handwritten letter by Bar-Jonah was printed on the Internet site www.mansonfamilypicnic.com)

Dear Casey,

Well, Casey I don't know why you lied about me. You know I didn't touch those kids. You know, Casey, I lied to the police for you about that girl who accused you of raping her but I know what the truth is. I saved your ass many times and prevented you from committing suicide. You lied man and you know it. Just remember that if something happens to me my blood is on your hands. I thought we were friends.

Nathan

P.S. No matter what Casey, I forgive you and I'm praying for you.

With this letter, Bar-Jonah was charged with witness-tampering, but the charges were later dropped to press on with more serious issues.

From the Cascade County Jail, Bar-Jonah wrote a suicide note to his family and mailed it to Massachusetts:

Hi Mom, Lois, Bob, Lee and family,

I am writing this first of all to say I love you very much and to let you know I'm tired of this place. I'm here for crimes I didn't commit and as I look at the possible time I could receive-3 life sentences is more than I can take. I don't want to have to kill someone in defence [sic] of my life. I've been there and done that and still live with the nightmares of it. I also know if by some miracle God works as he did before that Bellusci, Burton and Cameron will try something else and I just can't take going back to prison for crimes I didn't commit. I did my time-14 years. Although God was there for me, I see no future for me as it's going and I'm tired of the struggle of everybody's prejudice toward me because of my past. All I want is to have friends and a normal life but I don't see that anymore. I know I should of left Great Falls when I had planned to instead of listening to Bob because of the 2000 scare. I [sic] also tired of the pain and agony I feel in my innermost being. It's time to go home, yes, it is, it's supper time. I love you all very much. Be happy for me.

Love ya, Nathan

It wasn't clear if he was serious about dying, but his family worried. They notified the jailers. Bar-Jonah immediately received a lot of attention especially after he mailed a copy of his last will and testament to the *Great Falls Tribune* newspaper in March of 2000. Jailers searched his cell and found an elastic bandage tied into a noose. They placed him on suicide watch.

The rambling "will" gave an overview of his thought processes as he waited for trial. The following is a copy, unchanged from the original, as reported in the *Great Falls Tribune*:

I, Nathanael Bar-Jonah, being of sound mind and a great sense of humor requests the following done on my behalf after I'm gone or incapacitated.

1.My family will not assume any financial responsibility for any of my debts.

2.If I'm paralyzed and on feeding tubes, these feeding tubes will be removed and you will let me die. If, I'm on life support, you will pull the plug and you will let me die.

3.I wish to be cremated and my ashes scattered in the mountains.

4.At my memorial service I would like these songs played or possibly sung by Russ Michaels. The are as follows:

1.Mama Tried by Merle Haggard (for my mom)

2.Time in a Bottle by Jim Croce (for my family and friends)

3.These are a Few of my Favorite Things (A song from the Sound of Music, one of my favorite movies)

4.He the Pearly Gates Will Open (my favorite hymn)

5.Front Seat, Back Seat by Love Song (Christian music 1970's)

6.Through it all by Andre Crouch (This song is the one that saved my life when I was about to commit suicide in 1977)

7.I Pledge Allegiance to the Lamb by Ray Boltz

8.The Sun will Come Out Tomorrow-Movie (Annie)

My final wish is that no one mourns for me. Instead I want you to celebrate my death. I mean party on dude for I'm going to a place where there is no more pain or sorrow. Gee, it sure sounds like heaven time. Ooops! You know what? It is Silly me! You know Pastor Russ, I can remember when you visited me in jail in that little booth and you said that you didn't think you could hold up as well as I did. Well, the truth is that for 14 years that I spent in prison, God never left my side. I saw Big miracles and small ones and I expected at least one miracle a day from God. He always came through. I witnessed a full pledged Satanist give his life over to God and a guard known for his cruelty toward prisoners and he showed compassion towards me. I had an inmate rip my Bible in half to get back at me and 3 days later in the mail I got a brand new one. I've been raped by several guards on the same blood mat where they had killed an inmate just hours before while they videotaped the whole thing for training purposes. So, I guess you could say I made my first porno flick although an unwilling participant. I've seen the good and the bad in people.

Yet through it all, God kept me safe and he has always been there for me. He never faltered in his love for me. That's quite a comfort in a time of turmoil. God cares enough about a little sparrow, so, how much more does He care about you and me. So, What did I have to worry about? I've seen God take a hopeless situation like when all avenues were closed it seemed and I'd never be released. Yet God told me I would and I believed Him even though the evidence of my release was not there. Then totally out of left field I got 2—Yes, 2—Christian psychiatrists who believed in me. That was a miracle in itself to find 2 Christians in that profession in Massachusetts. The state had a lot of evidence on there [sic] side, yet the judge sided with me. Another miracle for sure and even when I had to stay in prison 4 additional months due to a clerical error I still believed God's promise to me even though my friends told me I was crazy. So, just keep your eyes on Jesus and he'll always be there for you no matter what. Just keep expecting that miracle. Well, with that I'll close.

Love ya'all,

Nathan Bar-Jonah

Bar-Jonah was worried about his fate for good reason. There he sat, locked up and isolated. If convicted on the Zachary Ramsay abduction and murder charges, he could receive the death penalty. For crimes against the neighbor children, he could get life in prison. There wasn't even a public defender willing to take on his case. His first lawyer assigned by the Prosecutor resigned after he learned his own child was on a Bar-Jonah potential victim list.

Placing Bar-Jonah behind bars gave FBI Special Agent James Wilson great satisfaction. Three years of toil following Zachary Ramsay's disappearance had paid off.

In their investigation of Bar-Jonah as a suspect in the case, Wilson and police detectives had read information from the Massachusetts Department of Justice and Bridgewater Treatment Center. They also received details of the Shrewsbury abductions and attempted murder charges that sent him to prison for fourteen years. The investigators pored over the records.

Bar-Jonah had already been convicted of stranger-abduction and attempted murder. Most importantly, they found mental health documents describing his fantasies and interest in torture and cannibalism. This information confirmed their worst suspicions after more Great Falls people came forward and described in sickening detail the odd-tasting meat dishes Bar-Jonah served them.

Detectives John Cameron and Tim Theisen were relieved by Bar-Jonah's arrest, too. They had taken over the investigation from Detective Bellusci in 1999. Near obsessive dedication to solving the case took a toll on their lives. Cameron, Theisen and Special Agent Wilson worked as compatible partners with complimentary crime-solving capabilities. Very different in many ways, they were alike in their fervor to bring the case to a close.

John Cameron was known as "Cold Case Cameron" because of his dogged successful work on unsolved murders. The skilled detective had closed some difficult files, but he was haunted by the eyes of two missing children. Zachary Ramsay's smiling school photo and a sad-faced little girl named Dolana Clark stared down at him from pictures over his desk. Daily, they reminded him that his work was not done.

Dolana had disappeared without a trace before Zachary. Years after her disappearance, Cameron found her killer and put him in prison and now he'd found Zach's. He began talking about retirement. Soon he'd have twenty years in, but would need another profession because he was only in his forties.

Cameron's busy desk was cluttered, a study in organized chaos. Even though it looked like a mess, he knew where everything was located. He accomplished an immense amount of work from his small office cubicle on the second floor of the Great Falls Police Department. Surrounded by his files and without a window to peer outside, he had few distractions. On his laptop computer he kept dates, names, phone numbers and details of investigations, all carefully organized and just a key stroke away. Around him he displayed interesting mementos like Bar-Jonah's name tag from Hardee's restaurant, "Nathan, Biscuit/Chicken Man" and a childhood photo of Nathan in a bikini.

Thin, energetic and athletic, Cameron rode his bicycle endless miles along the Missouri River path on lunch breaks looking for clues. He kayaked the river during off-time hours searching the banks for possible evidence. He couldn't get the case off his mind. A swimmer and a concert pianist, too, Cameron had many things he enjoyed, but his passion to solve this case and others got in the way. When he did get home, he took his work with him. Over dinner he'd talk to his artist wife. She was a good listener but his kids finally asked him not to talk about Zach anymore. It was too upsetting. His marriage fell apart as a result of his total commitment to work and the Ramsay case.

Dealing with the tough cases they investigated left both detectives stressed. Cameron could relax and lose himself for a while playing piano. You might find him unwinding with his buddies and eating spicy chicken "buffalo" wings at The Sting, a bar popular with other officers and owned by a former vice detective. Cameron said he used to like beef jerky with his beer but couldn't stomach it after Wilson deciphered Bar-Jonah's writings about human dishes. Jerky reminded him too much of a recipe in Bar-Jonah's apartment for pemmican, a dried meat and nut combination used by coastal Indians to preserve meat. Thoughts of jerky and pemmican reminded Cameron of the awful smells that emanated from Bar-Jonah's apartment and what might have happened to Zachary.

Tim Theisen changed his eating habits, too. After working on the case, he said he stopped eating beef all together.

Different from Cameron, Theisen's desk was barren. Lucky to be next to a window, he looked out over a tree-lined street. From his desk, he could almost see the Hardee's where Bar-Jonah worked when he first moved to Great Falls. Sunlight glinted off the polished surface of Theisen's desk. Part of it was covered by a calendar and a blank pad ready for notes. He liked things orderly. At the end of each day, he cleared his desk, filed everything and was ready for the next onslaught.

Theisen's stress reducer was jogging. At five miles a day, he stayed fit. His neck had been broken in an altercation with a suspect and following a surgical fusion, he paid attention to his health. It had taken a long time to recover mobility and strength. He didn't want to lose it again. Just as driven as Cameron, Theisen hid it better. He, too, decompressed after work and told his wife about cases he worked on. "If I came home and said nothing, I'd have an ulcer," he explained. Theisen is very protective of his children and even with his crushing responsibilities at work he remained involved in their sports and school activities. The former sociology major, an expert on polygraphs, loved his job. At it for about twenty years, like Cameron, he thought about retiring.

Special Agent James Wilson had no eye on retiring. He was right where he wanted to be. With three young children, he had years before thoughts of retirement. Before applying to the FBI, Wilson was afraid to tell his parents what he wanted to do after his brother was shot in the military and nearly died. When he finally talked to his father about the interest, he learned his father had wanted to work for the FBI. His parents encouraged him to do it.

Wilson's interest in cryptography came in handy. In the Ramsay case, he swiftly solved some of the Bar-Jonah encrypted writings but spent many sleepless nights pondering others. FBI Agent Corey Dunstan from the Butte office, worked on the coded writings with him. Wilson also received help from Tom Malzbender at Hewlett Packard Labs who used high tech procedures and interactive digital enhancement in an attempt to interpret indented notebook writings.

After months of work, late one night at the Salt Lake Regional FBI Office, Special Agent Wilson said he was "dog-tired but couldn't quit." Suddenly, some of Bar-Jonah's writings that were indented on blank pages and projected onto a huge IMAX-like screen came into focus. With tangential lighting, magnification and enhancement, the words were finally readable. Growing information on the content of Bar-Jonah's personal notes and encrypted writings troubled Agent Wilson even more. The content contained abductions and violent acts: *"He was 10. Once I got him near my home... put him into a box. I then carried him into the house. I then ... his clothes... we had sex together... I brought him some company ... he's 10, too ... I captured a young boy with a puppy ... him into my car ..."*

It wasn't until four years after Bar-Jonah's arrest, when Wilson was en route to a Special Task Force meeting in Washington D.C., that he solved one of the most telling collections of word jumbles. Wilson didn't like travel or being away from his children and wife, but he was pleased to be part of the FBI Task Force trying to correlate Bar-Jonah evidence with other missing children in Massachusetts and Connecticut. Troubled with back pain and hating air travel, James was lying on a bed in an Amtrak sleeper-car headed east when he realized what the letters said.

Bar-Jonah claimed the dedicated team of investigators and prosecutors had framed him. In a statement he made to the *Great Falls Tribune* he said: *They are indeed Great Fall's finest who believe they will always get their man either by hook or by crook. That if they can't prove it legally, they will set them up and bully people into making a false statement. These cops remind me of the Borg in Star Trek, 'WE ARE THE LAW, Resistence [sic] is futile.'*

During this time, prosecutors who were overwhelmed with cases in addition to usual business had to devote long hours to the Ramsay case. Prosecutor Brant Light, Assistant Prosecutor Susan Weber, and Legal Assistant Sarah Hollis, often worked late into the night. They pushed on with the detectives and focused on the molestation case. Prosecutor Light decided to try Bar-Jonah first on the molestations, while intensifying research on the Ramsay murder investigation.

Before Bar-Jonah was charged with Zachary's homicide, Prosecutor Light met with Rachel Howard, Zach's mom, and her family. He wanted to give them support and understanding because of the grisly details that led the legal team to their planned action against Bar-Jonah.

Light showed the family a computer slide presentation which detailed the investigation. He showed photographs and Bar-Jonah's incriminating writings. It included all the evidence that supported the abduction and murder charge. They were sure Bar-Jonah killed Zachary and used his flesh as food.

Since no trace of Zachary had been found, they were faced with trying a murder case without a body and knew it would be difficult. Trying a molestation case where victimized children would testify provided a high likelihood of conviction. The case was strong, with massive supporting evidence: Photos, Bar-Jonah's collection of pedophile paraphernalia, classic grooming behavior and his calculated choice of vulnerable boys.

Both Brant Light's and Wilson's daughters were in Bar-Jonah's collections. Wilson's was even labeled with a wrong name and coded in the ledger with the correct one. It appeared Bar-Jonah might be planning to target children of the law enforcement community.

Ultimately, two high-profile trial lawyers experienced in death penalty cases agreed to represent Bar-Jonah, Greg Jackson of Helena and Donald Vernay of Kalispell. Both astute in defense procedures, they did their best to delay the trial. They also tried to limit admission of damning evidence. In a pre-trial hearing, they were adamant Bar-Jonah would not get a fair trial in Great Falls because of voluminous negative publicity. They demanded the trial be moved to another location because news about the murder charge and international frenzy over the cannibal aspect made obtaining an unbiased jury nearly impossible. Besides, they needed more time; they had a late start and twenty-eight boxes of evidence to go through.

A *Great Falls Tribune* article covered the hearing held before Judge Kenneth Neill and reported the analysis of defense jury expert, Seattle psychologist Alan J. Cohen. He said local and national news covered Bar-Jonah's criminal past and time in a mental hospital for sex offenders; all information that would probably not be admissible. Per the newspaper, he said, "It's a lot easier to discount what the defense might say if the defendant is a monster. The inflammatory nature of the reports tended to demonize Mr. Bar-Jonah." Cohen believed postponing the trial would decrease the negative impact of news reports and allow selection of a less biased jury pool.

Even though Jackson and Vernay wanted more time to sort through the mountain of evidence, Judge Neill refused another delay. He had already moved the trial two hundred miles away to Butte.

Dr. Cohen said that was too close. He suggested the trial be moved far from Great Falls to the eastern edge of the large state, to Billings. There, Cohen said, Bar-Jonah would be more likely to get a fair trial with a less biased jury pool.

Judge Neill denied the request.

Prosecutor Brant Light complained the defense team had not provided them with a list of people who would be testifying for Bar-Jonah. Nor had the prosecutors been informed of what evidence the defense lawyers planned to use. How could they prepare their approach without key information?

In the meantime, Bar-Jonah's lawyers did their best to delay both the molestation and murder trials as long as possible. The Defense pushed to proceed with the murder trial first. Judge Neil listened carefully to both teams. But the Prosecutors won that time, the molestation trial proceeded.

In the end, the judge excluded a lot of evidence from the molestation trial because it played no part in the charges. It was difficult to sort it all out. Much of it was inflammatory and would have weighed heavily against Bar-Jonah. Some evidence overlapped both cases. Bar-Jonah's previous convictions, lists of victims and many other pieces of evidence obtained from his apartment in the search warrants were excluded by Judge Neill. Even the arrest at the school yard in a police-style jacket was not allowed.

While all the legal bickering was going on, Bar-Jonah sat in his eight by eleven foot cell under a $2.2 million bail, praying for another miracle.

Chapter 15 Western Justice: The Trial

Butte, Montana 2002

Despite many delays by defense lawyers, the most expensive trial in Montana history moved to the small old mining town of Butte. On a harsh subzero morning it opened February 12, 2002, in a historic courthouse high on a hill in Uptown Butte before Cascade County District Judge Kenneth Neill. Huge weathered greenish copper courthouse doors, remnants from past tumultuous mining days, opened to an interior of swirled pink marble floors and columns. Diverse cultures still make up the population of this old town. Tinsel and colored lights left from Chinese New Year celebrations draped over banisters and dangled along the three flights of worn stone stairs leading up to Judge Neill's courtroom.

Portraits of former statesmen and copper barons ringed an elaborate stained-glass dome. They stared down on a modern metal detector. The high-profile trial necessitated unusual security. Police inspected bags for weapons and cell phones. Uniformed Butte police on courthouse duty checked identification and directed each individual past wooden barricades, through the metal detector.

Once inside the austere court room doorway, I saw Nathanael Bar-Jonah. He focused on each person as they entered. His eyes locked on mine in a cold stare. I felt what others had described. One eye so pale it looked like an opaque blind eye, the other eye brown. Together, they had a piercing sinister effect. Like the little boys, I couldn't look away. I walked past and sat close behind him to his left. He slowly rotated until our eyes met again. Expressionless, eyes locked for a few long seconds—then, in slow motion, he turned away.

Bar-Jonah sat at a table nearest the entrance and to Judge Neill's left. Thinner than pictured in photos at the time of his arrest, his still-bulky form filled a metal cushioned armchair. His appearance differed sharply from the Manson-like press photos taken two years earlier. Bar-Jonah didn't resemble the front-page arrest photo of a man with long dark greasy hair and bushy beard wearing a jailhouse-orange jumpsuit. In court, his hair trimmed and that fearsome face clean-shaven except for a small narrow mustache, he was hardly recognizable.

Thinning brown hair stuck out in unruly sprigs along his collar. Large gold-rimmed reading glasses perched low on his nose. Wearing navy blue slacks, white socks, dark shoes and a pale sweater with wide horizontal yellow and chartreuse stripes, he sat expressionless. His sweater colors cast a jaundiced luster to his sunless face. Greeted warmly by his lawyers when they entered, Bar-Jonah visibly relaxed in their presence, leaned back in his chair, and concentrated on proceedings.

Nearly motionless pudgy hands stirred occasionally to take a few notes or raise raisins and cookies to his mouth. The attractive female legal assistant supplied him with the snacks his mother would have given him if she could have been there. Occasionally Bar-Jonah spoke quietly with his lawyers. On breaks, he laughed with their assistant. Otherwise, he seldom moved except to cross or uncross his legs, or to blink his eyes. He looked benign, incapable of performing the acts of which he was accused.

By the end of one week, half of a pool of over two-hundred potential jurors had been questioned by both sets of lawyers. Following a one-day break for Presidents' Day holiday, the final twelve jurors, plus two alternates, were selected. None of them had been on jury duty before.

To assure Bar-Jonah's safety, Sheriff's Officers from Great Falls transported him from the Cascade County Jail to Butte locked in the back of a police cruiser. In transit, a video camera was focused on him at all times. It made a full indisputable record. Should anything go wrong, the video would document any occurrence and avoid conflicting stories. Lt. Jim Bruckner drove Bar-Jonah and remained alert for trouble. With his cohort, Deputy Chuck Gailey also of the Cascade County Sheriff's Department, they guarded the pedophile through out his trial.

One day during a lunch break, Bar-Jonah and the officers sat at opposite ends of the table. Officer Gailey talked to Bruckner about buying a small pressure cooker for his wife as a surprise, exclaiming she was a great cook. Without looking up from his food, Bar-Jonah entered the conversation and commented that he preferred using large pressure cookers. One wonders what he was cooking.

During the trial, with support of Butte police, the Cascade County officers guarded the prisoner and entrances to the court room. Their alert stances and scanning eyes made it obvious they took their jobs seriously. Concerned about spectators and potential trouble, one officer always hovered near the defendant. At the end of each day, they transported Bar-Jonah miles north of Butte to the Boulder jail for safe-keeping. In this remote jail, they believed the prisoner was safer from potential turmoil in Butte.

Assistant Prosecutor Susan Weber, striking in appearance with blonde-streaked shoulder-length hair and dressed in a flattering dark suit, addressed the jury candidates in an easy informative manner. She thanked them for their patience through the tedious selection process and instructed them to be fair to both sides.

Based on the preponderance of evidence presented, she stressed, they would determine the defendant's guilt or innocence. After she explained the importance of maintaining security of evidence, she told them the State did not have to prove a motive but had to prove the charges beyond a reasonable doubt or to a moral certainty. Only after hearing both sides, the jury had to decide who was telling the truth.

When his turn came, suave Defense Attorney Greg Jackson strolled back and forth in front of the jury box. His silky grey suit matched his thick, perfectly coifed silvery hair. Looking like a Hollywood star, he spoke directly to them and stressed the "presumption of innocence." He told them of the Innocence Project releasing people from death row and how twenty percent of those inmates had confessed, yet evidence proved they didn't do it. The jury must weigh all testimony and beware that an officer's zeal could influence his and other's statements. Jackson cautioned, too, that children might not tell the truth especially if they are afraid of getting into trouble. He instructed the jury to watch for inconsistencies in testimony and accept the fact that memories could be inaccurate, especially the longer it is after the happening.

Judge Neill then instructed the jury. He told them not to talk about the case among themselves, to keep an open mind and not form an opinion until all the facts were in. Only after all the facts were presented and his specific instructions were given, should they begin their deliberations. They were not to talk about the case or even talk to each other to pass the time of day and should research nothing independently. He instructed them not to watch television, listen to a radio or read a newspaper. If any rules were violated, he asked jurors to inform him and he would interview the jurors involved.

There were no infractions. All twelve members of the jury remained throughout the week-long trial.

Before opening statements, defense lawyers implored Judge Neill to exclude information regarding the stun gun, badge and police impersonation. They argued the evidence did not specifically pertain to the charges Bar-Jonah was on trial for. Jackson stated, some information should not be allowed because it is "uncharged conduct." For example, there was no allegation of stun gun use; it was prejudicial. Nor did the defense team want the jury to know about any "prior bad acts," because the information was "highly inflammatory."

Judge Neill allowed presentation of photos from the undeveloped film in disposable cameras found in the search. The photos of Calvin, Eddie, Buddy and the naked Bar-Jonah, were key pieces of evidence for the prosecution. Prosecutors entered enlarged photos into evidence.

Judge Neill also allowed the stun gun data but excluded the impersonation of a police officer charge and an incident in which Calvin was handcuffed to a pole outside Bar-Jonah's apartment.

During proceedings, the court room itself became a character. The large stark white room rimmed in pale wainscoting was heated by old radiators that spoke to each other. They hissed and clanked like ill-behaved attendees, but Judge Neill couldn't ask them to leave. Skylights edged by squares of green and yellow stained glass matched Bar-Jonah's sweater. Rows of metal folding-chairs cordoned off behind a rope draped around the Court, creaked and groaned when occupants moved. Except for the last day, spectator chairs were nearly empty.

Students from a high school class attended en masse a few times. One day a class of twenty-five third graders (the age Bar-Jonah liked the best) observed.

No young students were present when the molested children testified.

Every morning, an attentive gray-haired male slid into a chair behind Bar-Jonah. The retired man said he was interested in the court process. Other daily attendees included journalists, FBI personnel from around the country, Special Agent James Wilson, and Detectives Cameron and Theisen. None of Bar-Jonah's family was present.

In his opening statement, Cascade County Chief Prosecutor Brant Light, walked close to the jury. His forceful attack grasped their attention. "This is about a man, a man aged forty-two, with one ambition—to meet, groom with intent to abuse, three boys, ages five, nine and fourteen, all Native American.

"He took his time, pursued, became a friend, and then successfully sexually abused them. Calvin and Buddy, half-brothers, lived with their mother upstairs from Bar-Jonah. Eddie, their cousin, lived with them for a while. Calvin, a freshman, large for his age and shy, sensitive and immature, played with younger children. Buddy was only five years old. Eleven people lived in their two-bedroom apartment. Their mother, on welfare, did her best. Cousin Eddie came to live with them for a number of months.

"They met him (Bar-Jonah) in December of 1998. Before long, the boys were spending all day at Bar-Jonah's; eventually they were allowed to spend the night. Their sisters were never invited. Bar-Jonah took numerous photos of the boys inside and outside the apartment. At times they played on the bed with Bar-Jonah when he was just wearing underwear, skimpy jockey shorts. Bar-Jonah was usually friendly, but the boys saw his other side, a bad temper if they didn't do exactly what he wanted.

"Bar-Jonah got Calvin in his bedroom and locked the door, made him pull down his pants. Bar-Jonah fondled Calvin's penis. Eddie knocked on the door. Bar-Jonah allowed Calvin to leave.

"Calvin saw Bar-Jonah rubbing Buddy's butt. Bar-Jonah threatened Calvin to never tell anyone. Calvin was scared, confused, and embarrassed.

"Calvin kept the secret.

"Nine-year-old Eddie said he was sitting on the couch when Bar-Jonah grabbed his penis. He pushed Nathan's hand away and left. Eddie also told of the terror of being hung from the kitchen ceiling, a noose around his neck choking him. He was released and ran upstairs. His father pounded on Bar-Jonah's door, but he didn't answer.

"Eddie's family moved far away. He kept the secret.

"In the first police interview with Calvin, he denied he'd been abused. After about an hour and a half, he began sobbing and described what had happened.

"During the first interview with Eddie, the audio tape didn't work. He was angry and didn't want to repeat what he had said. Ultimately, with his mother present he told some of the story again so his testimony could be recorded."

When Prosecutor Light began to present information from the search warrants, Jackson and Vernay jumped to their feet and requested a sidebar with the Judge.

Prosecutor Light continued. He said a search of Bar-Jonah's apartment uncovered a yellowish braided rope. There was an article on knot-tying, including how to make a noose. An article on autoerotic asphyxia discussed heightened sexual arousal through self-choking. However, instead of using the method on himself, Bar-Jonah was sexually aroused by choking others, not only Eddie and Calvin, but previous victims too. After choking incidents, Calvin reported Bar-Jonah went into his bathroom and closed the door. Was it to ejaculate away from the boys' view?

Attorney Jackson's opening was short. He made it sound like the boys, their parents, and Bar-Jonah, were one big happy family. They were all on friendly terms. He said when Bar-Jonah was arrested in an unrelated case, Calvin and Buddy's mother was very upset. She questioned her children about inappropriate behavior between them and the defendant. They denied it. Even when police first asked the boys about inappropriate behavior, they said Bar-Jonah had done nothing to them.

Jackson pointed out the boys' stories were contradictory. The stories changed. The boys even said they'd lied.

Jackson implored the jury, "Nathanael Bar-Jonah did not do any of these things. Return a not-guilty verdict."

After opening statements from both sides were completed, Prosecutor Brant Light called Great Falls Police officer William Bellusci to the stand. Bellusci had expertise in handling sexual assault cases, years of experience; he had done the initial investigation regarding Bar-Jonah.

Bellusci explained to the jury that is common for molesters to be trusted by parents. When Light began to question Bellusci about items obtained in the search warrant, Jackson and Vernay jumped to their feet and asked permission to approach the bench. There was evidence about to be disclosed to the jury that the Defense did not want submitted.

Judge Neill had the jury removed. After hearing the opposing teams, he allowed the stacks of photo albums in their entirety. The judge deemed them closely related and explanatory to the events of the case.

When Jackson had his turn, he asked Bellusci about the initial interviews with the boys and their mother. Bellusci stated the mother and children denied anything inappropriate had happened and he let it drop. At that time, he had not seen evidence to trigger further investigation.

Brant Light questioned Bellusci after Jackson's cross-examination. For the jury, Brant emphasized a known fact. "In your experience as an investigator with five years experience, is it unusual for victims to initially deny sexual abuse?"

"No."

The prosecutors called their second witness, Sgt. John Cameron.

Appearing professional and relaxed, sporting a new mustache, the experienced Lead Detective, calmly answered Light's questions. Asked about his job history and skills, he presented an amazing background of advanced training in special law enforcement certifications, interviewing techniques, investigational skills, and courses in understanding the criminal mind.

Brant questioned him about evidence and how difficult it was to sort through and identify the children in the photo albums. Cameron explained to the jury how Bar-Jonah had labeled the pictures with the wrong names but had coded them to the correct ones in a journal.

Cameron said it was on June 29, 2000, when he and agent Wilson went to Bar-Jonah's apartment building and talked with Calvin and his stepfather. A few days later, on July 4th Cameron returned, this time with Detective Theisen. The two men talked with Calvin and his mother, and then Calvin went down to the police station with them to give a statement. When asked about details of his interview with Calvin, Light asked Cameron why Calvin was crying. Vernay and Jackson objected but the judge allowed Cameron to answer.

Cameron said simply, "Because he had disclosed the abuse."

Light questioned Cameron about their troublesome interview with Eddie when audio was lost on the first try. Special Agent Wilson and Cameron had driven six hours, to the northeast corner of Montana, to interview Eddie. He lived with his family on the Fort Peck Reservation. Cameron explained, after the interview was completed, they discovered there was no audio record. All of them were frustrated. Eddie didn't want to go through it again. He was agitated and sad, but agreed to do it again only if his mother could be with him.

In the presence of parents, interviews may be more constrained because the child is embarrassed and does not want to disclose sexual information in front of them. But this time, without his mother, Eddie didn't want to go on. With her there for support, and the second time through the information, his affect was flat. Cameron said there was less content and spontaneity, but they had a record of the details in Eddie's own words.

In his cross examination of Cameron, Attorney Jackson pointed out discrepancies and poor technique used in the interviews. Instead of open-ended questions, Jackson said the children were led in their responses. Another problem was the detective's delay in questioning the children. It would have been much better to question the kids right after the event, not months later, especially true in children with learning disabilities. Jackson accused officers of having an agenda. He noted on the video tape, investigators implored Calvin to help. "Everyone else has helped," they said. "We need your help. Tell whatever happened."

Jackson told the jury detectives said things like, "Nathan's a scary guy." He contended the interviews were biased and badly flawed.

The court room was dead silent when each of the boys was called to the stand.

Calvin was first. Dressed in black, he looked like a weightlifter but vulnerable in demeanor. The large adolescent entered slowly, eyes downcast. He appeared frightened when he glanced at Bar-Jonah who sat far to his left. Calvin diverted his eyes quickly. After he sat, Calvin leaned back and hid behind the edge of the Judge's podium. It partially blocked his view of Bar-Jonah. It had taken a great deal of courage to talk about the abuse the first time, now he had to do it in front of a court room full of strangers, and the perpetrator he had once trusted.

Prosecutor Light was gentle with Calvin. Easy questions came first. Bar-Jonah sat motionless, no fidgeting, his face like stone. When tough questions came, Calvin dropped his gaze to the floor. Answers came in whispers.

"What did Nathan do?" Light asked.

"There was holding and hugging," Calvin said.

"Did he touch you in a manner you didn't like?"

Calvin glanced up and said, "He told me to take my pants off." Quickly, he looked down at his hands, a leg jiggled nervously.

"What happened?"

Silence.

The large teen trembled. His facial expression turned sad, snuffling, he cried. His broad shoulders shook. Quietly he said, "He touched my crotch...in the front."

Bar-Jonah showed no expression but blinked a few times. More questions. "What did he ask you to do?"

"He asked me to but I didn't."

"What?"

"Touch him."

"Then what happened?"

"Eddie knocked on the door and I left."

Light asked about other specific situations. When it came to Buddy, Calvin said, "He touched Buddy's butt. I got mad and took him home."

Light changed to another topic. "Did you get a letter from Nathan?"

"He wanted me to write a letter for him. I didn't know how to write. My sister wrote to him for me. I was in special education classes and couldn't write when I was fourteen."

Calvin said one time when he was at the Cascade County Jail visiting someone with his sister, Bob Brown was there and asked him to visit Bar-Jonah. When he did, he said Bar-Jonah ordered him, "Don't talk to anyone."

Prosecutor Light asked, "Are you afraid of Bob?"

"Yes."

On Jackson's cross-examination, Calvin became more nervous, his left leg jiggled continuously. His face flushed.

Jackson asked, "Did you like Nathan? Wasn't he a nice guy? He took you out to eat, to movies, you even went to the Christmas party with him at Malmstrom Air Force Base."

Calvin agreed.

Jackson talked about the letter Calvin's sister wrote for him. It said:

Hi, Big Guy. How are things going? Good, I hope. You were like the Dad I never had. Thanks. You never harmed me. You treated me good.

Jackson explained to the jury, Calvin only became afraid of Bar-Jonah after the television news.

Calvin sat jiggling his leg and looking down at his hands.

Jackson emphasized the "Big News." He pressed this issue even though it was the defense team that said any mention of the arrest for murder or cannibalism to the jury would not allow Bar-Jonah to get a fair trial. They had succeeded with Judge Neill excluding the information from this trial, yet both Jackson and Vernay referred to it many times in the course of the trial.

Calvin shook his head, upset and flushed, he slouched farther in the chair, as if trying to look small and just disappear.

Bar-Jonah remained motionless during Calvin's entire testimony. His breathing barely evident as the boy answered questions.

Eddie was next. The thin twelve-year-old was dressed in bright clothing with hair trimmed short, walked stiffly, and appeared tense. He listened carefully to the questions. Cautiously, behind half-mast eyelids, he watched Bar-Jonah.

Prosecutor Light began gently, and like with Calvin, he asked easy questions first. Eddie told the jury he was living in Billings and was enrolled in special-education classes. When asked how often he visited Bar-Jonah when staying with his cousins in Great Falls, he responded, "All the time."

"Did you sleep at his house?"

"Just one time, sir. Both Calvin and Buddy spent the night."

"Did Nathan touch you in a way you didn't like?"

"Yes sir, on the couch."

"Where was this, on his couch?"

"He touched my penis and butt. He tried to touch me again. It made me feel bad."

"Why didn't you tell anyone?"

"I was afraid to."

"Did you ever see a rope?"

He glanced at Bar-Jonah. "Yes sir. He put it around my neck. He was behind me."

"Was it with a pulley?"

"The pulley was on the ceiling. He started pulling it. I started choking. I went up. I was scared I might die."

"At first did you think he was playing?"

"Yes, sir."

"Was it hard to breathe?"

"Yes, sir."

"What happened?"

"He let me down and I ran out of the apartment. I told my Dad. He went downstairs and knocked. He didn't answer."

Don Vernay took over on cross-examination. He started abruptly, "Remember me?"

Eddie said, "No, sir."

There were few questions and then Buddy was called to the stand. The chubby little boy enjoyed himself playing with the microphone, giggling and wiggling. He tapped the microphone and tested the sound. Then he spoke loudly into it and laughed when it echoed in the court room. He entertained the jury. Their laughter encouraged him and he played more.

Some of Buddy's answers were inconsistent but he stated clearly that he had bad dreams and had to sleep with his mother sometimes because he was afraid.

Waiting his turn, defense lawyer Vernay appeared nervous. He had a difficult job cross-examining the distractible child. Vernay clenched his teeth repeatedly, as if chewing on something he couldn't crush. He listened intently to Prosecutor Light's questions, and with eyes magnified by myopic lenses, he observed Buddy's antics.

Vernay had to ascertain if the child could separate fact from fantasy. Pleased with Buddy's response to his first questions, he started by asking the child if his (the lawyer's) dark curly hair was pink.

Buddy assured him it was pink.

Jurors chuckled.

With an audience on his side, Buddy became sillier. He leaned forward and laughed loudly into the microphone.

The jurors laughed with him.

Vernay had accomplished his goal. Buddy was a useless prosecution witness.

Next, Calvin and Buddy's mother was called to testify before the jury.

Bar-Jonah listened intently.

Calvin's mother said, "Nathan is a good and generous person...when he got grouchy with the kids, they would run upstairs."

She explained, "When Nathan was arrested, it hit Calvin hard."

When asked about a letter, she confirmed a letter in February 2000 arrived from Bar-Jonah. He requested letters of support from her and Calvin.

In her letter she wrote: *Calvin's doing good, and he is missing you a lot.*

She wrote letters to Bar-Jonah in March and April, both before she knew her children had been molested. When a friendly one from March was read aloud, she blushed and sank into her chair like her son had done earlier.

Bar-Jonah continued to write letters to Calvin.

A later letter from Calvin's mother had a different message. She told Bar-Jonah she wanted Calvin to have nothing to do with him.

After Calvin revealed the molestation on July 4th, the family moved far away, to the Fort Peck Indian Reservation, but the move offered no escape. Serious problems at school for Calvin occurred when he was bullied by other children and teased when they learned of his friendship with Bar-Jonah. He became very ill and was hospitalized, diagnosed with diabetes.

After learning to give himself injections of insulin, Calvin was discharged. Still suffering from low self-esteem and unrelenting teasing from the children, he was in desperate need of counseling. He started getting help, but the family didn't have enough money for gas to drive him to the counselor. He only went a few times before they all moved to Billings. She said, in the larger city, he did much better and even found a girlfriend.

When each of Eddie's soft-spoken parents sat before the jury, they said they were upset over their son's abuse. Both appeared uncomfortable and gave few details before being dismissed.

The next witnesses were counselors and clinical psychologists. Anita Plann met with Calvin four times after he moved back to the Reservation. She said Calvin's IQ was sixty-four, in the mildly mentally retarded range. School was difficult for him. He was fearful and experienced flashbacks about Bar-Jonah, afraid it could happen again. He was even afraid in his own neighborhood. He couldn't sleep.

The counselor said Calvin tried to block his emotions, avoid feeling. She found him bashful, honest and suffering from a reactive depression, with elements of Post Traumatic Stress Disorder. After he developed diabetes, he wanted to quit school, but in the end, things improved for him. The two boys who had teased him about being friends with Bar-Jonah, became his friends. His grades improved and he went to summer school to make up a failing grade.

Defense Attorney Vernay badgered Calvin's well-meaning counselor about her credentials. He emphasized that she was not a psychologist. He attempted to make her conclusions appear invalid to the jury. She countered that the testing done on Calvin was interpreted by a clinical psychologist. Though he made a good effort, Vernay did not successfully discredit her strong testimony that established how severely Bar-Jonah's abuse had harmed Calvin.

The next witness called by the prosecution was Dr. Kimberly Poyer, a young attractive woman with stylish dark hair. An FBI expert in forensic interviews of children, she was there to defend the problematic interviews investigators had with Calvin, Eddie and Buddy. Employed by the FBI in the Crimes Against Children Unit, Dr. Poyer teaches officers how to interview children. With this background, she reviewed important techniques with the jury. One essential aspect was the need to develop a therapeutic relationship, to make children comfortable enough to divulge secrets. It is very important to avoid leading questions with children, because they might say what they think the questioner wants to hear. Her analysis, after listening to and watching taped interviews with the children, was that there were problems, but the officers were not coercive.

In her evaluation of Calvin's interview, she emphasized he made unsolicited statements and described events in his own words. In the end, she said, no interview is perfect. Her final analysis was that the interview with Calvin was "not great, but not so damaging to have problems."

Her evaluation of Eddie's repeat interview was more negative. It was not as good as the initial botched one would have been, but he made the profound statement that Bar-Jonah hung him with a rope around his neck and thought he was going to die. At that point, she said Eddie's flat affect changed abruptly. He was animated and acted like he was "reliving the event."

Dr. Poyer spoke of an interview technique used for children under six. They have trouble being asked questions over and over, and then asked to determine, "Is it truth or a lie?" (The technique Don Vernay had used on Buddy.) She said children will often change their answers. They can't cognitively sequence events. Interviewing props and pictures are helpful.

She confirmed, many victims liked and had trusted their abusers, abusers who were usually family members and friends. Abusers often satisfy emotional needs of children that are not being met elsewhere. If parents encourage the relationship, it creates more conflict and ambivalence in the child.

Vernay's cross-examination did not go well. He questioned Dr. Poyer about problem areas in the police interviews. He attempted to emphasize the importance of obtaining accurate information, information that was a key issue for his client's defense. She agreed with the concept and stressed the importance of gearing interviews to the child's intellectual level, especially a child with learning disabilities.

After making little headway with the female prosecution witnesses, Vernay was frustrated. Outside the court room, he exploded in pressured staccato speech with a New York accent, "I always get the ones that hate men!"

Throughout emotional testimony from children who trembled and cried as they spoke, Bar-Jonah was wooden. When their parents and counselors revealed the toll Bar-Jonah's actions had taken on the kids, he sat passively, without evidence of pain, change of expression or even a drop of perspiration on his brow. Other than nibbling on a cookie, his only movement was an occasional blink. But when Detective Tim Theisen took the stand, Bar-Jonah changed. He leaned forward and listened intently.

Prosecutor Light asked details about items seized from Bar-Jonah's residence and about Theisen's interview with Buddy. Theisen said it was hard to keep Buddy focused, a very difficult interview candidate because of his short attention span. Just as Theisen began to describe a hole found in Bar-Jonah's kitchen ceiling where a rope had hung, Bar-Jonah leaned over and said something to his lawyers, Jackson and Vernay jumped up and abruptly approached the bench.

Bar-Jonah was having chest pain.

Judge Neill announced a recess until after lunch while Cascade County guards rushed the over-weight defendant to the Butte hospital emergency room.

Bar-Jonah had already had a heart attack that required placement of a coronary artery stent to keep the vessel open. His complaint of chest pain got action. They knew he had a diseased heart. Although he hid his emotions well, the morning's testimony troubled him. From what the witnesses had disclosed, his future looked grim. The jury heard details of his assaults from the mouths of children, children with learning disabilities, who were tearful and frightened on the stand talking about it and having to face their abuser.

The jury listened intently, and Bar-Jonah had seen hope for his release fade.

The thought of a life sentence can induce erratic behavior. Some will do anything to escape. A trip to the hospital for feigned illness is a common ploy. Officers not only had to guard Bar-Jonah against possible injury from irate parents and relatives, but they had to foil any escape attempt. Did Bar-Jonah just want an out, a temporary escape from the emotionally painful court proceedings, or was he really having cardiac pain?

The afternoon session of court was delayed less than an hour while ER staff cleared Bar-Jonah medically. Electrocardiograms showed no evidence of a heart attack. Laboratory tests, performed to look for heart muscle injury through elevated enzyme levels in the blood returned with normal results. After his evaluation, Bar-Jonah entered the court room smiling. He walked rapidly to his chair, with no sign of chest pain. His temporary escape didn't end Detective Theisen's testimony as he'd hoped. Theisen's damaging answers continued when Prosecutor Light asked him again about the rope and tying knots.

Theisen said investigators found instructions on knot-tying, specifically on how to tie a noose. With that, suddenly Jackson and Vernay approached the bench. They did not like what they were hearing.

Judge Neill allowed Theisen to continue.

Theisen said they also found an article in the apartment on adolescent autoerotic deaths and a letter that had come to Bar-Jonah from bereaved parents in Scottsdale, Arizona. It concerned autoerotic asphyxia and their son's death. If things go wrong and choking is too prolonged, lack of oxygen to the brain results in death. Instead of heightened sexual arousal, life ends.

Bar-Jonah had contacted them!

Survivors who find a loved one dead under these circumstances often believe it was suicide. When they realize it was unintentional and related to aberrant sexual practices, some have even more difficulty dealing with the death. Bar-Jonah's interest in this appeared voyeurism related to his practice of choking young boys.

Light asked Theisen about interviews he conducted with the molested boys' mother. He said she'd told him that Bob Brown, Bar-Jonah's brother, had warned her to say nothing against Bar-Jonah or he'd notify the Department of Family Services and have her kids taken away. She feared Bob would take action against her for telling the truth.

When the potential obstruction of justice and intimidation by his brother were revealed, Bar-Jonah's affect remained flat. He had known Bob tried to help him. Bar-Jonah had also done his best to keep the boys from telling anyone what he had done to them. As he listened to Theisen, he leaned forward and spoke to his lawyers. This prompted another interruption.

Bar-Jonah was hungry. He'd missed lunch during his trip to the ER.

Judge Neill authorized a short recess.

When court continued, Vernay questioned Detective Theisen's competence and training to handle sexual abuse cases. Vernay stressed Buddy's reports were the result of "cross-contamination" that occurred because of family discussions and his exposure to television reports.

Next, Dr. Philip Rector, a Clinical Psychologist and forensic interviewer who investigates child abuse cases, took the stand. Dr. Rector worked with Indian Health Services in Lame Deer, Wyoming. The prosecution had consulted him because of his expertise with Native American children. He strengthened their case on the difficulty of interviewing children, especially these children. Many factors affect a child's ability to disclose what happened to them, especially talking to a stranger; embarrassment and self-blame are common. He also said because some of them do experience states of hyper-arousal, fear and other symptoms of Post Traumatic Stress Disorder when they talk about what happened. They feel as if it is happening again as they speak.

The children fear a breakup of the family if they speak out. Their attachments and loyalties are mixed allegiances. Even with chronic and severe abuse, they still won't tell. It is not worth losing the other things important to them. Dr. Rector also stressed the age of the child made a big difference. In an adolescent with sexuality in evolution, after being molested a male may worry that he is homosexual. In the Native American culture, they don't talk about sex. Individual needs are secondary to group needs. Personal shame is hidden to protect the family.

Dr. Rector critiqued the interview between Detective Cameron and Calvin, when Calvin confessed the abuse. He noted Calvin was initially open and unguarded. As Calvin became aware of where the interview was headed, he felt compelled to talk but became very emotional. He experienced "emotional flooding and intense fear." Fear that something else might happen. Rector said, "Kids don't tell the whole story the first time. The big secret needs to come out first, once the big piece is out, other things come out."

In traditional Native American communities, it is the job of the community to raise the children. Dr. Rector said children are often left with extended family members and friends. Leaving the boys in Bar-Jonah's care would not be unusual. There is fluidity of caregivers and less division between adult and child activities.

He agreed with Jackson and Vernay that there were some problems with the interview but emphasized the spontaneity of many of the boys' responses. Many questions were open-ended and did not direct their responses. In Vernay's cross-examination of Dr. Rector, he focused on officers imploring Calvin "to help." This was coercive and did not follow the recommendations for an untainted interview.

The prosecution had hired a consulting psychologist to evaluate the children before the trial. Dr. Janet Hossack met with the three boys twice. After the first interview, the trial had been delayed. After many delays, she met with them again.

This very effective witness wore large-framed studious glasses. The thin older woman explained her findings to the jury in a grandmotherly fashion. Like other witnesses with experience interviewing abused children, she softly stated that children are often reluctant to tell. They are much more likely not to tell, than to make something up. Protection is very important. If they feel protected and believed, the consequences of telling won't be as bad as the fear they'd lived with. Until a traumatized person can feel safe, no other work can be accomplished. Shame is a big problem. Resolving emotional issues of abuse and embarrassment before peers is difficult, too. Abused children often develop doubts about their own sexuality.

Dr. Hossack had watched the taped interviews between the children and the police. In court, she described Sgt. Cameron in his interview with Calvin. Cameron had said, "This must be awfully embarrassing for you." That's when Calvin began crying and after sobbing for about half an hour, he told his story spontaneously. She said it wasn't pulled out of him. Dr. Hossack believed Calvin finally trusted someone enough to tell what had happened. Something he had been painfully holding in.

She believed Calvin was finally doing better because he felt safe. He was more willing to talk than Eddie who remained detached. Eddie said he keeps remembering bad smells in the apartment. When she was talking to him, he said he was "mad and sad." He had bad dreams. "I remember it all and sometimes when I don't want to." He wandered and "went away" in thought, then said, "I don't want to talk about it."

When she talked to Buddy, he said school was going well and that he didn't want to talk about anything bad. His mother said he was calmer but watched television a lot. "I watch cartoons all day long," Buddy said. "I'm sad all the time. I wake up in the morning sad. I wake up crying and go to my mom."

Both Calvin and Eddie had ambivalent feelings toward Bar-Jonah. They had many good times together. He had played games with them and had taken them out to lunch. They spent hours munching snacks and watching television. They knew Bar-Jonah had done wrong, but they said they did not want to be the ones who got him into trouble. They liked him and yet at the same time they were fearful. It wasn't clear if it was because they feared Bar-Jonah would come through on his promise to harm them if they told or if they still had fond feelings for him and hated to see him in prison.

On Attorney Vernay's cross-examination of Dr. Hossack, he was less abrasive than he had been with other female witnesses. He used a calm, friendly tack and looked kindly at the jurors and observers as he spoke. Vernay explained, "Many people have vilified the accused. Calling Nathan a scary guy is certainly not a compliment."

With that, Bar-Jonah stopped munching raisins and smiled.

Attorney Vernay tried to dispel the notion that Calvin, Eddie and Buddy had developed Post Traumatic Stress Disorder. He said the perpetrator was in jail. The threat had been removed. And why would Calvin continue to have contact with Bar-Jonah such as visiting him and writing letters to him if he felt threatened?

Adam Kingsland, a friend of Bar-Jonah's and a former roommate who visited the apartment often, was next on the stand. The prosecution said Adam's name was also on the victim list. The thin nervous young man said Bar-Jonah's apartment was always messy and the kitchen blocked by a hanging sheet. He said "the children from upstairs" were there watching television while Bar-Jonah sat around wearing only his jockey shorts. Bar-Jonah even answered the door in the same attire. Adam thought it was odd a man would dress like that around kids.

On the last day of the trial, under blue skies at eighteen degrees below zero, snow crunched underfoot. The old courtroom filled with observers in spite of the icy weather.

The defense team called their only witness. Dr. Phillip Esplin, a Freudian figure with a white trimmed beard and photo-chromatic glasses darkened by court room light, presented extensive credentials. The forensic psychologist and expert witness with experience in forty states was a hired gun for the defense. In fact, in eighty percent of cases he was hired by the defense.

His testimony emphasized children were taught to be deferential to adults, to acquiesce to adult wishes. By age ten, the normal child's memory capacity is equal to that of an adult, but younger children provide unique problems to an interviewer and must be treated differently. If the child is developmentally delayed as these children were, you had to gauge your questions to accommodate their levels of understanding.

If a child is a reluctant witness, he said it was essential to get the child to know truth was important. They should be instructed to say, "I don't know," if they don't know the answer. The best information is obtained if they're able to explain in their own words, "Everything that happened from the beginning to the end."

Dr. Esplin educated the jury. He said it is best not to confront a child, but instead say, "I don't understand." An interview can be contaminated and not valid if the child feels you don't believe him. A three-year-old can be a reliable witness, but under the age of ten, a witness can more easily be influenced. A high-status interviewer, such as adults, police and parents, affects the child's perception and increases his desire to please. Information obtained may be tainted by the way questions are asked and by the interviewer's status in the child's eyes.

With this information, defense lawyers intended to show the jury that the police interview with Calvin was tainted and not truthful. The police had encouraged him to confess what had happened. They were in a position of power, some of them wearing uniforms. Dr. Esplin stressed they were coercive and overpowering to the young man. He noted it was a full hour of talking before Calvin broke down in tears and told about the touching and choking. He said Calvin's relationship with the defendant was complex. His shift in demeanor after such a long period could have been associated with betrayal of their friendship and embarrassment when he told of sexual maltreatment.

In Dr. Esplin's opinion, Eddie's interview wasn't to be trusted either. Not only did it have to be redone, but his mother was present during the second interview, and she was pressuring him to talk. He strongly recommended a parent not be allowed in an interview room. Eddie didn't want to talk. He showed avoidance behavior and nearly void of expression. With such a flat affect, he looked depressed.

Likewise, Buddy was a "marginal informant". He wondered if Buddy even understood what was being asked. The doctor did not believe the information could be considered accurate. He also stressed that a child with a learning disability is more difficult to interview.

It makes sense that the interviewer's choice of words and questions must be gauged to the child's level of understanding. If more than one child in a family is abused, like these children, their answers could be contaminated by family discussions. There had been more than a two-year delay between arrest and the trial. The extended time delay made recollection of specifics for the young boys hazy.

Based on many documents in the apartment, Bar-Jonah had specifically chosen the boys because of their learning disabilities. One article noted the tendency for predators to molest children with learning disabilities—because they made bad witnesses. There would have been more victims but for astute screening at the Easter Seal Society. Bar-Jonah had filled out an application to work as a childcare attendant where children with disabilities would be less able to defend themselves or report abuse. Bar-Jonah also attracted adult "friends" who had limited intellect, mental problems or unusual beliefs. Like the women who didn't go to police right after Zachary's abduction when they thought Bar-Jonah might be involved in a murder.

In the end, the two older neighbor boys did a superb job of explaining what he did to them.

In summary, the only defense witness concluded, there were "major serious flaws in the interviews" with Calvin, Eddie and Buddy. If you believe the flaws affected the validity and reliability of the information investigators obtained, then the data was compromised and not believable.

After Dr. Esplin's testimony, Prosecutor Brant Light's redirect was aimed at discounting the forensic psychologist's views. He needed to convince jurors the interviews, though flawed, provided solid believable information. He also attempted to show this defense witness was nothing more than a hired mouthpiece who did no ongoing clinical psychological care for patients. His income was almost exclusively from appearing in court. However, clinicians may not have the detailed experience in forensic work as evidenced by the psychologists who authorized Bar-Jonah's release from Bridgewater treatment center. The lack of a clinical practice does not detract from expertise on forensic matters.

Light emphasized there is no standardized approach to interviewing children. In fact, there is no national protocol used as a standard for interviewing children.

On redirect questioning of Dr. Esplin by the defense they emphasized Calvin's functional age was between that of a first and third grader's. His social age was well below that of a fourteen-year-old. In other words, he was suggestible, and the interviews were "fatally flawed"—sufficiently flawed that the jury should find Nathanael Bar-Jonah not guilty.

In the short closing arguments, the prosecution called one rebuttal witness, Lead Detective Sgt. John Cameron. He reviewed evidence obtained from the two search warrants which included a key journal article that noted minority, developmentally handicapped abused children made the worst witnesses. Bar-Jonah's three victims correlated with the pattern described in the article and he may have believed they would be poor witnesses against him.

Prosecutor Light summarized and explained all the charges against Bar-Jonah to the jury. Aggravated kidnapping charges regarding Calvin and Eddie stemmed from Bar-Jonah purposely restraining the boys— "isolation for commission of a felony." He tied them both with ropes and locked Calvin in the bedroom.

Assault with a weapon was charged as a result of hanging Eddie from a noose in the kitchen. For unknown reasons, Calvin's reported choking incident in the bedroom, tied to a board, had been omitted in the charges.

By law, a weapon is defined as any article or substance that is used to restrain or cause injury to another or any object that is used purposely, knowingly, "to create substantial risk of death or decreased function of a member or organ." In Bar-Jonah's case, he used handcuffs, ropes and his hands to choke them, but his primary weapons were his weight and eyes. His stare unnerved children and adults. Beginning with his first known sexual assault, he crushed them with his weight so they couldn't breathe.

Bar-Jonah was charged with sexual assault on all three. To bring these charges, three components must be present: the perpetrator must have had sexual contact, without consent and acted knowingly. Sexual contact is defined as touching for the purpose of sexual arousal or gratification. Consent is not valid even if the child agrees, if he is under the age of fourteen or if the perpetrator is three or more years older than the victim.

All of Bar-Jonah's offenses were voluntary acts against children. There were several charges related to Calvin and Eddie but only sexual assault against Buddy.

Prosecutor Light reiterated that even while Bar-Jonah was in jail he coerced Calvin and told him not to tell anyone. Embarrassed, threatened and powerless, Calvin was attached emotionally to his abuser. He had enjoyed the advantages and friendship Bar-Jonah had given him. Calvin didn't want that part of the relationship to stop. He wanted the abuse to stop. Calvin was old enough to understand some of the sexual aspects of the abuse, but Eddie was at an age where sexuality was just evolving. Eddie may not have understood what was happening, but he knew the choking was dangerous. He believed he was going to die.

Nathan Bar-Jonah said he was not guilty. Under the law, he is innocent and must be found "guilty beyond a reasonable doubt."

The jury must decide.

Defense Attorney Vernay had the difficult responsibility of providing closing arguments, to show the jury there was reasonable doubt, that they should let Bar-Jonah go free. Vernay stressed conflicting statements. Calvin's mother even said Calvin enjoyed visiting Bar-Jonah in jail. Would Calvin have gone to the Cascade County Jail if he felt threatened? Vernay made a comparison. He said, "You don't go into the yard of the dog that has bitten you."

"The children were abandoned to him," Vernay said. Bar-Jonah had unlimited access. He also tried to dispel the notion that Bar-Jonah had groomed the children with his treats and movies, gaining their confidence and friendship before molesting them.

The defense lawyers stressed the children were frightened and confused because of media contamination. They'd heard of Bar-Jonah's other charges. Even though the defense wanted all comments regarding Bar-Jonah's previous convictions and charges related to Zachary Ramsay's disappearance excluded from the jury's ears, the lawyers repeatedly insinuated events had occurred.

When Psychologist Hossack performed a pretrial evaluation of the children, they waited in a room together, disabled and frightened children who could influence each other. Vernay instructed the jurors, "The law requires more than just suspicion." He ended vociferously, "One drop of dye in the water spreads. It contaminates all the water." He contended the interviews were flawed and therefore contaminated the validity of the outcome of the trial.

The jury left to deliberate about three-thirty p.m.

The worn marble stairway opened to the dome of the old courthouse, echoed with the sound of footsteps. Media and other observers walked around and waited impatiently for the jury's return. They were afraid to leave and miss the verdict. Everyone expected a verdict that day.

Six hours and a pizza dinner later, the jury returned.

On Calvin, they found Bar-Jonah guilty of aggravated kidnapping and sexual assault. On Eddie, they were deadlocked on the sexual assault charge but found him guilty of assault with a weapon. For charges related to Buddy, they found him not guilty.

Bar-Jonah's lawyers were furious with the verdict and immediately spoke to reporters of an appeal.

Prosecutors and law men were ecstatic with the verdict. Cameron, Theisen and Wilson's faces portrayed a medley of satisfaction, joy and tears of relief. They celebrated with the prosecution at a popular Butte nightspot.

Chapter 16 One-Hundred-Thirty Year

May 23, 2002

Nathan Bar-Jonah spent the next three months awaiting sentencing while sitting in administrative isolation in the Cascade County Jail. Isolated to protect him from other prisoners, now that he was found guilty, he prayed his lawyers could convince Judge Neill he would benefit from confinement in the state mental facility at Warm Springs. He did not want to go to the state prison at Deer Lodge.

Warm Springs brings to mind the image of a spa, a resort with natural hot springs, a great place to recover. For Bar-Jonah, the austere old mental facility was miracle oasis and opportunity for release.

In some ways, Warm Springs is similar to Bridgewater hospital for the sexually dangerous in Massachusetts where Bar-Jonah spent twelve years, following two years in Walpole prison. Warm Springs is not as austere as Bridgewater. Instead of asphalt and razor wire, Warm Springs hospital is located in the foothills of the Rocky Mountains surrounded by large ranches. If sentenced there, Bar-Jonah thought he would have a good chance of convincing the doctors he would sin no more. Maybe they would believe he'd learned his lesson. After all, the crimes weren't really violent ones. Choking was just for a little while, no permanent damage.

The stun gun and handcuffs were just for fun. Besides the kids liked him; they said so. To children, parents, adults and even doctors, Bar-Jonah knew he could be nice and very convincing when it benefited him.

The sentencing hearing held May twenty-third proceeded during a freak snowstorm that closed freeways around northern Montana and made travel nearly impossible. None of Bar-Jonah's family was present but the bad weather didn't stop one of his victims from attending.

The unannounced surprise witness for the prosecution flew in from the East Coast. When he'd learned his name was on the Lake Webster victim list and learned of Bar-Jonah's extensive history of violence against children, the man felt compelled to do something. He contacted the FBI and offered to tell the story of his abuse at the hands of David Brown, AKA Nathanael Bar-Jonah.

In his emotional testimony, Jason Mercer described the fear he had felt when David had sat on his chest, nearly suffocating him under the weight, and forced "oral sex" on the five-year-old. David had molested him again. Jason was so frightened and mortified he told no one about either incident. He had thought Bar-Jonah was still in prison in Massachusetts and unable to harm children. With him freed and harming other children, Jason felt responsible. Battling with tremendous guilt for not coming forward sooner, he now risked his professional and personal privacy in hopes that he might stop Bar-Jonah. He said, "Over thirty years, his behavior has progressed. He is violent. There is no therapy, no medication that will help. He needs to be where children will not be harmed."

Two psychologists for the defense, Drs. Paul Beljan and John Espy, evaluated Bar-Jonah and presented their professional opinions. They did their best to convince listeners he was not a pedophile and would benefit from hospitalization and medical treatment. They stressed he would be safer in the hospital and would not need protective custody as he would in prison where other inmates would likely try to kill him.

They said he was "developmentally impinged" at the age of about two-years-old due to "disruption with his maternal figure." To a non-psychologist, it's not clear what this terminology means, but they believed his psyche was harmed at an early age.

The psychologists said Bar-Jonah had an "organic brain disorder" with psychiatric features of Borderline Personality Disorder, and Obsessive Compulsive Disorder. His mother had confirmed obsessive behaviors including collecting names and recipes beginning in grade school. Psychological testing showed Bar-Jonah misinterpreted internal and social cues. He had never learned to function socially. He wasn't capable of interacting with another individual in a meaningful way.

Because he is "profoundly disinhibited and impulsive," people are not real to him, they are objects. With rigid and circular thinking and a tendency to fabricate elaborate stories, after years, the stories had become reality to him. One example is his description of a childhood rape told in "very elaborate detail" when defense examiners talked with him. It was a fantasy repeated over and over in his head. Even if the story were true, it wouldn't explain his behavior. Would that incident produce a violent predator who abducted young boys, forced them to undress in humiliation, and then choke and try to kill them? Something pushed him to violence. His early victims, Richard O'Connor, Billy Benoit and Alan Enrikaitis, were fortunate to have survived.

The prosecution aired audio-taped interviews of Enrikaitis and O'Connor at the sentencing hearing. The men described the violence, abuse and fear they experienced as children under his power. Both victims begged Montana not to make the same mistake Massachusetts did. They did not want him released to add more victims to his list. Alan Enrikaitis commented, "I got a life sentence, why shouldn't he? A day doesn't go by that I don't think a about it."

In their final analysis, defense psychologists said Bar-Jonah required a highly structured environment and could not function in "the outside world." Unable to control impulses, they thought new neuroleptic medication might be helpful in controlling his obsessive behaviors. Maybe cognitive behavioral therapy could give him better skills and insight into interpersonal interactions that would help him become more aware of how his behavior affects others. They concluded, even these treatments would not make him capable of independent living.

Supported by research, the prosecution accurately contended Bar-Jonah was fully capable of appreciating the criminality of his conduct. He intimidated Calvin from jail and tried to force him not to tell. Even though Bar-Jonah understood his conduct was wrong, "once in the moment, he can't control his impulses."

Brant Light pointed out that even though defense psychologists said Bar-Jonah couldn't think ahead and organize behaviors, had poor judgment and insight, his past crimes of predation and abduction were well thought out and executed. He planned ahead, dressed like an officer, carried weapons, a badge and handcuffs and then prowled until he found a victim and carried out his plans.

In a report for the prosecution, Dr. Michael Scolotti, a Montana expert on sexual offenders, said that Bar-Jonah is an "extreme danger to society. He has shown chronic compulsive sexual patterns over years, uses physical force and harms his victims. He is a pedophile who attacks strangers."

When Scolotti asked Bar-Jonah about his notebooks filled with lists of names, he said he was going to write some books and they were potential names for characters. When asked about the photos found on rolls developed by the police, Bar-Jonah said it was a new camera that he wanted to try out; he was testing it for scenes to use in books and business.

The pictures were of the boys he molested and pictures of his genitals.

Bar-Jonah was a high-risk offender. Dr. Scolotti said repeat offenses were likely and he could not be in the community without being dangerous. Based on repeated violence and lack of cooperation during fourteen years in Massachusetts facilities, he had no rehabilitation potential and Warm Springs State Mental Hospital was not appropriate.

Dr. Scolotti recommended Bar-Jonah receive the maximum prison sentence.

In his closing statements, Brant Light stated Bar-Jonah was not mentally ill and restated how he had duped the psychologists at Bridgewater who freed him. Note, pedophilia is a paraphilia, a mental illness related to sexual practices, but Bar-Jonah was not psychotic or delusional. He did not carry a psychiatric diagnosis such as schizophrenia.

With six prior felony convictions showing sexualized rage, under Montana law, Nathanael Bar-Jonah was classified as a Level III sex offender at high risk to re-offend. He was deemed a preferential child molester who will use force.

Judge Neill did what Bar-Jonah's victims begged him to do—protect the children, protect society. He sentenced Nathanael Benjamin Levi Bar-Jonah to one-hundred-thirty years in the Montana State Prison at Deer Lodge without the possibility of parole.

Chapter 17 Deciphering His Codes

With Nathanael Bar-Jonah behind bars forever, there are still many unanswered questions. What about the stacks of notebooks with coded writings? What about the multiple photo albums with victims noted? What about the indented writings describing abductions, murder, and cannibalism? What about recipes for human flesh and the unidentified wrist bone of a child?

Mixed with yearbook pictures mounted in photo albums were those of his victims from Massachusetts. Even Jason Mercer, the five-year-old boy he molested when he was just ten years old, stared back. Jason looked out from the page at Bar-Jonah, just as he appeared when he was molested. Jason is an adult today but for Bar-Jonah, in his mind and in his photo album, he remained a grade-schooler. Zachary is there too; his gentle brown eyes stare back. When Bar-Jonah looked at the photos, he remembered. He fantasized.

Bar-Jonah used many methods of hiding his words, his deeds and his thoughts. His coded writings prevented people from casually looking at his work and understanding his notes. There were at least seven different writing methods Bar-Jonah used to conceal his thoughts. He obviously enjoyed and studied ciphers, then put it to personal use. His codes have not all been broken.

The FBI has had experts work on them. One unusual string of numbers and letters found in Bar-Jonah's notes matched writings found in the margin of Zachary's school notebook. Those turned out to be related to a video game. Bar-Jonah denied he knew Zachary, but this finding would lead one to believe otherwise.

Former fiancé Pamela Clark said when Bar-Jonah was angry or stressed he would write. Compulsively, he wrote strings of letters with no spaces, in some ways similar to the letter Green River serial killer Gary Ridgway sent to police to throw them off track. Bar-Jonah's letters were written in a string without spaces, too. Sometimes the writing made sense; he had just left out the space and so the words were readily discernible.

Other times, he used simple codes to hide words, placing the letters a few spaces apart with nonsense letters in between. He varied his coding methods to conceal the meaning. In some, he zigzagged letters between lines or skipped groups of letters between the correct ones. In others, he replaced letters with numbers he had substituted in the alphabet. He also alternated lines and spaces.

Pam said when he focused on writing, it lowered his stress. Bar-Jonah literally buried his thoughts on paper. Detective Tim Theisen also thinks he buried Zach, at least parts of him.

It would have taken Bar-Jonah a great deal of time and effort to come up with some of the concealed messages. People have said he was not very smart; that isn't true. He was intelligent, enjoyed writing and playing with codes.

Special Agent James Wilson was successful in solving many of the ciphers. Because of his success and FBI interest in the case, Headquarters invited Special Agent Wilson to present a seminar for other law enforcement members involved in cryptography investigations. The earliest method Wilson solved was one of the most simplistic Bar-Jonah used, but it exposed telltale text. In a photocopy of his handwritten script (at the end of the book), there are other hidden words you can find if you try. Most of his writings are more difficult to decipher.

Shocked investigators solved these writings and feared the worst. They feared the encrypted words confirmed why Zachary's body had not been found. The flesh had been consumed. By the time some of the writings were interpreted, Bar-Jonah was already behind bars. Although he'd been released after his initial arrest for carrying a stun gun and impersonating a law officer, he was only free for a couple days before investigators read writings with the cannibal references and acted.

Zachary's name was on the victim list. The last word on one list was "died."

Bar-Jonah's complex assumed name carries special meaning for him. He would not elaborate on how he chose his new name, but if you look at it like a word jumble, it too may carry coded meaning. Nathanael Benjamin Levi Bar-Jonah could be interpreted to mean, I'm an evil son of Jonah. "Bar" means "son of." From childhood he had a fixation on man-eating fish and terrible nightmares. God ordered the Biblical Jonah to preach repentance to the sinners of Nineveh. Jonah disobeyed and was punished by being swallowed by a whale. After living in the whale's belly for three days, Jonah repented and was saved. Knowing the value of repentance from personal experience, he went to Nineveh and delivered a sermon.

Being in prison is termed <u>In the Belly of the Beast</u> in a book written by maximum-security convict and killer, Jack Henry Abbott. Bar-Jonah believed in miracles and being spewed out of the belly of the beast of Bridgewater to sin again was a miracle.

However, there is yet another angle, at <u>www.jonah-web.org</u>, there is information regarding the JONAH organization which is acutely related to Bar-Jonah's life. Taken from the website: It is "a nonprofit international organization dedicated to educating the worldwide Jewish community about the prevention, intervention and healing of issues causing same-sex attractions." The name itself comes from <u>J</u>ews <u>O</u>ffering <u>N</u>ew <u>A</u>lternatives to <u>H</u>omosexuality, JONAH.

There is a collection of words that appear many places in Bar-Jonah's notebooks. They were finally deciphered by Special Agent Wilson. After he solved the initial word, Agent Wilson knew Bar-Jonah was using a method termed slipping. By hand, Wilson tested his theory against the alphabet and solved the puzzle. He cringed at what he found.

Thes strange sounding message consists of coded word fragments in shorthand. It could have been Bar-Jonah's way of recording and reliving his secret by reading a message only he could interpret. It might be a work in progress where he hadn't finished the encryption. The partial words shown are the only findings from the coded words using the slipping method.

Taking the alphabet and slipping letters the designated number of spaces breaks the code. In some words, the vowels (a,e,i,o,u, plus or minus y's), are omitted and not slipped. No other iteration of the twenty-six letters of the alphabet produced readable word segments. They appear to say a "young-aged boy was killed and buried in the dirt floor of the garage."

The interpretation is speculation but interesting, and if correctly deciphered these are damning to Bar-Jonah, too.

A coding formulated by slipping letters looks like gibberish but is a common simple shorthand way of keeping concealed records. For Bar-Jonah, it was a way to recall and savor his achievements without anyone being the wiser. What other reason would drive a person to do this tedious task?

When Bar-Jonah was asked to interpret the words, he said he'd never seen them before, yet they were in his handwriting.

The FBI has extracted detailed records of violent acts and abductions from other personal records. These notes took experts months of tedious work to interpret. Using tangential lighting, computer enhancement and other methods, the images were extracted from imprints left behind on notebook pages. Where the actual written notes above had been ripped out, what was left behind on the blank pages underneath were indentations, one atop the other.

The stark and frightening words provided a window into Bar-Jonah's secret thoughts. He wrote of many abductions...including abducting boys, even one with a puppy, and locking them in boxes before carrying them into the house. Then knives to throats and sex between him and young males, "and he's ten, too." Age ten is Bar-Jonah's chosen age of eroticism. Once convicted, most SVPs reveal two to five times the number of victims they were prosecuted for.

Police found dog bones buried with human bones in Bar-Jonah's garage floor. These notebooks could be fantasy ramblings but maybe they are true. None of the missing pages were found. Investigators wondered if he sent them to Massachusetts or had them hidden in a secure location for safe keeping, possibly with other explicit criminal details or photos.

Bar-Jonah continued to claim innocence in the abduction of Zachary Ramsay. Even without a body, the accumulated evidence from his journals combined with other circumstantial evidence appeared compelling enough to convict him of murder.

Prosecutors proceeded with the murder trial while the FBI formed a special task force to investigate other child abductions.

Chapter 18 Evidence and Witnesses

According to former FBI profilers, sexual predators often strike victims at the height of a personal stress state, such as when they are tormented by external stressors and internal turmoil. It is then their fantasies accelerate to the explosive point. They begin prowling. The predator has learned from past experiences that carrying out their fantasies calms them, if only temporarily.

In Bar-Jonah's earliest abductions, he followed this pattern. His stress was high when he abducted, disrobed, choked and nearly killed little Richard O'Connor. Bar-Jonah's father had recently died, and his mother expected him to help support her while he attended high school. They were financially strapped and had to move from their home because they could no longer afford it. While his sweet religious mother was devastated by her circumstances, her hapless son seethed with rage and feelings of injustice.

Immediately preceding Zach's disappearance, circumstances in Bar-Jonah's life during the winter of 1996 would support his unstable mental state. A stressful disordered existence without his mother to calm him could have precipitated a crisis which accelerated fantasies and led him to act.

Being strapped for money was not unusual for Bar-Jonah, but this time he was destitute and emotionally drained. His job working with a man and his teenage son delivering bulk newspapers around Great Falls ended abruptly when the young boy committed suicide by hanging himself. A few months later, in December 1995, the father killed himself, too. He is the same man who had been living with Rachel Howard, Zachary Ramsay's mother.

One would wonder if Bar-Jonah had discussed autoerotic asphyxia with the boy. Bar-Jonah used ropes on the children in his apartment. He hanged the boys bringing them to near asphyxia for his enjoyment. In any case, Bar-Jonah not only lost two close friends, but his delivery job also ended, and he lost the security of steady money.

His dismal financial situation worsened when Social Security Disability checks reportedly stopped. Being a pedophile did not qualify him for compensation, nor did obesity, bad teeth or the fact that he had developed diabetes and had sores on his feet from so much walking. Without a steady income, he was in real trouble. His minimum wage part-time job at a fast-food restaurant paid little. His job was now across town, too far to walk, and he had no personal means of transportation. His old Ford Fairlane had stalled downtown. Abandoned on a city street on January 16, 1996, it was towed away. He had no money to retrieve it at the time and no way to get to work unless Tyra drove him.

To make things worse, his mother's sister in Massachusetts died. Tyra had to leave Great Falls and attend the funeral. She couldn't drive her son to work and she forbade him to use her car. Her Toyota Corolla sat in the garage. In the past, she'd let him use it on a limited basis, usually with her along. With Tyra away, Bar-Jonah had no transportation unless he defied his mother's orders.

On top of his grief and financial problems, his relationship with Pamela Clark had deteriorated. They met at work and attended the same church as Zachary Ramsay. Bar-Jonah had actually asked Pam, an attractive Black woman, to marry him. They had set a wedding date. Pamela visited him often, but they had not been living together. On February 2, she moved in with a former boyfriend after being evicted from her apartment.

Bar-Jonah and his mother lived in his brother's duplex, but they were expected to pay rent. His elderly mother had no money to help him during this time of financial need, but probably more important, she was in Massachusetts and had left him without her stabilizing influence.

Later, Tyra told police she had taken her two sets of car keys with her. Over the years, she had recognized his anxiety states and learned how to calm him. Without her, Bar-Jonah's stresses grew overwhelming. Without her watchful eyes, his activities went unhampered. Police know he drove her car while she was gone. He had made his own set of keys to her car. Maybe he drove it even when she was home. She was nearly deaf. His brother Bob had noted things could happen "right under her nose" and said she would not realize it.

A series of suspicious events unfolded in Tyra's absence.

Even though Bar-Jonah had little money, on January 29th he rented a car. It cost him $175 a week. He postdated the check because he had no money in his account to cover it. He'd asked that the check be held until after his next paycheck from Hardee's was due. Curiously, during the week he had the rental car, he was not working yet he drove 510 miles.

Bar-Jonah had a rental car as well as his mother's car sitting in the garage but on February third, he took a taxi. Why would he do that when he had two cars at his disposal? Records showed he used his mother's car and put gasoline in it. The day before Zachary's abduction, on February 5th Bar-Jonah returned the rental car after school hours.

Where did he go covering over five hundred miles that week?

He said, "I probably just drove around town...probably went to antique stores. I had to get around. It was awfully cold then."

There are a dozen antique shops in Great Falls. The city is fifty blocks north to south and seventy blocks east to west. Not much distance to accumulate all those miles.

Investigators traced his steps during those days by tracking his purchases. With Bar-Jonah's hoarding tendency, he had kept receipts and cancelled checks dating back to the early 1970s. Part of the tedious job investigators had was to sort through boxes of his papers, then organize the receipts and cancelled checks by date. Once accomplished, they could analyze them in reference to a timeline and determine if there was a correlation with Zachary's abduction.

Bar-Jonah probably hadn't saved all his receipts but there were so many of them, even for small purchases, that it was an excellent overview of his transactions during the period of interest. He wrote checks for almost everything, sometimes even for a two- dollar purchase. With his check register, cancelled checks and receipts, a paper trail of his activities emerged.

February's atypical totals jumped off the sheet in contrast to those from January, March and April. During the short month of February, he had doubled his gas expenditure from the January total. His food cost was seventy-five percent lower than January's. His taxi rides were up sixty percent. What was also striking, he worked much less, sixty-five percent less than in January. He earned only $250 and spent $175 on a rental car. All the while, he took more taxi rides than usual while bouncing checks. With his food bill decreased by $120, what was he eating?

Bar-Jonah maintained his innocence but based on gathered evidence, the following scenario is what investigators believe happened.

When he faced trouble in all aspects of his existence, like in the past, he drove to calm his nerves. Bar-Jonah, forbidden to use his mother's car, didn't want to be seen driving it, but his compulsive driving urge had set him in motion. He rented a car even though he had no money. He couldn't help himself, fantasies under the surface churned and in the cold of winter, they boiled to the top.

He drove and drove.

Based on photos of neighbor boys he molested and a young boy who lived next door in the duplex, he may have developed a liking or fetish for dark-skinned boys. Even back in Massachusetts, on his Lake Webster list, he had targeted boys who were black. He organized child photos in his albums according to skin color. Pages of darker-skinned and black boys smiled back at him. Shorthand codes beside names in a log book carried a description of their skin, hair and eyes. In other notebooks were columns of names that were classified by age and race with "B" noted before some names, presumably designating Black.

The *Missoulian* newspaper clipping dated August 13, 1996, stated, "Lack of witnesses and evidence kept child killer free for years." Other articles about killings, murder, and newspaper clippings of Rachel Howard, Zach's mother, were found. There were photos of Zachary in an album and like other victims, labeled with the wrong name. He kept news articles about Whittier School events, (Zach's school), and about Zach's disappearance. Unless he was acutely interested in the disappearance, why would he have collected them in the first place and why would he have the three-year-old newspaper?

Zachary disappeared on his way to school on the sixth of February while Tyra was in Massachusetts. On the day of the disappearance, Bar-Jonah went to his doctor's office complaining of pain in his leg, the leg with the large scar he liked his victims to rub. He had previously said the scar caused him to become violent when he had pain and was stressed. He received a non-narcotic prescription for pain medication.

Organizing receipts from the time of Zachary's disappearance took investigators on an interesting ride and produced many unanswered questions. They compared Bar-Jonah's checks with the check register. He had altered dates! The changes made it look like he was covering his tracks on February sixth. On the seventh he wrote a check to pay for a cab ride. He altered it to show February sixth. Was it done to appear that he had no access to a car on the date of the abduction? Was he riding around the area to check on what the investigators were doing to find Zach?

The check bounced a week later.

He took a taxi twice on the eighth, once on the ninth, and twice on the tenth. He wrote individual checks for each ride. These trips were probably to and from work. He may also have wanted to ride through the neighborhood without appearing suspicious. It's common for perpetrators to be curious and even return to the crime scene to see what was happening. Some try to involve themselves by offering to help police, but not Bar-Jonah, he avoided them.

A receipt from Sun Dry Cleaners from February twelfth, six days after the abduction, showed he had a navy-blue jacket cleaned and its torn zipper repaired. Bar-Jonah was slovenly, usually wearing dirty clothes. Why did he spend money to clean and fix a jacket when he had no money and was overdrawn at the bank? Police wondered if the jacket might have been damaged in a struggle with Zachary—if he was abducted by Bar-Jonah. Did he put up a good fight and rip it? Was Zach's blood on it?

On Valentine's Day, Bar-Jonah got a new driver's license. In that picture his hair is short. His only facial hair is a small, trimmed mustache, but just prior to that he looked like he did in cooking class, long haired with a full beard. Why did he cut his hair and trim his beard? Was he trying to change his appearance at the time of the abduction? In the photo he looked like a cop. He has accused "a cop" of abducting Zachary. Maybe the cop was Bar-Jonah. Maybe he was just getting cleaned up to have dinner with his family. On February fifteenth, Bar-Jonah celebrated his 39th birthday with his brother and sister-in-law.

Initially, police thought his former roommate Sherri Deitrich and fiancée Pam Clark would be very strong witnesses against Bar-Jonah. Combined with eyewitness information regarding Zach's clothing and supporting written materials, prosecutors believed the two women would be instrumental in convicting Bar-Jonah of Zachary's abduction and murder.

Sherri told police she'd found clothing like Zach was wearing when he disappeared. She even tried on the high-top black tennis shoes that were in a bag with the clothing. The details made the investigators think she was telling the truth. But then, unfortunately, she rambled on into disorganized thoughts and said she was helping solve murders in another state.

If she had mental problems or delusions of solving crimes elsewhere, Sherri was not a reliable witness. A jury would have trouble believing her tales about Zachary and the clothing she said she found in Bar-Jonah's apartment. The defense lawyers would have no difficulty discounting her testimony.

Pamela Clark, too, turned out to be an unreliable witness. She had unusual beliefs and practiced "black magic." Police interviewed an acquaintance of Pam's who knew her well. She and her "ornery daughter" had stayed with him for a while. He liked Pam but didn't agree with her practices. Pam had introduced him to her fiancée, Bar-Jonah.

The friend explained, "He [Nathan] was working on the same business. She did black magic to help him...People would come to her for readings. I was worried about the black magic stuff. I didn't believe it. She was always burning candles and incense. She kept people out of the kitchen and bathroom. Those rooms were off-limits. She was mixing stuff, liquids, in the bathroom. She worked magic and could cast a spell. People gave her money, like an evangelist. They even sent her money by mail. She'd put her hand on my head and tell me to do this and that."

In a taped police interview, he went on to say that in Pam's apartment there was a "powerful liquid potion. She would dab it on your neck. It was deep red colored, like blood with fragrances in it. She prayed over it, said scriptures."

He said, "Then she'd say psychic things like, 'Now a person can't tell you no.'

"Or she'd say, 'I see this person coming into your life...'"

She was evicted from the apartment near Bar-Jonah's after she had painted the walls black and other tenants complained to management because her water was running all the time. The friend told police she wasn't paying her rent and "always left water in the bathtub running to keep bad spirits away." He said the bad spirit was the landlord trying to collect his money.

With this additional information regarding both women, the prosecutors knew they'd be no help in the difficult murder case without a body.

They had hoped Bob Brown would have given them more information, especially after he cleaned out the duplex garage his brother had left in a mess when he moved. But Bob had thoroughly cleaned the garage three years earlier. He had a positive image in the community and was concerned about his brother's notoriety. He didn't want his name tarnished further. Bob had told police if they suspected his brother had killed Zachary, he would recommend they look in the garbage or the river, but he couldn't believe his brother was capable of the crime.

Chapter 19 What About the Bones?

Ultraviolet light on walls and floors inside Bar-Jonah's former haven produced an eerie purple darkness as police searched his brother's garage at the duplex. After Bar-Jonah had moved out years earlier, Bob emptied the garage, raked the dirt floor and painted the interior walls. The walls had looked clean in natural light but in purple light, strange words in Bar-Jonah's handwriting jumped out from beneath the paint. Yellowish fluorescent letters glowed forth, "The Land of Tito .... In a land far away...."

Investigators had found a "Land of Tito" story written on grid paper in Bar-Jonah's handwriting. It detailed an idyllic setting where a clan lived together in the Village of Tito. In this land, pairs of individuals were happy until someone entered their lives "and spread lies and deceit." One boy stood in the town square and yelled that his love could not be bought. However, the clan discovered they could buy happiness.

Most of the names were unisex like River, Rainbow, and Phoenix, but one obviously different pair was Trinity and Zach. When I interviewed Bar-Jonah in Deer Lodge Prison, I asked him about the Land of Tito. He said, "I've never heard of it."

Bar-Jonah lied. He clearly wrote details about this Land, not only on paper but on the walls of the garage!

Denny Adams with his bloodhounds, Calamity and Otis, had searched for Zachary right after his disappearance. Three years later, police called Denny again. This time they wanted the dogs to search Bob Brown's property. A video tape of them working at the residence showed the trio covering the garage, duplex and grounds in an amazing show of systematic thoroughness. They found nothing suspicious.

In an odd coincidence, Police Officer Mike Stimac used the same garage as Bar-Jonah. He lived in the duplex with a roommate in the late eighties before Bob bought it. The two boarders had found a tombstone in the yard back then. Stimac recalled he hated the garage because of the consistency of the dirt floor. Although the ground was nearly rock-hard, it had a light powdery surface that left a layer of dust on his car, his clothes and his shoes.

Before the garage became a crime scene, Officer Stimac went back to look at his old garage. He commented on how an area of the formerly hard dirt floor had changed. This soft section had a bouncy consistency to it. The area even looked different. Instead of the hard clay-like soil covering most of the ground, a section was covered with a layer of sandy soil. Investigators began digging in the ominous area of new soil.

About six inches down, they found a piece of Bar-Jonah's teddy bear stationary. Did he bury it on purpose, or did it just fall in the hole and get covered without him realizing it? At the same depth they began finding bits of bone. They dug deeper and sifted piles of dirt. A Great Falls Tribune article stated three excavations and two tons of dirt later, investigators found twenty-one bone fragments that had been crushed into little bits.

Forensic evaluation of the bones showed some of them were parts of a dog skeleton. Why had the dog bones been pulverized? Whose dog was it? Where did the bones come from? Could Bar-Jonah have practiced on a neighborhood dog with a stun gun? The cell mate in the Cascade County Jail who Bar-Jonah had intimidated and subdued by sitting on him told jailers Bar-Jonah had said they'd find dog bones when they dug up the floor. He hadn't mentioned the other bones. The rest of the bones were human!

The largest piece of human bone was from a child. It was a radius, a wrist bone belonging to a child between the ages of eight and thirteen. Age estimates are possible in pediatric bones by analyzing growth plates. At birth, sections of bones known as growth plates are open. It is from these areas that growth takes place. When maturation occurs, the plates fuse and growth stops. The age of the child at the time of death was determined by comparing the radius fragment with bone samples of known age and development.

Now they had evidence to seal the murder case of Zachary Ramsay. Believing them to be Zach's, they sent the bones to a lab for testing. Since none of Zachary's DNA was available for genetic comparison, they tested the bone DNA against his mother's mitochondrial DNA. This portion of genetic material is only received from the mother. A match would mean the bone was Zachary's.

It was not a match.

This doesn't mean the bones weren't Zachary's. It could have been a false negative finding, meaning if the material tested was an amplified contaminant cell adhering to the bone, such as from another person, then the test would not be valid.

Maybe the bones had been boiled, destroying most of the cellular structure but leaving a small contaminant. Or, most likely, the bone belongs to another dead child.

The test process at Mitotyping Technologies of Pennsylvania began by cleansing each bone fragment with an enzyme solution and sonication (ultrasound agitation), followed by a bleach rinse. The bone fragments were thoroughly cleansed to remove the risk of contaminating extraneous cells. If the fragments had been larger, a grinding tip might have been used to remove surface material. The lab processed and powdered each bone individually. Using less than one gram of powdered bone from each fragment, they extracted mitochondrial DNA (mtDNA). All of the controls were free of contaminants which confirmed pure mtDNA. Some tests were inconclusive because the fragments were too small and degraded. Taken as a whole, profiles from eight fragments proved the remains were not those of Zachary Ramsay.

With no DNA match, Detectives Cameron and Theisen sent out a missing person notice to law enforcement in the Northwest Region. It said, "This agency has recovered remains of an adolescent human being during the search of a garage owned by Nathanael Bar-Jonah, 2-26-57, AKA David Paul Brown, white male, 250 pounds, brown hair, one blue eye, one brown eye. We are investigating Bar-Jonah in regards to the disappearance of a 10-year-old boy named

Zachary Ramsay. His preferred victims are adolescent males. The bones we have recovered have been tested for mitochondrial DNA and contain human strands of DNA. The bones do not match our victim. Bar-Jonah traveled the flea market circuit and is known to have been in Wyoming and surrounding states. Bar-Jonah is originally from Massachusetts. Bar-Jonah has been out of prison since June of 1991 and was incarcerated December 1999. Any agencies that have unsolved homicides with adolescent victims, where all the remains have not been recovered, please contact Sgt. John Cameron, Detective Tim Theisen of the Great Falls Police Department, or Special Agent James Wilson, FBI..."

Wyoming authorities called the Great Falls and reported a young female, Amanda Gallion, had disappeared in 1997. Bar-Jonah's apartment contained a Wyoming road map and receipts from the state. He had told friends he was planning to move there and already had a job. When I asked him about those plans, he denied ever being in Wyoming.

Investigators alerted Canada. Law officers there began searching their records for missing children. Bar-Jonah had tried to enter Canada, but the Border Patrol had turned him back because of his felony record.

Stymied by dead ends, the dogged Great Falls investigators pushed on. They hoped to find other DNA and continued sifting through the boxes of evidence.

Because the bone fragments were small and the testing process had consumed the entire sample, they needed more DNA for any further testing.

When a DNA sample is minimal as in saliva and lip imprints on a cigarette butt, the cells obtained are processed and the DNA is amplified to produce many copies. If DNA extracted from the bone fragment was a contaminant, even from the person doing the procedure or a faulty lab process such as dirty equipment, the result would be inaccurate. There is no indication the tests were unreliable or improperly performed.

Mitochondrial DNA is one of two types of DNA found within a cell. DNA typically discussed is from within the nucleus of a cell and contains twenty-three pairs of chromosomes. Both parents contribute to the makeup of the chromosomes. Mitochondrial DNA does not come from the nucleus. Instead, it is found outside the nucleus in cellular protoplasm within tiny structures called mitochondria. The mitochondrial powerhouses make ATP (adenosine triphosphate) cellular energy that runs our bodies. These structures contain hundreds of DNA copies. When forensic scientists cannot compare nuclear DNA because the specimen is too small or too degraded, or if they only have maternal DNA to compare against, they use the mitochondrial source.

Blood typing started about 1900 but genetic testing has revolutionized identifications. Blood is a great source of DNA and a preferable specimen. The type of blood is identified and then compared with crime scene blood evidence.

The FBI has the database CODIS (Combined DNA Index System) with the genetic code of over 250,000 convicted felons. The system also stores thousands of samples left at the scenes of unsolved crimes and is used to compare with perpetrators of other crimes that are similar. CODIS software is used internationally. The DNA Identification Act of 1994 formalized FBI authority to establish an index for law enforcement use. The National DNA Index System (NDIS) provides the ability to link biologic evidence from crime scenes and can identify serial offenders.

DNA identifies individuals with such a great degree of accuracy that many old cases have been solved and death row inmates have been cleared. Serial murderer Gary Ridgway, the Green River Killer from the Seattle area, was a man who avoided arrest and continued killing prostitutes over many years. His "normal" life was a good cover but his propensity to pick up prostitutes, and a saliva sample taken by police in a stop, led to his eventual arrest. He had been questioned previously and was a suspect for years. Technological advancements allowed DNA from his saliva sample to be tested and matched with DNA from semen found on some of his long-dead female victims. During the intervening years, he killed at least fifty women. Technology finally won and placed him in prison for life without parole.

The pulp from the central portion of teeth and microscopic bits of skin can be used as DNA sources. A licked postage stamp or a single hair follicle may contain enough material to match with a perpetrator. When Great Falls investigators found a portion of a Negroid hair in a meat grinder in Bar-Jonah's possession, it raised their hopes of solving the case. Unfortunately, without the root follicle where DNA is located, they could not use it for testing.

In Zachary's situation, none of his DNA was available to test against bone fragments. Mitochondrial DNA was their only choice; they had to use his mother's for reference and comparison. More sensitive than nuclear DNA testing, mitochondrial testing is only done in a few laboratories. It is more time-consuming and costly compared to nuclear DNA profiling but just as valuable.

After initial testing had been accomplished using Rachel Howard's mtDNA as the comparison sample, Zachary's father recalled saving Zachary's dried umbilical cord tissue as a keepsake. He gave this to the police. It is now in storage and available as a sample of Zachary's DNA should they find further human body parts to test.

Using the mitochondrial DNA method, profiles of the bones found in Bar-Jonah's garage floor were tested against both Amanda Gallion in Wyoming and Janice Pockett in Connecticut. None of them matched.

In 1976 Angelo Puglisi vanished in Lawrence, Massachusetts, not far from Webster. Pedophile Charles Pierce confessed to both Janice's and Angelo's murders. He told police where to find their bodies. He even led them to the spot. They found no grave, no remains. Sentenced to life in a Florida prison, Pierce confessed on his death bed to Detective Norm Nault that he had duped the police. He said he'd confessed to killing the children just so he could get out of prison for a little trip to break the monotony. Pierce is deceased. The cases remain open. There are many missing children with possible links to Bar-Jonah. Because of the complexity of this case, an FBI special task force was formed to continue the investigation.

Chapter 20 Lost Evidence

The summer following Zachary's abduction, a woman walked the Missouri River shoreline in her affluent neighborhood south of Great Falls. Just downstream from an isolated public access to the Missouri, she found an object that gave her concern. Sticking out of the sand was a piece of thick translucent plastic sheeting with writing on it. She carefully removed it from the sand and examined it.

Indented in the plastic were easily readable ballpoint pen writings. Although there was still some ink present, she could have read it just with the indentations in the plastic. The content gave her a chill. Letters compressed together formed words that begged forgiveness, begged for mercy, for sinning and "doing it again." Black Negroid hair like Zachary's adhered to heavy plastic sheeting, heavy enough to wrap a body in. She wondered if it could be related to the missing boy.

On numerous occasions, she had seen Bar-Jonah near the hidden boat ramp. Nearly immobile, he stood on the river's edge and gazed at the moving water. At the time, there were no adjacent homes. Few could see him standing in this isolated place.

After finding the plastic piece, she thought Bar-Jonah might have disposed of Zachary's body in the Missouri River. She remembered the man standing beside an older model white four-door car like the one Bar-Jonah drove. She carried the plastic piece home and called the Cascade County Sheriff's Department. An officer chided her for picking up such stuff but took her find with its writing and black hair specimen. Records showed it was properly catalogued and filed in the County evidence locker. Great Falls Police were never told.

Later, the same woman's dog carried home a small pelvis bone. She took it away from him and threw it in the garbage. At the time she assumed it was from a small deer. Later she realized she had not looked at it closely and wondered if it could have been human, part of a child's skeleton. Years later, after Bar-Jonah's arrest in 1999, one night she couldn't sleep. Her mind activated by his photos and the news, she kept seeing images of Bar-Jonah standing for hours not far from her home, next to an old light-colored car at the river's edge. She also recalled riding past him one day on her horse. He stared at her, a stare she couldn't forget.

The next morning, she called Detective Cameron to ask about the bit of plastic she'd found. The two had been high school classmates. Cameron was excited to hear from her and about a possible DNA specimen. The hair and a writing sample to compare with Bar-Jonah's handwriting could clinch the case. Cameron rushed to the County evidence room.

In 1999-2000 when the new jail opened, "dead evidence" had been discarded. Records showed a writing sample on the plastic and the hair were destroyed. Cameron was horribly disappointed. After all the elapsed time, the likelihood of any remaining evidence is miniscule, but with Cameron, the woman and I searched the shoreline.

The Missouri boils with the spring melt and run-off from mountain snows. Even in mid-summer when water levels are lower, it is still a deep daunting river in that location near the boat ramp. The only hope would be if skeletal parts lodged in the whirlpool area known to be just downstream from the area Bar-Jonah frequented. With grappling hooks or divers, we might find something. But after so many years and so much money already spent putting Bar-Jonah behind bars, the State of Montana was not inclined to spend more money for such a search.

If the hair and plastic samples had been given to the investigators and hadn't been destroyed, the whole story might have played out differently.

At Bridgewater, Bar-Jonah had spoken of the "trash bag murders." Some think he disposed of Zachary's body parts by merely dropping them in garbage cans. Police considered looking in the city landfill but determined it would not be a worthwhile effort since any evidence there would be under three years of accumulated garbage from a population of about 70,000 people. The dump covered four square blocks with the area of interest buried about sixty feet down. The expensive time-consuming task was unlikely to produce the information they needed.

Looking back, investigators had more questions and concerns. Police discovered plumbing in the older duplex where Bar-Jonah lived when Zachary disappeared had completely plugged. Bob had to replace all of the pipes from the bathroom to the alley. Old pipes were capped and cemented beneath the basement floor of the house. There was ominous speculation about what might have blocked the pipes but after so much time, any biological evidence stuck in the pipes would be too degraded for DNA determination.

Chapter 21 Homicide Defense

Exhilarated by the guilty verdict in the molestation case, the prosecutors moved forward with their challenging case against Bar-Jonah for Zachary Ramsay's murder. There have been numerous murder trials with successful convictions where no body was found; but based on circumstantial evidence alone they are more difficult to prosecute.

Cascade County Prosecutors worked diligently preparing their case. With the evidence and witnesses, it looked like a strong case. Bar-Jonah, already in prison for more than a lifetime without the possibility of parole, awaited trial again, this time Brant Light asked for the death penalty.

Defense Attorneys Jackson and Vernay claimed Bar-Jonah could not get a fair trial with all the negative publicity and sensational reports of suspected cannibalism. His photo appeared in newspapers across the U.S. and Europe. News media featured the story and television specials on sexual predators talked of Bar-Jonah and his crimes. The psychologist instrumental in releasing Bar-Jonah from Bridgewater was interviewed, the doctor who had believed he was no longer sexually dangerous and would be unlikely to re-offend. Great Falls neighbors and friends believed they'd been made cannibals by eating his meals. How could an unbiased jury be found?

Before the molestation trial the defense team searched through twenty-eight boxes evidence; they knew of the heavy evidence they'd have to counter, but claimed prosecutors had nothing upon which to convict Bar-Jonah for abduction or murder. While they plowed on, prosecutors did the same.

Prosecutors constructed large posters and organized all the receipts showing Bar-Jonah's activities around February 6th, 1996. These jury props provided a clear timeline on the day of Zachary's disappearance showing his travel progress minute by minute along the boy's usual route to school. One depicted all the witnesses who had seen him that morning and their exact locations. Another large poster showed Bar-Jonah's receipts and checks for the months of January, February and March. As part of discovery, defense lawyers were given copies of the posters. Both teams worked from the same evidence but looked at it from different perspectives.

Prosecutors emphasized the damning evidence while the defense lawyers looked for holes to cast doubt. They looked at all the witnesses, examined their backgrounds and tried to find something to discredit them.

Bar-Jonah's personal writings excluded from the first trial would be key evidence in the murder trial. With the ominous content in his handwriting, the words were damning. They even included Zachary's name. On a list of known victims, "died" appears at the bottom. Prosecutors believed deciphered messages would put a needle in Bar-Jonah's arm.

Prosecutor Brant Light and Deputy Prosecutor Susan Weber were both busy with an unending stream of cases. Salaried attorneys, they worked usual hours on cases that poured in through their doors. Then, in the evenings, away from their families, they kept on working. Their long after-hours schedules continued as they prepared for the Bar-Jonah murder trial.

Paid by the State on an hourly basis to defend Bar-Jonah, Don Vernay and Greg Jackson spent hours on the case and lots of the State's money for time, consultants and their own investigations. In action, the two men are a team to behold. Very different in appearance and approach, together they are complimentary and effective in their defense of death penalty cases. Vernay, more flamboyant, outspoken and accustomed to living on the edge, is aggressive and vociferous. Jackson is just as aggressive, but his smooth manner disguises it. He softens Vernay's approach. A theatrical team, they skillfully played "good-guy, bad-guy" in the molestation trial.

Vernay gave up sailboat racing on the Atlantic coast and took up motorcycle racing. Dangers in both sports and his penchant for risk-taking, his legal work also left him wary. Much of his law career had been defending people who made serious enemies. As a result, he has enemies himself. Even when he is out to lunch, he sits with his back against the wall.

Bar-Jonah liked his lawyers and believed they worked hard to defend him on the molestation charges. He hoped they would be more successful on appeal and get him released.

Bar-Jonah gave me written permission to access his defense files through Don Vernay. He explained, "I know Don Vernay would never compromise my appeals. That is one thing I like about him...his honesty about the many players in the case. Greg Jackson is more conservative than Don Vernay. Don is more like me and fights the fight needing to be done. I thank God for both. They do complement each other which make them an unbeatable team."

Vernay and Jackson waded through discovery material presented to them by the prosecutors. They scanned thousands of items in evidence and hired their own investigators to scout for countering witnesses and evidence. In their approach to defending murder charges, they interviewed the same people the prosecutors had interviewed and searched for discrepancies in their statements.

Human bones exhumed from the garage floor were a huge problem. How could they defend that? They thought they had a way to cast doubt on the finding when they first learned a tombstone had been found in the back yard of Bob Brown's duplex. Maybe the bones were really from an old grave unrelated to any of Bar-Jonah's activities.

The old tombstone Officer Stimac saw when he lived in the duplex turned up the second time police searched the Brown duplex premises. They found it next to a pine tree in the back yard. The origin of the broken worn stone engraved with the name Kay Morrisen 1925-1930, a dead five-year-old is unknown. The find raised more questions and suspicions than it helped. Had a grave been robbed? Could it somehow explain why a child's wrist bone had been buried with a piece of Bar-Jonah's personal stationery?

Sgt. Cameron learned the headstone had first been brought to police attention in 1988 when Officers Jack Allen and Mike Stimac rented half of the duplex. Back then, officers were unable to determine whether a burial had even taken place. Now Cameron pondered the bones. Did they belong to Bar-Jonah or not? Maybe they were from an old grave disturbed in construction of the house and garage, broken, scattered and rearranged by unsuspecting builders. Cameron sorted through old records at the courthouse and finally located a deed to the house. Both the home and the garages behind it were constructed prior to 1920. A photo showing both buildings eliminated the possibility that bones from a grave dated 1925 were scattered during their construction.

Cameron was unable to locate anyone with the last name Morrisen, who lived there. Death certificates from the years 1925-1935 held no record of anyone with that last name dying in Great Falls.

The Montana Granite Company located at 1216 First Avenue South is just a block and a half from Bob Brown's duplex. If an engraving error on a stone occurred, it was their practice to discard the piece. The Granite Company had been at the same location since 1900 and the Kay Morrisen headstone could be one of their mistakes. Maybe it had been used as doorstop and then carelessly tossed into the back yard. Cameron made sure the stone was not an explanation for the bones.

With the "tombstone defense" shot down, the defense lawyers would have to look elsewhere.

Another defense issue was the stun gun Bar-Jonah carried at the time of his arrest at Lincoln School. He had talked about fantasies of electrocution and electric beds at Bridgewater. Was this part of a fantasy he'd decided to put into practice? Ordered on November 13, 1995, Bar-Jonah received the device in December, less than two moths before Zachary disappeared. Was he planning to use it to control victims?

The powerful stun gun he purchased could incapacitate an adult with its high voltage, low amperage electrical charge. When pressed against a human, even through heavy clothing, it temporarily paralyzes. The person can breathe but is unable to move. Effectiveness depends on the contact, size of the jolt and size of the victim's body. A half-second jolt would startle a person, two seconds causes muscle spasms and the person is dazed. After three seconds of contact, the person loses all muscle control, falls to the ground and becomes disoriented. This dramatic effect is generated by a weapon the size of a small flashlight run by nine-volt batteries. It's like a phaser on stun-mode used on Star Trek, one of Bar-Jonah's favorite shows.

Police now use stun guns regularly in the line of duty. When used properly, they are a non-lethal method of restraint. Unfortunately, criminals are also using them. A rapist in California controlled his victims with one. The women were rendered unable to move, yet awake, aware and unable to resist his assault.

Stun guns are easy to order off the Internet and from catalogs. Because they are so small, stun guns are easily concealable and so effective that some cities and states have banned them. They are outlawed in Bar-Jonah's home state of Massachusetts. In the Montana jail, he talked to his cell mate about how effective it was in controlling children. How would his attorneys counter that?

His lawyers listened to audio tapes made by police and watched hours of video witness interviews. They had come to the conclusion prosecutors had a very weak murder case. The molestation case with three victims testifying had stronger evidence against Bar-Jonah than the murder case. The defense believed they could easily win and wanted to try the murder case first. Without the molestation conviction, Bar-Jonah might have been freed.

Vernay and Jackson espoused that Bar-Jonah "is childlike and narcissistic. He lives totally within himself." Vernay said he thought the molestation charges were excessive for "just touching, like playing doctor." He also commented, "Detective Cameron's actions are unconscionable." Stating the case against his client was "built on beliefs, not facts." There was "nothing to link him to Zach. The case was completely misrepresented by the police."

Just days before the murder trial was to start, prosecutors worked late and ate at a local restaurant. It was the night before they were scheduled to meet with Zachary's mother, Rachel Howard, to go over some details. Deputy Prosecutor Susan Weber and two others from her office stopped in for dinner at Dante's. To their shock, they saw Rachel in the upscale dimly lit restaurant having dinner with her attorney, Sunday Rossberg. With them were Bar-Jonah's attorneys and their legal assistant.

Susan Weber tried to hide her surprise. She greeted them and let them know their secret was out. Weber immediately called Brant Light and told him what she had seen.

The next day, Rachel stormed into Brant's office with her attorney at her side. Light said Zachary's mother was angry, said she never believed Zachary was dead and had a video tape to prove it.

The video she had was made in 1997, taken in Italy where a military family with a son named Zach that looked like her Zachary had been stationed. It was filmed on an Air Force base. Like other leads, the Great Falls Police had followed up on that one, too. They had even told Rachel about it. The boy was not her son, but she had clung to the hope that it was her Zachary anyway.

The scenario of the two Zachary's is almost unbelievable. They are both mixed African-American-Caucasian children that looked alike. Both were born on the same date in Montana, December 18, 1985. The other Zachary was born in Butte. The resemblance was shocking but the dental records did not match. They were not the same child.

That morning following Rachel's outburst, Prosecutor Light reminded her of the warmth she'd shown and a hug she had given him in the past. At a pre-trial evidence hearing, she had thanked him for all the work he'd done.

This time, she snapped back that he had misinterpreted her actions. She also stated investigating officers had told her to shut her mouth.

Light told the *Great Falls Tribune* reporter, "It was all lies." They had told Rachel the video tape of a boy who looked like her son was not her Zachary. She'd hoped for a miracle and had maintained that her son was alive.

Rachel announced to Prosecutor Light she would testify Bar-Jonah was innocent and the police had threatened her to be quiet.

When interviewed later by Kim Skornogoski of the *Great Falls Tribune*, Light exclaimed, "We'd been ambushed." He said he'd never seen it before, "The defense and the victim together!" Prosecutor Light verbally attacked Vernay and Jackson; he believed they had intentionally misled Rachel and sabotaged the case. How could a jury find a man guilty of murder when the victim's mother proclaimed her son was alive and that the murderer was not guilty?

The defense team said it was not their responsibility to educate Rachel Howard about the video. While formulating their defense, she made an unexpected visit to their office. She carried a video with her that showed a boy who looked exactly like her son. She was convinced her son was alive and prosecutors had quit looking for him because they "had their man." Believing her son was alive, she thought Bar-Jonah's defense team might be interested in helping her look for him.

It is almost unheard of for the defense team to meet with a prosecution witness, a victim herself. The covert meeting would not have been known to the prosecution if Susan Weber had not happened on them that night. They would have found out in court.

Based on strong circumstantial evidence, Prosecutor Light had been ready to try the murder case without a body, but the victim's mother being called as a witness for the defense derailed the case. Combined with Rachel's attack on the police officers, Light didn't think he could win. He called a press conference and angrily announced that he was dropping the murder charges and why.

Police slammed Jackson and Vernay for leading Rachel astray regarding the video tape. In a *Great Falls Tribune* article, John Cameron was quoted: "We get used to being hammered on by the defense attorneys...they are never held accountable. They (Bar-Jonah's attorneys), quite frankly, owe this community, this department and Rachel Howard an apology." Cameron stated the Great Falls Police had always been upfront with Rachel. Both Theisen and Cameron said with her announcement, the case was too damaged to proceed.

In the same article, Vernay was quoted saying, when Rachel Howard had come to them in 2001 asking for their help in locating her son, they had just taken the case. She thought they would be motivated to help her. At that time, they did not know the police had ruled this child was not Zachary Ramsay. Several months later, they knew it had been ruled out, but Vernay stated it wasn't their job to tell Rachel about the police investigation. In response to the accusations by the prosecution team, Vernay was quoted saying, "We don't hang out with the victim's mother, you know. If they think we did something so wrong, why don't they file a complaint against us?"

Prosecutor Light dropped the murder charge, "without prejudice." This means he can re-file a case against Bar-Jonah in the future should compelling evidence like DNA or body parts be found. He sincerely wanted to try the murder case as a backup to keep Bar-Jonah off the streets in case the Montana Supreme Court overturned his molestation conviction on appeal and freed him. Special Agent James Wilson, investigating police officers and Prosecutors were angry and disappointed at this turn of events. Light felt there was no other choice; they had forced his hand.

The defense accomplished their goal and undermined the case. How could a jury convict a man of murder when the victim's mother proclaimed her son alive? Her psychics said he was alive. Bar-Jonah couldn't be guilty of murder if her son was alive, now could he?

Bar-Jonah voiced great relief and awaited his appeal. He denied ever meeting Zachary Ramsay, but his friends have testified otherwise. They say he talked about Zach. He also knew personal things that would be difficult to know had he not talked with Rachel, Zach or someone close to them.

There is no question Bar-Jonah knew Zach. Many items support the fact. They had attended the same church. The boy shopped at toy sales in his garage. Bar-Jonah took a photo of Zach clowning in front of Whittier School in After School Scouts and had it in his collection of child photos. He also told a pen pal that Zach had come to his sales and that he had befriended "little Zach." A boy named Zach lived in his "Land of Tito" writings. Bar-Jonah claimed he didn't know the boy and was innocent of his abduction.

In Bar-Jonah's defense, Vernay commented, "Nathan is a strange man, but you don't try someone on personality. The police lied. The charging document lied. There was a rush to judgment based on a bizarre history and a fantasy life."

Chapter 22 Cannibalism and Recipes

Bar-Jonah's rambling coded writing about various entrees made from human flesh may have been nothing more than a morbid interest. He had told counselors back in Massachusetts when he entered the penal system at the age of twenty about his desire to taste human flesh. A focus on the subject has been with him much of his life, just like fantasies, electrocution, power and sexual stimulation from envisioning torture and control of his victims.

Many deviants have killed their victims, eaten body parts and shared the meat with others. Jeffrey Dahmer, notorious serial killer arrested in Milwaukee, Wisconsin, had wrapped and frozen human flesh harvested from young men he had killed. Ed Gein had a human heart in a pan on the stove in his farm home in rural Wisconsin the day he was arrested. His female victim had been shot, dragged to his pickup truck and transported to his home where he disemboweled her like a deer. Her beheaded body hung from the rafters in the back of the house. Ed shared fresh "venison" with his friends, though reports stated he had never hunted deer in his life. In 1897, Chicago butcher Adolph Luetgert killed his wife, made sausages of her flesh and sold them to his customers. There are many other gruesome examples including one in

Russia and a recent liaison between two men in Germany who met via an Internet chat room which ended in murder and cannibalism.

Based on writings, his coded lists of recipes, and comments he made, it sounds likely Bar-Jonah ate Zachary's flesh and shared it with others. His early fantasies may have evolved over years until he acted upon them. Then, like in the barbecued meat in *Fried Green Tomatoes*, he cooked up special meals and fed them to others.

In a television interview with Debbie Coty, a woman who lived in Great Falls, she stated she had met Bar-Jonah during the summer of 1996. Receipts showed she purchased a Mike Tyson doll from Bar-Jonah for her eleven-year-old son. Debbie recalled the case of Zachary Ramsay had come up in a conversation she had with Bar-Jonah. He stated police would never find Zachary. After Debbie's house burned that December, in a friendly gesture, Bar-Jonah came to visit her on Christmas Day. He brought a gift of homemade spaghetti with meat sauce.

In his writings, Bar-Jonah wrote about sharing and some of his favorite things.

It wasn't only Christmas when he shared his cooking. He brought food to many people. His shared stew, pot pie and spaghetti helped ingratiate himself with young mothers. A woman interviewed by police commented that the meat had tasted funny. She also said she was not comfortable with Bar-Jonah in her home but had let him in because he seemed so nice. Her concern increased after he appeared obsessed with her young son. Bar-Jonah tried to get him alone on many occasions. She wouldn't allow it.

In the Cascade County Jail during one of Bar-Jonah's discussions with a cell mate he bragged and said human flesh tasted like chicken. Maybe it was a story to gain recognition and look like a big criminal, someone the man should admire.

If you examine Bar-Jonah's writings, he was a coward. He intimidated children. Writings suggest he had eaten human flesh and enjoyed it. What tremendous deceit to have actually fed human flesh to unsuspecting friends and his mother, his wonderful religious mother who totally believed in him. He brought her and the others unknowingly with him into his fantasy world.

Other phrases deciphered from compressed coded writing detailed not only *little boy stew*, but also *little boy pot pie, French-fried kid, mince meat pie,* and *lunch served on the patio with roasted child*. He said his specialty is quiche; it's a form of pot pie. There were many other dishes noted. Why would he go to the trouble to write these in a hidden manner?

He served barbecued burgers to his mother and pedophile friend Doc Bauman. A note card found in Bar-Jonah's belongings showed a picture on the front of a Panda bear holding its little baby. Inside, Doc thanked him profusely for sharing venison burgers with him and Tyra. Later Bar-Jonah said they were from a Hardee's special. Hardee's fast-food restaurant has never served venison.

When asked about other strange-tasting meat, Bar-Jonah claimed it was venison he had hunted, "killed and butchered" himself. His brother Bob said Bar-Jonah didn't own a gun and had never hunted. Police verified he had not purchased a hunting license. So what does all this mean?

Police spoke with a Montana hunter and former roommate. Bar-Jonah stated the venison had come from him. The roommate unequivocally denied ever providing Bar-Jonah with venison. In fact, during the time he rented a room from him, Bar-Jonah had tried to charge him extra for food he never ate including *venison*. The roommate observed Bar-Jonah fixing meat that was dark and gelatinous, not like any venison he'd ever seen in all of his years of hunting.

Researchers have found that cannibalistic killers have pent-up rage that is satiated when they kill. They are exhilarated by the hunt but calmed in the end; killing releases the rage. No one knows why some predators develop the desire to eat their victims. Profilers have found that in some deviants an urge to kill meshes with the unusual desire to eat human flesh and they are driven to fulfill their desire. It becomes an addiction. Then, like other serial killers, the cannibalistic killers don't stop until they are caught. Jeffrey Dahmer is suspected of killing more than fifteen boys and eating their parts before he was finally caught and stopped. He believed eating their flesh made them part of him.

Cannibalism has been around for countless centuries and crosses all cultures. It is even found in fairy tales. The Grimm brothers, Wilhelm and Jacob, had set out to document German folklore. Their first edition of *Nursery and Household Tales* was definitely not a bedtime storybook for children. They included horrific tales of incest and child torture. In the story *The Juniper Tree*, a woman decapitates her step son, chops him in pieces and makes stew. She serves the stew to the boy's father who thinks it tastes great. In *Hansel and Gretel,* a brother and sister barely escape with their lives during a time of starvation when a witch wants to fatten them up and eat them.

In times of extreme hardship and starvation, cannibalism is understandable and more acceptable. Those are not the only incidents found in history. Lack of food was a common problem for early man in his struggle for survival. It made sense to conserve life by eating human remains. In more recent years, the famous Donner Party traveling in covered wagons heading west was marooned during a harsh winter in the Sierra-Nevada Mountains. Without sustaining themselves by eating those who died, they all would have perished. In a similar situation, after a plane crash in the Andes Mountains of Peru which killed many of the passengers, survivors decided to save themselves from starvation by eating the dead. Some lived long enough to be rescued and tell their story.

Dating back 100,000 years, fossil evidence from a cave site in France occupied by Neanderthals showed clear evidence they practiced cannibalism. Neanderthal skeletal remains bore cut marks exactly like those on deer skeletons. Marks from sharp stone instruments showed how they stripped meat from long bones and disarticulated joints. Similar scars on human bones seen in pueblo ruins at Anasazi sites in Arizona, New Mexico and Colorado showed meat had been roasted on the bone. The excavated limb bones bore evidence they'd been cracked for marrow extraction.

Hunger is not the only reason for cannibalism found in history. Some societies ate portions of their dead for religious and ritualistic reasons. A less palatable concept was described by E. Adamson Hoebel in his text book, *Anthropology: The Study of Man*. "Dietary cannibalism" was practiced by some tribes in the Congo of Africa and the South Pacific. They fattened up penned prisoners like cattle and consumed human flesh because it tasted good. In sacrificial offerings to the gods, Aztecs killed hundreds of thousands of people. They believed their world would be destroyed unless the gods were given enough human hearts. Onlookers shared portions of the flesh so they could identify with the gods. Vivid depictions show them dismembering bodies and chewing on limbs, holding them like drumsticks.

In Australia, ritualistic cannibalism occurred among the aborigines who believed eating parts of dead relatives would enable them to inherit the best qualities of the deceased. Body parts of dead warriors who possessed highly desirable hunting skills became a feast for remaining relatives. Australian authorities had supposedly outlawed the practice in 1947, but there was little contact with the area to verify the practice ended.

Until about 1950, the Fore tribesmen in Papua, New Guinea, practiced the same type of ritualism. Fore natives ate the brains of their elders. Primarily women and children developed a rapidly progressive neurological disease called Kuru, their word for tremors. The afflicted tribal members developed spastic weak limbs and difficulty walking. Within a year of developing symptoms, they became demented and died.

Today Kuru is known as Creutzfeldt-Jakob Disease (CJD). The debilitating disorder is caused by an abnormal protein, a prion, which concentrates in neural tissue. It can arise spontaneously, but a new variant of the disease emerged in 1996 in Europe (vCJD) and infected people who ate beef that had contracted mad-cow disease. The cows had become infected with a Kuru-like prion by eating feed that contained contaminants from sheep carcasses infected with a prion disease called scrapie. After slaughter, the sheep carcasses entered the food chain via rendering plants that supplied protein concentrates to animal feed manufacturers. Since prions are not killed by rendering, cooking or usual sterilization procedures, it was unknowingly passed on to the cows. But like Fore tribesmen who ate brains, cows became cannibals. They ate contaminated meat byproducts of other ungulates and developed the disease. Humans, in turn, are at risk for prion disease even eating a well-done steak when the muscle meat contains mad-cow prions.

American physician D. Carleton Gajdusek, who visited New Guinea in 1957, determined the Kuru disease connection with cannibalism. In 1976, he was co-recipient of the Nobel Prize for Physiology and Medicine with Baruch S. Blumberg for his concentrated effort to study the Fore people with Kuru and identify its relationship to eating infected brain tissue. On numerous trips to the South Pacific to study the disease, he worked with Vincent Ziga, district medical officer with the Fore people.

Along with great skills as a researcher, virologist and trained pediatrician, Dr. Gajdusek had demons. He was and is—a pedophile. In 1997, he was found guilty of child molestation after his arrest by the FBI in connection with an Internet child pornography investigation. Over a twenty-year period, he brought more than fifty children to the United States from the South Pacific to live with him. Most of them boys, he reportedly "monitored their development for scientific interests" but was charged with molesting some of them. Under a plea agreement, he ultimately served a few months in prison and was allowed to serve five years probation in Europe. Great achievements in medicine identifying funerary cannibalism as the cause for Kuru were overshadowed by his sordid pedophile practices.

Cannibalism is symbolically practiced in the Sacrament of Communion in Christian churches. Figuratively eating the body and drinking the blood of Christ has promise of purification and forgiveness.

During the fourth century in China, warriors ate their enemies' hearts as an ultimate act of revenge. In Native American culture along the Pacific Northwest Coast, there are stories of cannibalism. In *Hamatsa* the stories are detailed by Jim McDowell. The author carefully researched historical sources and concluded the ritual consumption of human flesh and corpse-eating had persisted into our time. In the Kwakiutl/Hamatsa societies it was witnessed and recorded by explorers.

In Bar-Jonah's apartment, there was a story related to Native American folklore, *Why the Salmon Is Respected*. It probably originates from coastal Indians where salmon provided a sustained food source for their people. The salmon was thought to have supernatural powers. Interestingly, the story talks of catching a child, clubbing and eating him, then being very careful to burn every bone and part you do not eat. If you do not follow the rules, the child (salmon) will come back crippled without the parts not disposed of correctly. If you follow the rules, good things will happen. The nature spirits will assure that all things will be renewed.

Bar-Jonah says he found the story in a cookbook and didn't like it, yet he kept a copy of it. In other stories of the Salmon People, they believed that after a salmon died, it returned home to be reborn in human form.

Along with instructions on how to gut a deer, Bar-Jonah's apartment had a recipe for pemmican, an American Indian food made from jerky, nuts and berries. In pemmican, the preserved meat with additives is a high protein food, long-lasting and nourishing. What a wonderful way to fix a variety of meats including venison or "long pork," as human flesh is termed. Bar-Jonah's compressed writings included roast pork.

As shocking as cannibalism sounds, it has been around for a very long time. From survival necessity to religious symbolism, it has had a place in society and has not always been the social taboo it is today. Of course, cannibalism is one thing, as distasteful as it is, but in this case, Bar-Jonah's case, we are talking about murder.

After Bar-Jonah was arrested in 1999 and the public learned some of the content of his writings, people came forward to tell police he had made a variety of dishes and shared with them. They uniformly recalled the meat tasted strange. Bar-Jonah's girlfriend Pam said the meat had a funny tasting "twang." His lawyer Don Vernay explained, "It's because he's a gourmet cook and uses a variety of spices. You know, the people in Great Falls don't even use much garlic. They wouldn't recognize good cooking."

Like his hoards of recipes and cookbooks, his collecting may simply be related to his obsessive-compulsive behavior but that doesn't explain why his writing concentrated on cooked human body parts. His mother said he began keeping recipes when he was in second grade. Along with all the garbage and junk, his apartment contained a large collection of recipe books he considered a treasure. He hoped one day to have them returned.

Bar-Jonah's propensity to cook started in childhood, continued through high school and during his years of incarceration in Massachusetts working in the Canteen. In Great Falls he worked in fast-food restaurants right up until he was arrested. In the Cascade County Jail, he demanded kosher food, but based on the piles of fast-food wrappers in his apartment, he wasn't above eating what he served to others at Hardee's and it certainly wasn't kosher.

The prison food in Deer Lodge left a lot to be desired. He said the flash-frozen entrees were edible but not great. Holiday meals were a little better, but he missed his good cooking. From details of his encrypted writings, one would wonder if "stir-fried penises" and "roast child" are fantasies, but they sound sinister and unappetizing.

In prison, his collecting continued. He assembled a cookbook with contributions from many acquaintances and pen pals. He hoped to have it published someday. He wanted to use the proceeds as a way to support himself after he was released on appeal. Law forbids inmates from making any money related to their crimes. In Bar-Jonah's case, it is very unlikely the cookbook or the book he was writing detailing his views on who might have abducted Zach Ramsay would ever be printed. He had also written a book of poetry and envisioned the cover on the book of poems showing the picture of a smiling heart standing behind prison bars, with arms wrapped around the bars as if hugging them. Bar-Jonah's thoughts about Zachary's abduction scenarios covered 1000 typed pages.

In the past, he said he had shipped some of his most important recipes to his mother in Massachusetts for safekeeping. He didn't want to lose them. Where are all the original ink-written notebook pages he ripped out leaving behind only indented pages? The FBI was finally able to decipher tales of violence from the indentations, but the original writings would be valuable evidence. He must have them hidden somewhere. If found, the writings would be telling evidence. Were they fantasies or tales of his activities? Of Zachary? Maybe he sent more than recipes to Massachusetts for safekeeping. It's too bad the Massachusetts judge refused to sign a search warrant for Montana detectives to search Tyra's house. In the end, maybe Bar-Jonah's family will be forthright and offer all his stored belongings to the police in their search for truth.

Chapter 23 Bar-Jonah's Appeal

In administrative isolation for his protection from other prisoners, Bar-Jonah sat in his cell in Deer Lodge hoping for a miracle release. First in the county jail, then prison since December 1999, he waited. He had waited for fourteen years for his release from the Massachusetts prison system before it happened. His faith was unwavering. He proclaimed, "Mark my words, I will be released. I guarantee it. God's always come through in ways I have never expected and always out of left field."

Immediately after conviction, Bar-Jonah's lawyers prepared an appeal to the Montana Supreme Court. They appealed on many grounds and Bar-Jonah was convinced he would be released.

The years following his incarceration passed slowly but he maintained a bright outlook. He filled his time writing books about finding who took Zachary, religious poetry and formulating a cookbook, all while awaiting the Supreme Court's decision.

Bar-Jonah staunchly claimed innocence of the molestation and assault charges that sent him to prison for 130 years. He was adamant he didn't molest or choke the boys who lived upstairs in his apartment building. "They lied about everything." He said, "I feel that once my book is published those kids who lied on the stand will come forward and admit they lied, and my present conviction would be overturned." He also emphatically denied he knew Zachary Ramsay and said he didn't abduct or murder him.

When his lawyers filed an appeal with the Montana Supreme Court they contested just about everything. The first was the District Court erred in denying Bar-Jonah's motion to suppress evidence. They said the investigative stop at the school that dark December morning was improper and that the police violated his right to be free from unreasonable searches and seizures under the Fourth Amendment of the US Constitution and Article II of the Montana Constitution. They argued that Detective Burton was familiar with Bar-Jonah's criminal history and of itself was not sufficient to justify an investigative stop. If that was thrown out, the entire trial would go because that stop opened the door to a search warrant and all the findings that put him in prison. If the stop was illegal, then the case might have been reversed.

The Justices saw it differently. Because Officer Burton had seen Bar-Jonah in the same area on two prior occasions the previous week, he requested a patrol unit to make contact with Bar-Jonah and find out what he was doing in the vicinity of the school. When Officer Brunk stopped to investigate Bar-Jonah, he had asked him to come in front of the car into the light and remove his hands from his pockets. Bar-Jonah refused even after a second request.

A second car arrived with Officer Badgley. Brunk asked Bar-Jonah if he had something in his pocket, and he responded that he had a stun gun. Bar-Jonah was then asked to place his hands on the car for a pat-down. Officer Badgley also found two cans of pepper spray, a toy gun and a badge. It was at that time Badgley reviewed Montana statutes regarding impersonating a police officer and carrying a concealed weapon with Bar-Jonah. Officer Badgley contacted his shift commander who advised him to file a report and release Bar-Jonah pending further review.

The State had argued that the initial contact between the officers and Bar-Jonah did not rise to the level of an investigative stop; rather it was merely a police-citizen encounter which didn't implicate the Fourth Amendment or Article II of the Montana Constitution. It was only after Bar-Jonah volunteered he had a stun gun in his pocket that the encounter became an investigative stop giving the officers grounds to not only believe that a crime was being committed but to conduct a protective search.

The danger to officer safety justifies a protective search.

Further, even if the initial encounter was a seizure, based on the totality of the circumstances, the officer had the suspicion prior to initiating the stop based on his knowledge of Bar-Jonah's past crimes against children. When he observed Bar-Jonah wearing a police-style jacket walking near an elementary school in early morning darkness, at a time when young children would be going to school, he was properly concerned.

The Supreme Court said the initial stop was not a mere police-citizen encounter because under the circumstances a reasonable person would not have felt free to leave. When a police officer who is armed and in uniform displays his authority by exiting his police car and approaches a citizen, the encounter constitutes an investigative stop, not just a police-citizen encounter. However, the police did not rely on a single factor alone to infer Bar-Jonah was involved in criminal activity. Burton had been involved in investigating an allegation of sexual assault on a youth by Bar-Jonah. Combined with seeing Bar-Jonah in proximity to a school and Officer Burton's extensive experience in criminal investigation, it led him to suspect Bar-Jonah was involved in criminal activity. With Bar-Jonah's history of crimes against children while dressed as a police officer, finding a concealed stun gun was sufficient cause for the pat-down search.

The Supreme Court stated the stun gun is a weapon capable of producing serious bodily harm and information gained from the pat-down that produced the pepper spray, toy gun and badge together with other facts formed the basis of the search warrants and was justified. The Supreme Court's decision that the officers' investigative stop was proper was key to establish the probable cause necessary to issue subsequent search warrants.

Bar-Jonah's next argument was that police went beyond the scope of the warrant which allowed seizure of items such as the stun gun, garments and badges that were clearly related to the offenses of Impersonating a Public Official and Carrying a Concealed Weapon. But when cameras, photo albums, film negatives and other items not related to the offenses were taken, it exceeded the scope and the searches were done under a false pretext. Bar-Jonah's lawyers felt the police were on a fishing expedition once they gained access to his residence. They wanted to search for evidence of more serious crimes.

The Supreme Court said the record did not support Bar-Jonah's contention that the searches were under false pretext. At the suppression hearing, Officer Badgley testified that the reason he did not arrest Bar-Jonah when he was stopped on December 13th was because he was not sure if a stun gun qualified as a weapon in Montana. On the advice of his superior officer, he returned the items to Bar-Jonah and let him go home until the police had a chance to investigate further. The Court determined the officer's intent in securing the warrant was irrelevant because probable cause existed for the issuance of the search warrant.

Another important contested issue was that any evidence gained as a result of the warrants must be suppressed because the searches were not only improper because they exceeded the scope of the search warrants but because the information supporting probable cause was "stale." The stale information was the fact that he had used a police badge in a crime twenty-two years earlier; and the 1993 arrest for sexual assault in support of the application was unsubstantiated because the case had been dismissed.

The Supreme Court stated the fact that the information of Bar-Jonah's prior offense spanned a time frame from 1977 to 1993 did not disqualify it. Instead, taken together, wearing a police-style jacket, carrying a badge, stun gun and pepper spray, and his sexual offender convictions using a similar "modus operandi" to gain the confidence of young children, supported a pattern of continuous conduct sufficient to support probable cause.

His lawyers said he couldn't possibly have received a fair trial because of a contaminated jury pool. The legal team was not satisfied that the trial had been moved to Butte, they wanted it moved a second time, all the way to Billings near the eastern edge of the state. Even the defense expert conceded that moving the trial again would increase media coverage and the Justices agreed with District Court that moving the trial a second time would have served no useful purpose. His lawyers also contended that jury selection was flawed. The record indicated the jurors decided the issues based solely on the evidence presented at trial and no prejudice or bias was revealed.

Bar-Jonah's lawyers also wanted the trial for Zachary Ramsay's murder held before the molestation trial, stating the molestation trial would prejudice the homicide trial. His lawyers were unable to show the order of the trials adversely affected him. The molestation case was filed first, and the alleged victims were children whose memories could be affected by further delay. The Justices determined the victims were entitled to a timely resolution of their allegations against Bar-Jonah.

A major contended issue was the admissibility of photo albums containing hundreds of photographs of children including pictures of the child victims in the case because they were highly prejudicial. His lawyers said among other reasons, the jurors would have prior knowledge of his criminal history or of the charges against him in the Ramsay case. They argued the evidence branded him as a pedophile and influenced the jury to convict him for "who he is, rather than for what he allegedly had done."

The Supreme Court concluded the facts of the case showed the probative value of the photo albums outweighed any prejudice to Bar-Jonah in introducing them into evidence. They were primarily introduced as a proof of Bar-Jonah's motive to befriend young boys and falls under the admissibility of character evidence.

Even testimony at his sentencing hearing was at issue. Former Massachusetts victims assaulted in years past presented testimony—two on tape and one in person. The Justices stated that Bar-Jonah's argument that his constitutional right to confront and cross-examine witnesses was violated at the sentencing hearing was ungrounded. His lawyers had failed to object in court and thereby waived his right to appeal on that issue. They explained that the Supreme Court may review claimed errors that implicate a criminal defendant's fundamental constitutional rights even if no objection was made, but they declined to do so in this case because their refusal would not result in a miscarriage of justice.

In conclusion, the Supreme Court affirmed the judgment and sentence of the District Court.

When asked about how he felt about the outcome of his appeal, Bar-Jonah said "That's no big deal. We now go to the US Supreme Court for a Writ of Certiorari which will cause them to review the State Supreme Court's decision which in my lawyers' opinion was erroneous. If the Court had properly decided my case, my case would have been reversed and dismissed. We also still have a State Post Conviction Action pending."

He hadn't given up on the idea of being released and based on his quick response with legal terminology, he had been listening to his lawyers carefully or doing significant personal research.

Chapter 24 Life in Deer Lodge State Prison

The small town of Deer Lodge sits just off Interstate-15 a few miles north of the Idaho border near Monida Pass. Scenic rolling foothills surrounded by impressive mountains are dotted with expansive cattle herds. Hot, dry summer weather changes abruptly in October to cold nights, heavy frosts and snow flurries. Green trees and bushes turn to brilliant colors, exaggerated against the white ground. Their leaves are driven away with sudden winter storms. Howling winds sweep the area and significant snow falls drift and close roads. A few miles out of town along Connelly Lake Road, fences topped by concertina razor wire surround sprawling buildings. They look out of place in an area where farmhouses should stand. Guard towers belie danger and high security is evident.

Deer Lodge State Prison houses thirteen hundred male adult offenders and employs nearly a thousand people. There are three compounds on sixty-eight acres inside the double-fenced perimeter. Four levels of restriction exist inside. For lower level offenders, a work-dorm situated outside the perimeter houses eighty inmates who work on a thirty-five-thousand acre ranch and dairy farm.

Bar-Jonah started in maximum security. Here he was allowed outside the building one day per week, but he didn't bother going. Fresh air didn't appeal to him and he was not inclined to exercise. He could go *nowhere* unaccompanied. Because of his "cho mo" designation, he was at risk of harm from other inmates. When en route somewhere, such as to see a physician, he left his building in shackles with guards. One of his trips outside was for retinal laser surgery to stop progression of damage to his vision caused by diabetes. Vision loss would be a terrible blow to him since television, reading and writing filled his time.

After I wrote and asked Bar-Jonah for an interview, he wrote back quickly and agreed. Visits to Deer Lodge are by invitation only. Prison officials were professional and especially helpful. After metal detector screening, and a transparent hand stamp, I was escorted to the maximum-security building.

Escorted in shackles, dressed in a tan jumpsuit, Bar-Jonah sat down for the interview behind a heavy glass separating us. A guard stood closely behind him and remained throughout the interview.

Bar-Jonah looked thinner than he had at the trial and wore a trimmed mustache like his drivers license photo. With no bushy beard and straggly long hair, he looked nothing like his arrest photos. Thin brown hair combed straight back made him look younger. His kind demeanor, vocabulary and personal presentation were incongruous in a man imprisoned for life for crimes against children. How could such a gentle soul become homicidal and choke little boys?

During our conversation he appeared comfortable, in control, but with guards hovering. In spite of no upper teeth and missing bottom incisors, his speech was remarkably clear. His distracting strange eyes darted about. He looked down or quickly looked away when I asked a question that made him uncomfortable or that he had no intention of answering. Most responses were quick.

When he didn't want to answer, he either said he didn't know or he couldn't respond because of his pending appeal. When I knew his answers were not truthful, I noted he'd fidget and look away. For example, when I asked him to interpret some coded writings, he said he'd never seen them before. They were in his handwriting, so I knew he was lying. When I asked him again, he looked away and said, "I've never seen it before in my life." These were part of the "alphabetic slip" method of coding in Appendix 1.

He talked comfortably and may have enjoyed having someone visit. I gained no solid information. He provided no insight into his life of crime except to say his actions stemmed from the childhood rape which he reiterated in detail. He denied having anything to do with Zachary Ramsay's disappearance and invited me to return anytime.

When asked about his rages, he said he no longer lost his temper. "I made up my mind that it isn't me. I don't hold it in anymore. Therapy taught me that much. I don't take my anger out on everyone. I take it up with the person."

Regarding his large photo collection, "I can't talk about it because of my appeal.

About cannibalism: "Somebody made it up." He wouldn't discuss his secret lists of various ways to cook human flesh.

A prolific writer and nothing else to do in prison, Bar-Jonah said he'd written three books related to the police investigations. Focused on various leads he believed they had not thoroughly investigated. Bar-Jonah spoke with pride about two books he hoped would one day make him millions: A pen-pal cookbook and 1000-page manuscript about Zachary Ramsay entitled "Justice for Zach and Me."

Prisoners cannot benefit financially from crimes, but Bar-Jonah remained confident his writing would bring him fortunes.

Chapter 25 Letters from Prison to the Author

I received numerous lengthy letters from him during his years in Deer Lodge. They were very up-beat, unusually cheery for a man in his situation. When I wrote and asked him specific questions, he responded within a few days.

Excerpts of a letter from Deer Lodge:

Hi Betty, I received your letter and I was really glad to hear from you. In fact, it made my day. I hope this letter finds you well. Also, I wanted to wish you a very Happy Thanksgiving. As for me? I'm doing okay, just a bit depressed. My friend, John, left and will be in Hobbs, New Mexico by Thanksgiving. I miss him and we use to talk about writing and all. He was very helpful in that area. He's already had two Westerns written and a coffee table book of Western trivia questions...Once I either sell my movie rights or my book, I'll join him at Hobbs. As to how I would get transfer? Well, if I do what John did, then I would be exchanged with an inmate in Hobbs or at least in New Mexico and pay $3,500 for that transfer but I have 4 male nurses and a doctor here willing to send me on a medical transfer because they can't meet my needs here and my safety issue. So, in that case I wouldn't have to pay for the transfer from what I've been told but I do want to go down with some money so I'll be able to get the things I need since they don't allow you belongings to go with you until a month later. Then they would *mail it to you. :(It is also illegal, the law states all belongings go with you so I'll have to sue Montana for the delay and all damage that occurs because they don't pack stuff well I'm told. So, there is a good chance my TV would be broken and maybe my typewriter. In Massachusetts prisons they offer nothing at all and they are alot more dangerous especially to people with sex charges. At Hobbs, they have a high profile unit and I would be safe. I'm allowed more property. There the canteen is 10 times better than here. You can go outside and soak in the rays in a large yard. Also you can utilize the library and the law library plus if you have a problem you can see someone at any time. Here in Close 3, if you have a problem it may take a person over a month or two. ...I usually wake up a 0500 hours & turn on the TV. Between 0630 to 0700 hours we are served breakfast. Depending on how I feel I'll either type, read, or go back to bed until 1030 or 1100. Lunch is served to me in my cell between 1130 or 1200. In the afternoon, I read or type while I watch TV. ...Meals are small and I basicly live on peanut butter and crackers due to my present money situation. I live on $30 a month. I buy three typing cartridges at $5.50 each, at least 15 stamps, toiletries and I might have enough to buy peanut butter and cracker. Also, typing paper costs me $2.80 per 200 sheets. ..I would of finished Chapter 7 but my last cartridge ran out so I got to wait until next month when my brother will send me some money. Although, once I sell my movie rights or book, then I can afford to do anything I want. I hate having to rely on other people. I've always worked even in prison or I created a job for me. In prison, I sold cards and gifts to the inmates and the guards. In Great Falls when I could not get a job, I mowed lawns. ..As for Thanksgiving, we'll get a typical TV dinner but* *usually they serve a little more food for the holiday. The inmate welfare fund will give us a 9"pie and a pint of ice cream. Also I ordered a pizza (meat lovers) on a food sale from Pizza Hut. I just had to do without some things. It's a large, I paid $10.00 for and it'll be delivered on the 29th. This will be the 1st time in over 4 years I had a good pizza. ...Well, not much else so I'll close for now hoping to hear from you soon. Have a Happy Thanksgiving! Your friend, Nathan*

That is a typical letter, generally newsy and friendly. He later began making personalized stationery by Xeroxing pictures he'd cut from magazines. Sometimes he sent recipes and drew pictures along the edges.

His letters revealed little of his past but told the exaggerated rape stories as a justification of his behavior. He looked toward the future and maintained hope for release. In one eerie letter he asked for "medical information" on how much force it would take to "crush a windpipe." He needed this for his research on Scenarios about what might have happened to Zachary Ramsay after a woman reported a vision of a man striking the child in the throat with the tail pipe of a car.

Food remained important to Bar-Jonah. Writing a cookbook while in prison made it impossible for him to try recipes as he wasn't allowed in the kitchen. It also made him dwell on food when he had little access. Deer Lodge meals are frozen selections provided in microwaved trays like TV dinners. Bar-Jonah said entrees and often canned fruit came in such small quantities that "kids in elementary schools eat more than we do." However, he said, "The food is tasty, better than the Cascade County Jail in Great Falls, just not enough of it."

He'd seen the inside of many cells. In his opinion, the prisons in Massachusetts were a lot worse. "Deer Lodge is like a kiddie kamp compared to them." He had no interest in transferring to the Massachusetts Correctional System to be near his family. "They offer nothing at all and they are a lot more dangerous, especially to people with sex charges." Instead, he hoped to move to a private prison in Hobbs, New Mexico, after an acquaintance moved there. "They have a high-profile unit where I would be safe." He believed he'd have access to a law library, a better canteen and a better living environment. To accomplish this move he said he would have to arrange to exchange places with a prisoner at the Hobbs facility.

Busy most of the time with writing, Bar-Jonah had numerous pen pals and worked on books he hoped to publish. One of his projects was to help his lawyers with his appeal and murder defense. In this endeavor, he'd been searching for "clues to Zachary's disappearance." Studying Zachary's health records provided to him by his lawyers, he learned the boy was troubled with Attention Deficit Hyperactivity Disorder (ADHD) and was off his medication at the time of his disappearance. He wondered if that might have caused Zach to just "run away."

With a new typewriter, Bar-Jonah was content to produce a compilation of leads he believed the police failed to follow up. "Scenarios" as he called them, contained his thoughts on reports he believed could have cleared him of the charges. He said he believed that if Zach ran away, these clues might help locate him. Dwelling on Zachary and coming up with possible reasons for his disappearance allowed Bar-Jonah to continue "touching" him.

Bar-Jonah said he was writing about the "twenty-ninth of thirty-four" suspects.

Another book he entitled "Who? Z.R.?" was written because, "No one knows what happened to Zachary Ramsay." Bar-Jonah believed one of the prime suspects was a Great Falls police officer.

In another letter, Bar-Jonah said, "I also plan on eventually publishing a cookbook of my favorite gourmet recipes...You know what people will think with my name on the cookbook and I have each book wrapped in cellaphane [sic], I bet in the first month I sell a million copies."

Chapter 26 The End of the Trail

On April 13, 2008, Nathan Bar-Jonah was found unresponsive in his prison cell and transported to Powell County Memorial Hospital in Deer Lodge by ambulance personnel. He was pronounced dead.

At fifty-one, he had been in poor health for years. Many of his problems stemmed from his lifelong obesity and the effects of diabetes. For years, he had refused healthcare within the prison system.

Diabetes, with its associated heart disease, vision loss and vascular narrowing, had progressed to devastating arterial problems in his legs. Even before that, Bar-Jonah was extremely inactive. After an amputation of one leg at a hospital in Missoula, he was severely disabled, and wheelchair bound.

Investigators searched the cell during his absence from Deer Lodge prison. They found no clues to other crimes. They found no confession of Zachary's abduction and murder.

State Medical Examiner Gary Dale, M.D. reported a pulmonary embolism as the cause of death. Although many people survive after a venous blood clot breaks loose from a distal point such as a leg and travels to the lungs, death is not uncommon. Once the clot travels through the heart into the lungs, it lodges in a vessel, blocking both blood flow and oxygen exchange. Large clots can result in cardiopulmonary arrest as with Bar-Jonah. Immobility contributes to the risk for this deadly disorder.

Following the coroner's inquest, his cremated remains were released to the Brown family.

FBI collected voluminous writings from his cell for scrutiny.

No additional information is available.

Until his death, Nathanael Bar-Jonah claimed innocence in Zachary Ramsay's disappearance. Coded and other notes told a different story. A list in his own handwriting names several victims, relatives and others, including Zachary Ramsay. At the end of the list "died" appears. Strong circumstantial evidence pointed to Bar-Jonah as both a murderer and cannibal.

Although never convicted in the Ramsay case, in the end, the people and law men of Montana stopped the violent pedophile from harming more children.

Chapter 27 Pedophile Traits

In the animal world, a predator lives by feeding on other smaller, weaker or maimed animals. Human predators behave the same way. They prey on vulnerable victims for perverse enjoyment, though usually not for food.

Imagine a cat that catches a mouse and plays with it, pouncing, tossing, injuring and enjoying every minute. In the final fatal act, the small helpless creature lies dead. Human predators look upon their victims much like the cat. Victims are toys they perceive as disposable.

Most sexual offenders are not psychotic; they don't hear voices or see things. They carry no psychiatric diagnosis except, perhaps, a personality disorder. That sounds benign but it is not. They are evil psychopaths that act without remorse for the terrible pain and terror they cause. In fact, what some of them enjoy most is the pain they inflict on others. Egotistical narcissistic offenders act out their fantasies because it pleases them. They enjoy it and—they can get away with it.

In the case of pedophiles, they preferentially target prepubescent children for sexual gratification. These young children, not yet showing signs of sexual maturity, are children they can intimidate and control. Instead of normal development evolving at puberty in combination with sexual interest occurring in the company of a similar aged person, the pedophile is sexually aroused by children.

Bar-Jonah's history and behavior correlate strongly with data compiled by the National Center for Missing and Exploited Children in their publication Child Molesters: A Behavioral Analysis. Here researchers report a pedophile's sexual preference for children usually begins in early adolescence. As he matures into teenage years, like with Bar-Jonah, it becomes more obvious there is a problem when he chooses to play with younger children. As their interests and fantasies become more compelling, they spend time, money and energy in their pursuits and ultimately commit multiple offenses.

In addition, researchers reported that the older the preferred child is, the more likely a specific gender individual is chosen. The younger the age of preference, the less likely the offender cares about the gender of the child. For example, a pedophile attracted to grade school children is more likely to prefer girls or boys exclusively. A pedophile attracted to infants or toddlers often molests boys and girls equally. Or like Bar-Jonah, a pedophile may have a specific age preference such as ten-year-old boys. Bar-Jonah's victims have ranged from five to fourteen, but his writings emphasized age ten.

Most sexual offenders are male. Their fantasy-driven behavior pushes them to collect theme pornography or "paraphernalia" such as souvenirs and videotapes to remind them of their desires or actions. They may take videos of acts and victims, tape television programs or purchase videos such as the junior boy workout tape found in Bar-Jonah's apartment.

As fantasy progresses to action, they want to record the fantasy as they act it out. It can then be savored time and time again. Bar-Jonah had thousands of child photos and boxes of videotapes. Some of the videos were shots of the neighbor boys he molested. Investigators did not find a video of Zachary but believe he had that specific "treasure" secured somewhere. It could tell the whole story of the boy's disappearance.

Now with advanced technical capabilities of small digital and cell phone cameras, videos and high-quality digital photos are possible. Because they are stored on a chip the size of a postage stamp, investigators have more difficulty finding them.

When boys mingle with children much younger, it is a red flag to watch for aberrant behavior. Another is, single men who never marry or live with their parents. They may also have difficulty interacting with adults. After failing at college and failing at jobs, Bar-Jonah lived with his mother for many years. Of course, spending fourteen years behind bars between the ages of twenty and thirty-four took a huge chunk out of his formative years when most young people are learning adult interpersonal skills. Instead of being with normal individuals, he was in a closed environment with other sexual offenders and probably learned less desirable skills by interacting with them and heard about their reasons for incarceration.

A way in which pedophiles access children is to choose activities or professions that enable them proximity to kids. They may become camp counselors, bus drivers, babysitters, foster parents, photographers, coaches, special education teachers and even school principals. Bar-Jonah specialized in childcare and garage sales that attracted children. In both Massachusetts and Montana, he acted as a Royal Ranger Christian youth leader. With his church affiliations, parents saw a benevolent, religious man who offered to take their children to church functions. In Bar-Jonah's handwriting, a poem to potential "girlfriends" spoke of being the marrying kind. He said children were okay up to the age of eleven. He should have added but "I prefer ten-year-olds."

From the time of his first abductions in high school, he dressed as a police officer, someone we are conditioned to trust. Later he hung around school yards ready to "help" the children. He seduced children by befriending them and by paying attention to them when their parents couldn't. He bought gifts and gave them treats. His house was filled with games. The Christmas of his arrest, Bar-Jonah's apartment was filled with stuffed animals, board games, wrapped presents and pictures of Santa with children. In his friend Doc Bauman's apartment all sorts of stuffed animals were stacked high against one wall. The men were ready to entertain little friends. Pedophiles learn what kids like and try to please them. Beware if an adult is paying unusual attention or giving your child gifts.

Photos don't have to show nakedness to be stimulating to the pedophile. Bar-Jonah's collection was not pornographic, but to him it was erotic.

Fourteen thousand photographs of fully clothed children must have provided joy to him otherwise why would he go to such great effort and time. Scattered among the pictures were his victims labeled with wrong names. O'Connor, Enrikaitis, Benoit, Calvin, Eddie and Buddy were all there. He could fantasize. He could stare at their pictures and relive his erotic experiences with them because they remained fixed in age forever. It didn't matter that they had grown. It was his treasure. He wanted the collection back if freed on appeal.

He had pictures of Zachary too.

Because their collections mean so much to them, offenders may spend large sums of money to support their special interests. With Internet access, they can download scores of photos and hide them away in a very small space with copies secure in a safe deposit box.

Some incarcerated offenders will go to great lengths to retain their collections. One reference noted a pedophile even offered to organize and file his collections in evidence for prosecutors. This way he could savor the pictures while pretending to be helping. Prosecutors were wise to his motive.

Pornography is not the cause of aberrant behavior. Actions develop from a much deeper stimulus. Pornography does fuel fantasies and may keep the inner fire burning.

Because Bar-Jonah was smooth, a seemingly nice man, easy to talk to and "engaging" even to a psychiatrist, he undoubtedly had gotten away with many molestations that went unreported. Most pedophiles molest numerous kids, sometimes hundreds, as revealed by cases against Catholic priests and others, including a pedophile pediatrician who video taped himself molesting his young patients.

Bar-Jonah was able to convince parents of the purity of his motives by helping with their children. After gaining parental confidence, he molested the children and intimidated them into silence. If intimidation didn't work and the child reported him, Bar-Jonah just denied it ever happened.

It was the child's word against his. Or he'd use the amnesia defense and claim he didn't remember. "I must have blacked out," he'd say.

Pedophiles are adept liars. They lie often and with such ease because they start early. By the time they reach adulthood, they are expert. The have no remorse, so with little emotional response to questioning, a polygraph exam is often meaningless for prosecution. If the subject being tested doesn't become nervous and sweaty, and his heart doesn't race, the polygraph cannot record telltale signs of anxiety and lying. Polygraphs may be useful in treatment programs.

When pedophiles bring presents, are ready to help with kids, babysit and take them to events, they mislead adults with their kindness. Sometimes parents are so taken by kind gestures that they encourage their children to participate even when the child tries to avoid it. If that happens, the child is placed in a terrible situation. He doesn't want to go with the molester, but the parent pushes him to continue a relationship he can't speak of due to fear of retaliation from the molester.

The situation is even more tragic if the molester lives in the household or has a relationship with the child's mother. The child may develop anxiety attacks, or post-traumatic stress disorder from being placed in a prolonged situation where they are trapped and there is no escape. PTSD can last a lifetime. The trapped child is vulnerable, weak and powerless. No one helps. They are abandoned and in the clutches of a pervert.

Predator skill comes with practice. But how does this overtly helpful person evolve to abduction and murder? There is no simple answer.

Fantasies play over and over in their brains like the words of a song they can't block. The fantasies accelerate to an abduction that is usually carefully planned and rehearsed. There may be no intention to murder but when something goes wrong, they may kill. Or realize the child will reveal what has happened, so they kill to avoid prosecution. Once a kill occurs, the feeling may be so thrilling the predator is compelled to do it again and again.

Predatory behavior is complex. Typically, it correlates with years of failed relationships and poor interpersonal development. Social bonding with a caretaker hasn't occurred. For some reason, significant people in their lives did not provide nurturing. Overlooked or ignored abnormal behaviors in adolescents may be rationalized by parents, allowing the monster to mature.

Researchers have found unprotected abused children who experience prolonged physical or sexual abuse will develop vivid frightening memories that replay in their brains. Helpless to stop the abuse, thoughts emerge that trigger nightmares, daydreams and eventually fantasies. Maybe the dreams are protective at first, an escape, but left undirected, they go awry. Dreams and fantasies become conflicted obsessive themes of helplessness or aggression. Without successful resolution, the aggressive fantasies aim at achieving the dominance and control missing in their real life.

As a child, Bar-Jonah was powerless at home. The large unhappy boy was mentally abused by his father and spanked with a strap at least until age eleven. His mother couldn't stop it. After his father's sudden death, there was no chance to resolve negative feelings toward the man. His grieving mother expected too much of him.

Young Bar-Jonah failed everywhere and was filled with helplessness and rage. He began taking his violence out on others long before his father's death. After bullying kids in elementary school, after growing bigger and older, he intimidated, molested and boldly abducted children in broad daylight. The emotional distress of his father's death cannot be used as an excuse for his actions.

Based on his behaviors, Bar-Jonah could have been sexually abused but sexual abuse isn't a prerequisite in this type of offender. It is common, though, and often denied, hidden by families refusing to face the truth. When Bar-Jonah visited the streetwise incorrigible boys in the reform school in his neighborhood, there were sexual encounters. Bar-Jonah denied sexual abuse, other than the far-fetched story of being raped at age ten by seven children younger than himself, one of them only three. Some of the children who he said were involved have no recollection of any sexual or physical assault and say he made it up. Psychiatrists agreed the story was not believable.

By age seven, he was physically and socially isolated from peers and had begun obsessive compulsive behaviors. He lived in a stilted fundamentalist religious household where dating, dancing and even card playing was frowned upon.

None of these factors alone produce monsters. But the repressive atmosphere is fertile ground for an internal life of unresolved emotions.

During an abuse episode, the abused individual may find himself physiologically aroused: fearful, heart racing, sweating. In the case of an adolescent, sustained emotional and sexual arousal can occur with beatings. Strong feelings interact with repetitive thoughts related to the trauma and physical arousal. The child's sexual development is altered. Normal development fails. Instead of imprinting and correlating sexual arousal with kindness and love, as in Bar-Jonah it is fused with violence.

With no attachment to caregivers, they lose control over the child. A child can be so psychologically deprived that he has minimal emotional response to normal events. With no role model on which to base appropriate behaviors, depression, lack of self worth and growing anxiety spiral. With no hope of escape, he isolates himself from the abuse. Isolation and fantasies calm him. There, in fantasyland, he is in control and safe.

Family dysfunction and abuse are common risks cited for developing sexual aberrations such as pedophilia. No one knows why some individuals become sex offenders under these circumstances and some do not. Childhood sexual abuse is a specific risk factor for developing pedophilia. Pedophiles then tend to choose their age-specific victims in accordance with the age of their own experience of sexual trauma.

Growing up with a feeling of trust, security and self-worth is supremely important for normal development. Children must establish relationships with others and develop personal confidence. Psychological growth begins in early childhood, playing with parents, with other children and learning to cooperate and share. Independence grows. If relationships are negative and children are not encouraged or supported, emotional maturity and self-sufficiency never evolve. Social isolation emerges along with fantasy.

Inner thoughts, schemes, plans and daydreams substitute for the lack of human interaction. Without positive human encounters, they do not learn how to interact and negotiate in everyday life. Pedophiles often stand out as shy, uncommunicative, backward, kids with poor interpersonal skills. When faced with conflicts, they have not learned acceptable behaviors, may become volatile, and just take what they want.

Sexual encounters based on pleasure, companionship and caring are nonexistent in their lives. They have no close friends. Evolving from isolation, sexual arousal occurs as a result of their violent behavior, fantasy and autoerotic activities. Examples of autoerotic activities include masturbation and autoerotic asphyxia (self-choking to enhance the intensity of orgasm). Sexual experiences become a confused mixture of isolation and aggression with no social sexual outlet. There are many variations on this theme, but evolution to molestation and abduction may occur.

Bar-Jonah thought the painful process of removing skin from his left leg and grafting it to his right was "cool." It may have been this unusual treatment, being held down and "tortured" with painful medical procedures and dressing changes, combined with beatings he took from his father at the same time in his life that triggered his fixation on control or bondage and violence. This fixation could accelerate into abductions of boys around the age of ten, boys his age when this violence was inflicted upon him. He may have experienced transference of explosive inner anger with no outlet except to impose his power on others. After he tried it out on someone he could subdue and humiliate with success, the positive feelings pushed him to expand his skills.

Bar-Jonah knew children were taught to respect police officers. Thus his charade as a police officer was very successful. He used it when he abducted O'Connor, Enrikaitis, and Benoit, and was arrested at the grade school in Great Falls dressed the same way twenty years later. He was prepared to overpower his victims with handcuffs, pepper spray and a stun gun.

For O'Connor, he didn't need ropes or handcuffs. All he had to do was sit on him to control him, just as he did the neighbor boy Jason. However, with O'Connor, he used the seatbelt, wrapping it around his neck after choking him with his hands. He used handcuffs on the other two but choked all three with his hands. He had choked a little girl when he was only six and had completely overpowered her. At a very early age he learned choking worked. Bruises ringed the boys' necks. On O'Connor, choking was so severe it broke blood vessels in his face and eyes.

Choking is a very intimate act of violence, not an impersonal act like shooting someone. He didn't have to sexually molest these children to get his thrill. Part of his payoff was control and the exhilaration from brutality that he found erotic. He also disrobed O'Connor and tried to force Benoit and Enrikaitis to undress. Voyeurism like "peeping Toms" peering in windows, visualizing young male bodies excited him.

Stress factors play a large role in a sexual pervert's life. Stress typically triggers behavior leading up to abduction. In a negative emotional state, frustrated, hostile and depressed, he searches for something to make himself feel better. Fantasies play in his brain. He knows acting them out will provide elation and relief. When reliving past activities, he experiences erotic replay in his brain and finds enjoyment. He "goes hunting." With fantasy fueling his search for prey, just like a hunter stalking a white tail deer, he experiences heightened excitement. He rehearses methods and uses those he has perfected. He may try new techniques like a stun gun.

Many abductors are compulsive drivers. Serial killer Ted Bundy was one of those; in ten months, he drove eighty-thousand miles. Bar-Jonah was also a compulsive driver. In Massachusetts, he walked in the woods to lower his stress and contemplate. When he could drive, even before he had a driver's license, he reported driving for hours to calm his nerves. Sometimes he didn't recall where he went. He drove aimlessly, prowling.

One week prior to Zachary's abduction, Bar-Jonah put over five-hundred miles on a rental car. When he didn't have a car, he walked. Friends say if he wasn't locked in the garage or his room, he walked for hours, sometimes along the Missouri River just blocks from his home and Zachary's.

When Officer Burton noticed him in 1999, Bar-Jonah was prowling. Dressed like a police officer as he had so many times in the past when he abducted other boys, this time he carried a badge, a realistic toy gun, and was armed with pepper spray and a stun gun. Circling the little grade school, he was hunting with an arsenal to back him up.

Another cold pedophile murder case in Great Falls, Montana, was finally solved with Detective Cameron's help seventeen years after nine-year-old sandy-haired blue-eyed Dolana Clark disappeared while riding her bicycle. In 1988, friends believed she was en route to purchase a kitten from a pet store across town from her home when she vanished. Wilfred Morrisey, a military retiree and neighbor, was not convicted until late 2005. The nice family friend spent extraordinary time in the dysfunctional Clark household. He brought money, gifts, food and shared meals with the family. Alcoholism plagued Dolana's parents. She was often left unattended and stayed over night with Morrisey.

By the time an elk hunter found Dolana's bullet-pierced skull, Morrisey had moved to Colorado. It was there he admitted hiding a dismantled weapon on his property matching the ballistics of Dolana's skull wound. Just before Dolana disappeared, friends said she had been trying to earn enough money to purchase the special cat. Morrisey purchased and kept the cat.

His behavior is consistent with the behavior of many pedophiles. He ingratiated himself to Dolana's parents, had few friends, spent unusual time with the little girl providing her gifts. He even stated he was waiting until she grew older so he could marry her. After rescheduling his trial numerous times, Morrisey was finally convicted to life without the possibility of parole.

His behavior could have been recognized by astute caregivers and her safety might have been assured, but pedophiles are wily. They often appear kind and generous and their motives are not evident unless you pay careful attention. After her parents reported her missing, as many perpetrators do, Morrisey helped investigators search for her in a ploy to detract attention from him.

An overview list of pedophile characteristics is found in Appendix 3.

Chapter 28 Protecting Children

There is no single effective way to keep our children safe from sexual predators. If you are able to recognize pedophile characteristics and refuse to allow your child contact with someone who fits the profile, you have a good start. But pedophiles are everywhere, so educating your children, friends and relatives is essential. If you are concerned about an individual's behavior, seek assistance from the police. Not wanting to discuss or expose molesters, families have concealed pedophile relatives for years, allowing abuse to continue while trying to protect the family name. A very important safety factor in stopping abuse is the willingness to report concerns to authorities.

Police Officer Mark Gado of New Rochelle, New York, compiled common traits which help identify the type of men children should avoid. In his experience, a pedophile is usually a single male over thirty years old. He has few or no friends his age and seeks systematic prolonged access to children through work and volunteer for jobs where he will be left alone with kids. Pedophiles are sympathetic listeners who target troubled or withdrawn children. Typically, their home or a room is decorated in a child's theme. Many of them collect toys. It is not surprising Nathanael Bar-Jonah had most of these traits.

If you are aware of a male lacking strong relationships with others his age or someone who has unusual collections or interests which attract children, you must be cognizant of their activities and not leave children in his care. Single adult males, living with their parents should trigger increased caution.

Children are safer if parents control who they socialize with, but even that is no guarantee. Just telling a child not to talk to a stranger or not get into a car with one is not enough. Stranger abductions are much less common than victimization by friends and family members. *Overnight pajama parties and hot tubbing can be high risk situations.*

The molester is often a family member or someone well-known to the family. If the perpetrator is a member of the household, such as a brother, father, uncle or grandfather, and if the molestation is reported, the family unit is divided. Incest is a horrible sex crime. A parent's responsibility is to the innocent child. In some cases, a family conspiracy to hide the shame goes on for years and in the process, children are abandoned to the rapist.

The negative impact of exposing a molester who is prominent in the community is immense. It takes strength to send a husband to prison and destroy the family name. But the child's life depends on it. Many pedophile rapists actually have the support of their spouse who covers rapes of their own children and participates in acquiring children for him. In these situations, the perpetrators live in freedom to harm children, all the while appearing to be a pillar in the community.

The only way to stop predators is to report them and be willing to testify in their prosecution.

Instruct your children to stay away from cars and vans parked along the sidewalk or road. Also instruct them to not help anyone.

Tell them it is okay to say "No" even to any adult, a policeman or a priest. If someone actually grabs them, they should fight to get away, kick, scream and bite. <u>Make as much noise as possible</u>. Yell something like: "*Help me! This is not my father (or mother). Help me!*"

Stranger-abductors use many ploys to get close to children. They don't usually use simple methods like offering candy or a ride. They become more creative. If an abductor tells a child their parents are injured or the parents said to give them a ride, the child is more likely to go with them. If an abductor asks a child to help find a lost puppy, the child would likely want to do it and would go along willingly. Some stranger-abductors are so brazen they don't trick their victims by ploys that will encourage a child to follow voluntarily. Instead, they grab children right off the sidewalk and whisk them away with people watching.

Two girls who were abducted and released in the 1970's near Bar-Jonah's home were both told by the abductor their mothers wanted them to take the ride home. Because of that, they got into the car with a stranger. Luckily, both girls were released. We don't know if the same ploy was used with Janet Pockett, the little girl who has never been found. It is doubtful. She wouldn't have left her bicycle willingly to take a ride with someone so close to her home.

The most important rule is: **NEVER let your children walk or bicycle alone.**

At times, Bar-Jonah was a stranger-abductor. That was his mode of operation with O'Connor, Enrikaitis and Benoit (and likely the two girls, Patty and Mary). Of course, that was not his only method; he adapted his techniques to the situation.

The friendly neighbor groomed Calvin, Eddie and Buddy. He offered them treats, played games with them and then after they learned to trust him, he molested and choked them. He threatened them with death if they talked. Calvin reported, "He said he'd have his brother shoot me then he'd chop me up in little pieces." The fearful boys didn't talk.

Encourage your children to say "No!" to photos and tell parents if this happens. Pedophiles take photos of kids for their collections. Children may not be aware they are being photographed or may be flattered and pose. Sometimes pedophiles place kids in sexually suggestive poses, like the child photo of Bar-Jonah wearing the girl's two-piece swimsuit and a wig. If the child poses, the photo could be used as blackmail to keep him from telling parents about molestation. Kids may believe posing is a game and have no idea what they are being asked to do. Seeing photos of other kids who have done it lowers their resistance and they go along.

In this age of videos and digital cameras, the child may not even know a photo was taken. Photos taken by strangers may be a benign interest or can carry ominous consequences. One of the photos of Zachary in Bar-Jonah's collection is a snapshot in front of his school showing him clowning around with a big grin on his face.

The helpful-policeman-guise is commonly used by abductors and works well because kids are taught to respect authority. Reported in the *Great Falls Tribune*, one little boy at the Lincoln School where Bar-Jonah was arrested, avoided abduction because he was suspicious and went back inside the school to wait for his mother. The boy said he was standing on the back side of the school near the playground waiting for his mother to pick him up when Bar-Jonah pulled up and asked him to get in the car. The boy got scared and ran back inside the school. He asked the teacher if he could wait inside until his mother arrived. When the pictures of Bar-Jonah appeared on television and in the paper, the boy told his mother, "That's him." After realizing how easily he could have been abducted, he told a reporter, "In nightmares he kills me and stuff."

That boy escaped. He escaped because he followed his instincts and did what his mother had told him to do. If he had taken the pleasantly-offered ride like other victims, he might be missing today.

Bar-Jonah told his cellmate he would wear his blue coat with a fake badge and drive, circling the school. Sometimes he'd sit in a car parked near the school where he could watch the kids. If one was in trouble, the child might approach him for help. He liked talking to them and openly admitted he was guilty of impersonating an officer and carrying handcuffs. He said he liked the stun gun because if he zapped a kid, the kid couldn't say anything.

Know what your children are doing on the Internet and their cell phones. Today there is an online subculture with Internet sites for child pornography and social networks for pedophiles. An abstract from the *Sex Abuse* journal noted there are five forums by and for pedophiles in the Web community. Child cyber exploitation has become an international problem with the Internet being the new pedophile playground.

A Florida sex sting recently resulted in arrests of 40 men seeking sex with children. Many of them were in positions of power in their communities and working with children.

International trafficking of children via Internet connections has made it easier for pedophiles to travel internationally to sexually exploit children. Travel to foreign countries to obtain sex with children is so prevalent that numerous world organizations have joined in an effort to protect children from traveling pedophiles. An ABC Nightline reporter stated, "Cambodia has become a magnet for pedophiles." Sex trade and access to children for sex is common there. An international crackdown involved local police, FBI, Immigration and Customs Enforcement (ICE) and International Law Enforcement. There is a concerted effort to protect children from pedophiles who will stop at nothing to gain access to kids.

Here, children and parents are becoming better educated because of public effort and recent extensive news media coverage of abductions and pedophile cases. On television, in school and at home, children are told about safety and how to protect themselves against abduction. But just as important, they are learning about proper touching and that no one should touch them on parts of the body that would be covered by a swimsuit.

Be suspicious if someone is paying unusual attention to your child. Molesters may not threaten violence. They confide in the child that they have a secret, an important secret that no other adult must know. They shower the child with gifts and then threaten the gifts will stop if they tell.

Child molesters are commonly live-in boyfriends and babysitters. The mother doesn't want to believe it and may discount a child's report. This attitude allows the abuse to continue. The child is confused, injured, frightened and in continual jeopardy. Vulnerable and unprotected, not knowing what to do, they are trapped in an untenable situation. The child must be rescued from the setting and given proper support and counseling. If the abuse continues, abnormal behaviors arise. If the child is male, he may become an abuser himself. Female abuse victims may become unusually fearful, try to run away, cry, and begin bed-wetting. As teens, rebellious behavior and prostitution occur.

Pelvic pain, rectal pain, bleeding and itching may be from sexual contact. A concerned woman brought her one-year-old granddaughter to me in the emergency room after she noted blood in the child's diaper. This little girl was not only traumatized vaginally but had developed obvious genital warts. She had been molested for months by her mother's boyfriend. Medical personnel bring these overt disgusting cases to the attention of police and the child welfare system, but it is the subtle cases we must be vigilant to identify.

Many cases are investigated on much softer evidence grounds, sometimes because the child is observed acting out with inappropriate sexual overtones or shows an unusual interest in sexual matters. I encountered an example of victimization when a five-year-old girl was brought to the emergency room after she was molested in a rescue mission. That wasn't her first time. Without emotion, she described the incident, then smiled and explained, "I know a lot about sex." She reached into the pocket of her tight little blue jeans, produced foil wrapped condoms and went on to explain how and why they were used. "I watched movies about it with my mother's boyfriend."

Your children should be comfortable talking to you so if a situation occurs in which they experience inappropriate touching or worse, they will tell you. However, while children "should be comfortable" talking with parents, they seldom are. Fear to report usually stems from a predator's threats and is a common reason not to tell. In addition, abused children may feel responsible or believe they'll get in trouble if they report it, so they keep it all inside. Sometimes failure to report stems from shame because the child experiences sexual arousal. They must be assured the feelings do not mean collusion with the molester. Instead, it shows that *the right parts work*. The offender knows this and takes advantage of the child's confusion.

Most important is to love your children and protect them with education and supervision.

You probably have a sex offender living near you. If that frightens you, you're not alone. Many people want them exiled for life. One of the most difficult problems for the court system is to accurately predict which sexual deviants will reoffend if released. In other words, who is "sexually dangerous?"

There is a broad range of sexual offenders. One has to be careful about reading statistics about offenders. Definitions vary and until recently, there was no standardized definition of rape. Statistically tracking crimes with accuracy has been problematic because of variable terminology. For example, consensual sex between a 16-year-old girl and a 19-year-old boy is *statutory rape* because of the underage girl. The boy is labeled a *sex offender*. A violent serial rapist is also a *sex offender*. There is a huge difference between the teens and the rapist. Most states have developed categories of sex offenders to designate presumed level of risk. A Level III offender like Bar-Jonah is more than an "offender," he is a violent repeat offender; a Sexually Violent Predator that should never be released.

The Justice Department's new definition of rape is: "The penetration, no matter how slight, of the vagina or anus with any body part or object, or oral penetration by a sex organ of another person, without consent of the victim." For proper reporting and statistical gathering, charges should specify exactly what type of sexual contact occurred.

Megan's Law is a federal law named after seven-year-old Megan Kanka and signed in May 1996 by President Clinton. The law requires state registration of sexual offenders and mandates community notification. Megan was raped and killed by a convicted sex offender. Unknown to her parents, he was living across the street from her home with two other sex offenders. This law has helped, but remember, <u>most sex offenders are people known to the family</u>, so Megan's Law is only part of the solution.

Take a proactive stance and contact local police for information about known sexual offenders in your neighborhood. Another easy source of information is the Internet to get public information on offenders in most states. See www.sexoffender.com

Police departments have information and tips for parents on how to treat the offenders who are friendly and helpful like Bar-Jonah. Officers usually encourage parents to be courteous to the offenders who may be trying to rebuild their lives but be wary of inviting them to any family functions. The children should be shown the offender's residence and given strict orders to steer clear of the location.

The fields of forensic psychology and forensic psychiatry are challenging. Imagine trying daily to evaluate violent sex offenders who are cunning sociopathic liars. These predators are convincing. Only seasoned forensic physicians should carry this heavy burden. Lives depend on their decisions. Is he sexually dangerous or not? Will he reoffend if released?

Predictability for reoffending is primarily dependent on: prior sexual offenses combined with antisocial behavior. Terminology varies somewhat from state to state. To qualify as a Sexually Violent Predator, SVP (as in Washington State), or as Bar-Jonah was termed in Massachusetts, a Sexually Dangerous Person, SDP, the individual generally: has been convicted for sexual violence, has a mental or personality disorder such as pedophilia and the offender is likely to reoffend unless imprisoned.

There are many guides to help in this determination, most with little accuracy in prediction. Experts agree the effective tools for predicting sexual violence risk currently are actuarial measures such as *Static-99A*. Multiple studies involving thousands of offenders were compared and tabulated over years. Risk factors considered are: Prior sexual offenses, prior sentencing, non-sexual violence, unrelated victims, stranger victims, male victims, perpetrator age less than 25, single. Higher scores predict higher risk to reoffend; above six is a critical cutoff and the individual should not be released.

Higher risk to reoffend is seen with positive findings of: young age, single, male victims, stranger assaults, and prior assaults.

Once classified as a Sexually Violent Predator (SVP), the perpetrator should be imprisoned for life because relapse prevention treatment does not work. The results from the California Sex Offender Treatment and Evaluation Project, SOTEP, found no significant difference among three groups of sexual or violent reoffenders over an 8 year period. This same result was found for both rapists and child molesters. The violent and sadistic ones are highly likely to repeat their offenses.

Psychologists and psychiatrists without experience and training in evaluating sexually violent criminals have a bad track record. Like Bar-Jonah's case in Massachusetts, he was released after two psychologists met with him, tested him and decided he was low risk for offending again. He duped them and was released without counseling or probation requirements. In forty-three days, he had re-offended.

In a Canadian study using the Sex Offender Risk Appraisal Guide for dangerous behavior prediction, they used a combination of: criminal history, a psychopath characteristics checklist and a measure of sexual arousal (penile plethysmography).

In 1997, Minnesota Department of Corrections developed the Minnesota Sex Offender Screen Tool, MnSOST. It was designed to help identify the most violent offenders and those most likely to offend again. Using the scoring system against 256 offenders released between 1988 and 1993, there was an overall recidivism rate of 41% but for those with the higher scores determined using the screening tool, 62% were re-arrested on sex offenses. Although the tool provides an increase in the accuracy of prediction, from these statistics we see how difficult it is to predict behavior in this population that already has a very high re-offense rate.

At this point there is no package of tests that measure offender recurrence risk with total confidence. Many behavioral tests have been developed to help determine whether a man will reoffend. The fact that there are numerous methods to calculate the risk shows the difficulty in producing an accurate prediction. If there was one great method, everyone would use it. The Static 99-A is currently the most reliable.

The prison psychiatrists with empirically based knowledge coupled with experience knew Bar-Jonah was high risk based on his behaviors. Predictions are improved if decision-making is based on a systematic use of factors from the individual's history rather than on the basis of clinical judgment.

<u>Risk analyses based on interviews alone are very superficial</u> <u>and carry little validity</u>. Offenders lie and learn from other offenders what they have to say and do to be released.

Characteristics strongly associated with recidivism are: being young, having a criminal history, sexual deviancy and having psychopathic behavioral features. Bar-Jonah had all of these.

Psychopaths are cold-hearted, impulsive, self-centered, and manipulative. They do not develop long-lasting bonds to people; they use people. With no empathy for their victims and without guilt or remorse, they think only of personal desires, use victims and discard them like trash.

Montana has as many sex offenders as elsewhere, but tolerance here is low and prosecution is perhaps greater than in some locales. There is aggressive monitoring and mandatory registration of sex offenders everywhere per federal law. When an offender moves into a neighborhood a photo with his address appears in local newspapers. The information includes the risk level for reoffending. Some have had to move after the announcement because of harassment by residents whose tempers flared, stimulated by intolerance and fear for their children. Knowing the location of sexual predators may not be enough. In Florida, more than one-hundred-sixty registered sex offenders lived within five miles of where a 7-year-old girl was abducted and murdered.

A new system of tracking sex offenders using implanted electronic chips and GPS, the Global Positioning Satellite system, is being used. Like the On-Star automobile system that can track the whereabouts of a vehicle or allow easy driving in an unfamiliar area, the new system puts the high-risk offender on a surveillance map. However, while wearing a GPS tracker, a recently arrested pedophile abducted an eleven- year-old and held her captive for years, raping her and forcing her to bear children. Police knew his whereabouts, but he persisted <u>with his wife as an accomplice</u>.

During the 1990's, many states enacted sex offender commitment statutes. Washington State was the first to pass a post-sentence civil commitment statute for sex offenders, keeping "sexually violent predators" off the streets indefinitely. The State of Washington must prove beyond a reasonable doubt that the individual is a sexually violent predator. The commitment is "until such time as the person's mental abnormality or personality disorder has so changed that the person is safe to be at large." Other states have fashioned their laws after this one.

In 2010, the US Supreme Court ruled that Federal officials can indefinitely hold inmates after their prison terms are completed if the inmate is considered "sexually dangerous."

A sexual predator is defined as a person who has been convicted of, or pled guilty to, committing a sexually oriented offense and who is <u>likely</u> in the future to commit additional sex offenses. The designation is for life and carries significant burden to the individual, including job loss, ostracism, harassment and even violence. It costs each state a large amount of money and places a grave responsibility on law enforcement for monitoring these individuals if they are released.

Statistics vary greatly and it is difficult to determine actual recidivism because so many cases go unreported. But with broad media coverage of failures after a violent offender is released and offends or kills again, the public becomes informed and enraged.

Recently the State of Minnesota came under fire as officials searched for ways to protect the public yet provide less expensive treatment for sex offenders than in two secure psychiatric hospitals. One option they considered was to place released sexual offenders in halfway houses. People who lived in the area were adamantly opposed. They did not want sex offenders released and living in their neighborhoods. Their view was reinforced after the violent rapist Alfonso Rodriguez was released after twenty-three years of incarceration. Within months, he abducted and murdered the beautiful college student Dru Sjodin.

Another controversy lies in Minnesota's commitment statute. When sex offenders have completed their prison sentences, as in many other states, some are given indefinite civil commitment until they are no longer deemed dangerous. Some offenders are enrolled in the Minnesota Sexual Psychopathic Personality Treatment Center. In essence, this is a life sentence. There is no cure. No one has ever been released from this Treatment Center.

The public needs to understand the differences between a sexual offender and a Sexually Violent Predator and how the SVP definition is determined and used. SVPs should never be let out. Many sexual offenders are "low risk." Once they have done their prison time, they must be monitored and allowed to rebuild their lives.

In Colorado, an unusual situation occurred when nearly 300 sex offenders were considered for release after the Colorado Supreme Court found legislators had enacted conflicting laws. Under new law, sex offenders are sentenced to indefinite prison terms and can be paroled only if they make progress in treatment programs. Even when they are paroled, they get lifetime supervision. The newer laws were intended to be tougher on sex offenders, but because the prisoners had been sentenced under the old law, they were exempt and could be paroled for no longer than the unserved portions of their original prison terms, or five years, whichever was less.

Many offenders were released from parole under the old law but the Attorney General appealed the ruling and placed a hold on further releases.

Wisconsin legislators had to quickly patch a hole in their sex offender legislation when they found a convicted Minnesota sex offender had decided to move in across from a playground. The Wisconsin law had failed to demand registration of convicted sex offenders from other states who chose to live in Wisconsin.

Numerous state laws have been challenged and deemed unconstitutional because they stigmatize the convicted offender without due process. However, these laws have been upheld with public safety in mind.

Instead of automatically assigning "sex offender" status, many appear before a judge who reviews the particular history and decides whether the individual is required to register as a sex offender. This process is wrought with difficulty and inconsistent application. Some offenders are very low risk and probably should not be required to register and have their photos in the newspaper. The designation is life changing.

In Oregon, sex offenders sued to block the state from posting their names, photos, addresses and details about their offenses on the Internet. The offenders claimed it was a violation of their rights and an invasion of privacy. Because of their suit, the State website was put on hold and the case appealed. Oregon legislators were trying to protect the public. Most states now post sex offenders on an Internet site and list their risk level to reoffend. The information is readily available on a public registry of state sex offender databases at the Internet address www.sexoffender.com.

Bar-Jonah, termed a Level Three sex offender, was the highest level. His designation became meaningless for the public after his one-hundred-thirty-year sentence and failed attempt at appeal.

The treatment of sex offenders is varied and expensive. Most are treated in a group therapy setting where urges and ways to avoid "doing it again" are discussed. A few offenders have requested surgical castration, removing their testicles thus stopping testosterone production. Without testosterone they become impotent, and their exaggerated sexual urges are decreased but not eliminated. Stopping male hormone production has never been shown to be "curative" or effective. The fantasies live on in their brains even with impotence. Hormonal suppression stops erections, but it is unlikely to stop other violent behaviors or molestation because sexual predators are not inactive even if castrated.

A source of their enjoyment is the power they feel from frightening, demeaning and humiliating others. Their minds remain active as they plan, target and gather material to fuel their fantasies. The thrill of doing it and getting away with it is part of the ultimate game of chase.

New hormone-blocking drugs designed to aid in the treatment of male genital cancer can be used to block testosterone production and avoid surgically removing their testicles. This is, in essence, medical castration. The drugs are only effective in high doses and have significant side effects other than impotence, but the effects are reversible if the drug is discontinued. Few offenders opt to take it. One chemically castrated sexual predator on the hormone suppressor drug asked a judge to allow him to take Viagra so he could have sex with his wife. That certainly opened up interesting possibilities and repercussions regarding the treatment.

A mandate of the National Child Protection Act in 1993 called for a study of offenders who committed crimes against children. The study found that eighty percent of prisoners convicted of sexual assault had committed their crime against a victim under the age of eighteen. Older violent inmates were more likely than younger inmates to have victimized a child.

There have been many failures in the legal system but some of the failures stem from protective parents who want to spare the child more stress and refuse to prosecute. Caring and supportive parents who have felt enraged and responsible when their child has been molested want to spare the child additional trauma of being interrogated in court and especially spared from facing their molester. Because of this common attitude and action, some sexual predators have been freed to prey on other unsuspecting children. Like Bar-Jonah, they will strike again.

Examining this parental concern another way, the child will likely gain emotional relief by placing the perpetrator behind bars and unable to hurt others. Testifying can be a cleansing experience. Counseling will help with recovery and prevent long term medical and psychological problems.

Nathanael Bar-Jonah corresponded with a number of inmates remaining inside the Massachusetts Correctional System. Among those was pedophile Wayne Chapman. A letter from Chapman found in Bar-Jonah's apartment was dated December 1998, a year before the arrest at Lincoln Elementary School in Great Falls. Chapman was one of the individuals featured in a television documentary on sexual predators. Described as a wizard at stalking children, he is believed to have molested over fifty boys. He had escaped the legal system for years but was finally locked up for life. Incest perpetrators, such as father-daughter, brother-sister or other close family-related offenders are less likely to reoffend after extensive treatment, but high-risk predators like Bar-Jonah and Chapman should never be released.

A pedophile's urge for sexual gratification from children is overwhelming. Pedophiles use victims for perverse enjoyment, then discard or kill without remorse. They rationalize their actions and record acts so they can reread and relive the erotic feelings. Pedophiles are evil. They are incurable.

As a physician in emergency rooms, I have seen what it means to be a powerless victim. In crisis situations, I have treated helpless children, damaged emotionally and physically. Both the children and their families are traumatized and need help.

There is help.

There is hope.

Beyond the initial crisis and acute situation, counseling remains the key to recovery. The beginning step is for the traumatized individual to be safe, in a trusting loving environment. Healing cannot begin until safety is assured.

If someone you know has been victimized by a sexual predator, help them obtain counseling from a skilled practitioner. In a therapeutic setting, discussing their abuse may reduce fears, allow them to regain self esteem and go on with life. The primary goal is to face the problem head-on and refuse to remain a victim.

An overview list of suggestions on protecting children is found in Appendix 4.

Key References:

Evaluating Sex Offenders: A Manual for Civil Commitments and Beyond

Author: Dennis M. Doren

Assessing the Risk of Older Sex Offenders: Developing the Static-99R and Static 2002R

Authors: Leslie Helmus, David Thornton, R. Karl Hanson,

Kelly M. Babchishin

The Psychology of Criminal Conduct

Authors: D. A Andrews and James Bonta

Diagnostic and Statistical Manual of Mental Disorders, 4th Edition, Text Revision (DSM-IV-R) Paraphilia section

Published by The American Psychiatric Association

ACKNOWLEDGEMENTS

First, thanks to the Massachusetts victims, neighbors, teachers, police and others who were willing to talk to me. They provided essential information about Bar-Jonah's (nee David Brown) early life.

Conversations with Detectives Cameron and Theisen and FBI Special Agent Wilson gave me a clear view of their dedication and competency. Knowing these men has engendered my utmost respect. They are a tribute to their field. Without their candid descriptions and assistance, this book would not have been possible.

The Cascade County Prosecutor's office and legal assistant Sarah Hollis were extremely helpful in providing me encouragement and assistance in learning the protocols for obtaining information and court documents.

Cascade County Coroner James Bruckner's friendship, coffee before dawn in the ER, and encouragement to write this book were instrumental in keeping me on track. His helpful discussions of crime scene investigation and clearance for me to attend the Montana Law Enforcement Academy-Advance Crime Scene Investigation Course contributed to accurately depicting Bar-Jonah's case.

Nathanael Bar-Jonah provided me access to his defense records. His attorneys, Jackson and Vernay, were helpful in clarifying details of their approach to his defense; a special thank you to them for allowing me hours of access to investigative video and audio tapes.

Dr. Gary Dale, State Medical Examiner, provided his medical expertise in details for this text and I thank him, too, for helping me decide how to "kill without a trace" in my fiction books. Thanks to Lori Hutchinson, Scientist with the Montana Crime Lab, for her assistance in sorting out DNA details.

Enthusiastic family members, Montana friends, Authors of the Flathead who are generous writers helping writers and our guru, author Dennis Foley, all provided support and critiques along the way. I especially thank Deb Burke for her friendship and editing from the beginning.

Again, I thank and commend Bar-Jonah's victims for their strength to go on after the ordeal they endured and the willingness to share their stories so others may better understand how to keep their children safe.

APPENDIX 1 CAREGIVER RESOURCES

Information regarding immediate response to locate missing children and some of the many national programs that have been instituted to protect and solve abductions are listed below. There are many other reputable sites.

AMBER Alert

Contact local law enforcement to activate an AMBER Alert to locate an abducted child. It will be broadcast immediately on the AMBER Alert network. They prepare the information and fax it to area radio and television stations and cable systems which interrupt programming and announce the alert. Television and cable systems run an information line with a photo of the child. The AMBER Alert is also a ticker-tape alert on the Internet and appears on electronic reader signs along freeways.

The AMBER Alert Plan was created in 1997 following the abduction of a nine-year-old girl who was brutally murdered in Texas. Outrage in the community stimulated local residents, radio stations and law enforcement to join together and develop an early warning system. This system was then set up as part of the "Protection Act of 2003" which legislated funding for a notification system along highways. It also implemented technology to improve broadcast communications when missing children are reported to law enforcement. For more information visit U.S. Department of Justice Office of Justice Program's AMBER Plan website.

Code Adam

A "Code Adam" alert is announced over the public address system when a customer reports a missing child to a store employee. A search is initiated immediately, and all exits are monitored to prevent the child form leaving the store. If the child is not found in ten minutes or if the child is seen accompanied by someone other than a parent/guardian, the police are called. This nationwide child-safety program is named in memory of Adam Walsh, son of John Walsh of America's Most Wanted. Adam was abducted from a Florida shopping mall and murdered. This alert method was created in 1994 and promoted by Walmart but is now enacted in many locations.

Jacob Wetterling Foundation 1-800-325-HOPE
www.jwrc.org[1]

Eleven-year-old Jacob Wetterling was abducted in 1989. He has never been found. The Jacob Wetterling Resource Center has excellent online educational information. The organization is dedicated to making the world safer for children by building community awareness, supporting law enforcement and helping the criminal justice system.

National Child Pornography Tipline 1-800-843-5678
www.cybertipline.com[2]

---

1.   http://www.jwrc.org

2.   http://www.cybertipline.com

Submit reports of sexual exploitation of children. Examples: child prostitution, online enticement of children for sexual acts, unsolicited obscene material sent to a child.

Crimes Against Children (CAC) Program
www.fbi.gov/hq/cid/cac/crimesmain.htm[3]

The Federal Bureau of Investigation designed and instituted this program in 1997 to provide a quick effective response to all incidences of crime against children. These include sexual exploitation, child pornography, abduction, domestic and international parental kidnapping and National Sex Offender Registry information. The priority of rapid response increases the safe recovery of victimized children and reduces the level of crime in which children are targets. It provides victim/witness assistance services and resource teams to investigate and prosecute CAC that cross legal, geographical and jurisdictional boundaries. A Child Abduction Rapid Deployment (CARD) Team consisting of 4-6 members responds to help local law enforcement.

FBI National Center for the Analysis of Violent Crime (NCAVC)
www.fbi.gov/hq/isd/cirg/ncavc.htm[4]

Located at the FBI Academy in Quantico, Virginia, NCAVC provides many services which include profiles of offenders, crime analysis, behavioral assessments, expert testimony, laboratory services, research regarding child abductions and serial homicides, and training for the law enforcement community.

---

3.   http://www.fbi.gov/hq/cid/cac/crimesmain.htm

4.   http://www.fbi.gov/hq/isd/cirg/ncavc.htm

National Center for Missing and Exploited Children
1-800-THE-LOST
www.missingkids.com[5]

Educational publications are available free of charge in single copies by contacting the Publication Department at Charles B. Wang International Children's Building, 699 Prince Street, Alexandria, VA 22314-317

> Request: **"Child Protection"** a pamphlet which provides an excellent detailed overview of child safety recommendations.

5.   http://www.missingkids.com

APPENDIX 2 PEDOPHILE TRAITS

The following are general descriptions taken from many sources which correlate with pedophile behavior. If identified as single actions, they should not be considered reasons to notify authorities. This is an overview of findings documented by researchers and law enforcement in pedophiles who have been apprehended.

Pedophiles are adept liars

Strives to be alone with kids

Males of any age, few friends his age, no close friends

Seeks systematic prolonged access to children through work and volunteer for jobs

Sympathetic listeners who target troubled or withdrawn children

Decorates area or room in a child's theme, collects toys

Collects theme pornography as a fantasy-driven behavior

Collects "paraphernalia" to remind them of their sexual desires

Saves souvenirs from encounters such as photos

Tapes TV programs or buys videos (ex. boys' workout tape)

Boys mingling with younger children—watch for aberrant behavior

Single unmarried men, don't date, may live with parents, and target children

Sexual encounters based on pleasure, companionship and caring are nonexistent

Shy, backward, with poor interpersonal skills

Volatile, withdrawn or hostile behavior

Difficulty interacting with adults

Seek girlfriends with children of their focused age

May marry women with children of their focused age

Church affiliations giving them access to children

Interest in guns, uniforms, handcuffs

Gifting and paying unusual attention to a child

Loitering around playgrounds

Excessive friendliness to parents

Takes videos of acts and victims

Photography, with an interest in kids

Psychopathic Triad: Missing or maimed pets, fire-setting plus bed-wetting = high risk

Lack remorse and empathy, may fake emotions

Childhood sexual abuse is a risk factor for developing pedophilia

Pedophiles tend to choose their age-specific victims in accordance with the age of their own experience of sexual victimization

Choose activities that enable them power and proximity to kids

Examples: Camp counselors, bus drivers, babysitters, foster parents, coaches, photographers, childcare, special education teachers, ministers, school principals

APPENDIX 3 PROTECTING CHILDREN

The following are general descriptions taken from many sources which may decrease abduction and molestation risks for children. Other items listed are sometimes seen in abused children and are provided to raise awareness that a child may be a victim who has been coerced into silence. If identified as single actions, they should not be considered reasons to notify authorities but may be a reason to contact your family doctor to discuss problems.

<u>**NEVER let your children walk or bicycle alone.**</u>

Your children should be comfortable talking to you about any topic.

The molester is often a family member or someone well-known to the family.

Tell your children it is okay to say "No!" to any adult, even a policeman or minister.

Remember the helpful-policeman-guise is commonly used by abductors.

Instruct your children to stay away from vehicles parked along the sidewalk or road.

If someone actually grabs them, the child should fight to get away: kick, scream and bite.

Be suspicious if someone is paying unusual attention to your child.

Pelvic irritation, bleeding and itching may be from sexual contact.

Observance of unusual behavior with sexual overtones requires investigation.

Bed-wetting after a child has been dry. (May be a bladder infection; see a doctor.)

Watch for behavior changes such as acting out, showing fear or avoiding a certain adult.

Avoidance of touching when child has been comfortable with hugs from family.

Girls who avoid touching or try to make themselves appear unattractive.

Encourage your children to say "No!" to photos without your supervision.

Child molesters are commonly live-in boyfriends and babysitters.

Be wary of Internet dating; the date may be targeting your child.

Know what your children are doing on the Internet.

Be cautious of any overnight invitations.

Praise for Eyes of a Pedophile

Dr. Kuffel approaches crime with a keen eye, just as she did as a hospital emergency physician, where she got to know the detectives working victim cases that moved through her ER. From that vantage point, initially as a doctor, then as a writer and researcher, she has brought to life the story of pedophile Nathanael Bar-Jonah, but from the heartfelt view of the lives of his victims. This is a must-read of an inside look

Cathy Scott True Crime Author, Las Vegas *The Millionaire's Wife, The Rough Guide to True Crime, Killing of Tupac Shakur, The Murder of Biggie Smalls*

When I first saw Pinero's play, *Short Eyes*, (prisoner's term for child molesters), I was stunned. After reading Dr. Kuffel's book, a recent update on child molesters, I was amazed and horrified in this compelling page turner.

Lavonne Mueller, Playwright and Woodrow Wilson Scholar, Chicago

Dr. Kuffel's true crime story should be read by every naïve parent and caregiver.

Barbara, Grandmother, White Bear Lake, MN

Eyes of a Pedophile helps the layperson get a better understanding of the mind of a serial molester of children. Although the subject matter is horrific, Dr. Kuffel handles it with such grace that even the most sensitive of us will find it very readable. Most importantly, this book educates us in ways that may protect our children in the future from monsters like Bar-Jonah

B. Palmer, Montana

Dr. Kuffel's book *Eyes of a Pedophile* is the chilling true story of Nathanael Bar-Jonah, a violent child molester. So many more are still out there. As a former journalist, I particularly enjoyed the doctor's in-depth research into the machinations of this maniac. Dr. Kuffel's book is a "must read" for every parent. Her guidance on the keys of recognizing pedophiles could save lives.

Constance See, Montana

In the 1990's the dark hand of a pedophile over-shadowed a member of our family. Someone my sister considered a trusted friend showed up on the nightly news one night - arrested for molesting several young boys. This could have been prevented if we had known what to look for. Betty's story will touch your life and help you learn how to protect the young lives around you. This well researched book will become a valuable read for your family and friends.

Peggy, Grandmother, Houston

Eyes of a Pedophile is a riveting, eye opening glance at the inner disposition of a serial pedophile and is a must read for educators and those working with young people.

Diane Hewitt Olson, Retired Educator, Grand Forks, ND

This book is a great resource for everyone, especially educators. As a grandmother, I worry about my own grandkids and shudder to think they could become victims.

Bonnie, RN, Minnesota

PHOTOGRAPHS

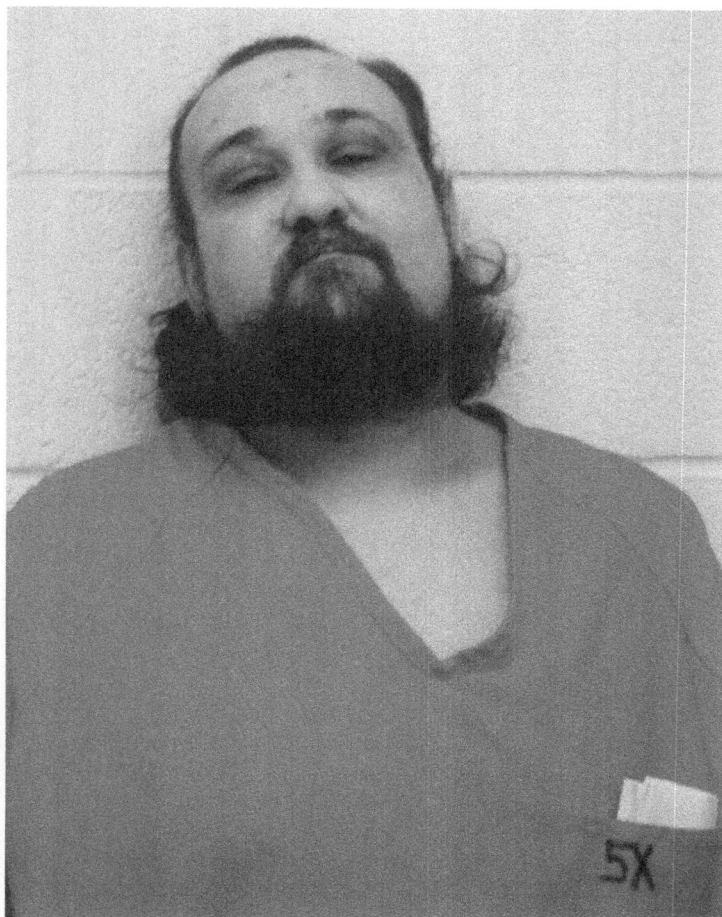

Bar-Jonah Arrest 1999

Bar-Jonah posing in wig and girl's swimsuit

Bates Family Cemetery – Webster, MA

Coded Writings

John Cameron – Lead Detective

Detective Tim Theisen

Nathanael Bar-Jonah Self Portrait

Bar-Jonah Apartment entry and interior

Tyra and Son

DISCUSSION TALKING POINTS

The topic of this book is sexual abuse, a topic most people feel uncomfortable discussing. In the past, sexual abuse was hidden. Protecting family names took priority over protecting children and stopping abuse. Because sexual abuse of children is so common, few families escape the problem. After reading about the missing boy, Zachary Ramsay and how sexual predators operate, are you better able to talk about abuse and how to intervene? Being more knowledgeable, what action would you take now? Would you have done the same before reading this book?

1. In recent years, victims of sexual abuse have been empowered by reporting their abuse and seeing their abusers prosecuted. For victims, reporting the abuse is difficult. Many adults have lived a lifetime of hidden shame and will never discuss childhood abuse. There is no shame in being abused; the shame is in not stopping the predator. What could have been done to stop Bar-Jonah from harming so many children?

2. When adults do not contact child protective services and law enforcement, the abuse continues. Pedophiles never stop. How has this book helped you feel more comfortable in teaching others what to do if they become aware of abuse?

3. Nathan Bar-Jonah grew up in an idyllic community on the shores of Lake Webster in rural Massachusetts. On the outside, his home-life appeared calm. His church-going mother loved him dearly. She provided food and comfort to the youngster after beatings by his father, but she did not stop the physical and mental abuse. What might a child learn from the conflicting adult behaviors he endured? How do think the home environment imprinted his young mind and affected his behavior later in life?

4. Most of us don't consider a ten-year-old capable of "rape" and one would wonder about his exposure to that behavior. Do you think Bar-Jonah was a victim? Is a ten-year-old capable of an erection? Without sexual abuse, discuss the impact of his father's beatings and any effect they may have had leading to Bar-Jonah's violence.

5. Bar-Jonah learned religious values, became a youth church counselor and throughout his life attended church. He joined women's church groups as the only male member and gained their confidence. Based on what you have learned about him, what do you believe his motives were? How did he accomplish his goals? Is his behavior common in pedophiles?

6. Twelve years in the Massachusetts Bridgewater facility for sexually dangerous people didn't seem to help Bar-Jonah. He failed to cooperate with counselors and psychiatrists in programs at the facility, yet he was released without monitoring. Based on available statistics, could he have been cured of his pedophilia? Why would two clinical psychologists decide he was unlikely to ever harm another child and recommend his release?

7. Why was Bar-Jonah released to Montana without notification that a violent sexual predator had moved into the community? Could the same thing happen today?

8. What actions might you take to keep your child safer if you knew a sexual offender lived near you? What if the offender was a Level One offender, would you be concerned about your child? How about a Level Three offender with a history of raping children?

9. From the files of many rapists and child predators, we see impersonation of a police officer as a common ploy to gain the trust of their targets. We know pedophiles in roles close to children can take advantage of their positions to harm them. Discuss how you might teach a child acceptable behavior to expect from superiors, such as teachers, coaches and clergy.

10. Discuss scenarios involving men you do not want your children to be with, such as: a male teenaged babysitter, a grandfather, uncle, father, boyfriend or neighbor who you question as being inappropriate. In any situation, the most important action is to be sure the child is safe and not allowed to be alone with the individual. Reports to both child protective services and law enforcement are essential.

11. Pedophiles can be found in any socioeconomic level and in all professions, no one is exempt. They are often believable, talkative, friendly, educated and in positions of power. Most are people you invite to your home. After they gain your confidence and trust, they molest your children. Based on the behavior of Bar-Jonah, how might you protect your children? Name some behaviors or signs you need to watch for?

12. Learning about behaviors commonly seen in psychopaths, you may find yourself wanting to diagnose people you know. Psychopathic behaviors include lying, exaggeration, narcissism (love of self), and using people—but these actions don't make them psychopaths. The diagnosis is complex. Based on Bar-Jonah's behavior, he was a violent psychopath, yet people trusted him, even psychologists. How does this happen? Do you think you'd be successful in identifying psychopathic behavior in someone like Bar-Jonah?

ABOUT THE AUTHOR

A medical School honors graduate and Internal Medicine specialist, Dr. Kuffel has extensive experience in trauma and emergency medicine. This work brought her close to many crime victims, investigators and perpetrators. Unique cooperation from Montana law enforcement, Bar-Jonah and his victims greatly assisted her search for accuracy in writing this educational true crime story.